The Networked Wilderness

The Networked Wilderness

Communicating in Early New England

Matt Cohen

 University of Minnesota Press
Minneapolis • London

The University of Minnesota Press is grateful for support from a University
Co-operative Society Subvention Grant awarded by the University of Texas at Austin.

Chapter 1 was previously published as "Morton's Maypole and the Indians:
Publishing in Early New England," *Book History* 5 (2002): 1–18.

The poem from *Off the Reservation,* by Paula Gunn Allen, is reprinted with
permission from Beacon Press, Boston. Copyright 1998 by Paula Gunn Allen.

Published by the University of Minnesota Press
111 Third Avenue South, Suite 290
Minneapolis, MN 55401-2520
http://www.upress.umn.edu

Library of Congress Cataloging-in-Publication Data

Cohen, Matt, 1970–
    The networked wilderness : communicating in early New England / Matt Cohen.
        p. cm.
    Includes bibliographical references and index.
    ISBN 978-0-8166-6097-1 (hc : alk. paper) — ISBN 978-0-8166-6098-8 (pbk. : alk.
paper)
        1. Communication—United States—History—17th century. 2. Communication—
New England—History—17th century. 3. Literacy—New England—History—
17th century. 4. Books and reading—New England—History—17th century.
5. Indians of North America—Communication. I. Title.
    P92.U5C55 2009
    302.209746´09032—dc22
    2009029589

Printed in the United States of America on acid-free paper

The University of Minnesota is an equal-opportunity educator and employer.

20 19 18 17 16 15 14 13 12 11 10   10 9 8 7 6 5 4 3 2 1

For Bridget

Contents

.

Note on the Text

Quotations from printed and manuscript sources are largely unaltered from the original spellings because the visual qualities of text are central to the argument of this book. Minor typographical normalization has been necessary for characters not in use today, such as using *s* for *f*, and words using diacritical marks to indicate the absence of a consonant have been rendered normally (for example, "then" for "thē"). As often as possible I have included images of the pages under analysis when textual configurations are difficult to reproduce in modern typescript. Unless otherwise noted, all emphases are in the originals.

Dates are rendered as in the original documents; most years are Julian. When significant, a modern rendering of a date is offered parenthetically. Biblical references are to the Geneva Bible (1587 edition). I use signatures (with the abbreviation "r" for recto or "v" for verso) to indicate page references in the case of volumes that are unpaginated and those whose pagination is unreliable or misleading.

English and Native American names are spelled according to (more or less) standard scholarly use. Algonquians often had several names over the course of their lives. For clarity I choose one, for example, Massasoit over Ousemaquin.

The nomenclature and capitalization of "Native" when used to refer to American Indians is chosen in part out of respect for those groups and in part to distinguish between native English and Native American audiences in the readings. The term "indigenous" is not capitalized in order to reserve it for application more broadly to indicate groups of people who consider themselves to have emerged from a land or to have been the first human occupants of a land. Exemplary of the persistence of the power of typographical distinctions to shape perception, the choice to capitalize or not, no less than nomenclature more broadly, is controversial. Native people of the area that became known as New England referred to themselves with a range of terms, from clan and family designations to more general terms that often translate to mean, simply but powerfully, "the people." My choice of usage is based on an awareness of the political importance today of such practices, but with an eye to keeping the terms of my argument clear.

Introduction

The early settlers of the northern English colonies in America, we are told, were people of the book. Devout Protestants, they insisted that those who would be godly must read the Bible for themselves. They were avid letter writers, they were more interested in writing down laws than were their relatives back home, and they seemed always to be reading or scribbling. Within a short time, the literacy rate among northern colonists was higher than that of the mother country. This was made possible, so the story has gone, by the colonies' isolation and linguistic uniformity. And such widespread literacy was remarkable in part because the people among whom the English had settled—the Algonquians of the northeastern woodlands and coastline—were *not* people of the book. Historians of communication and Native scholars alike have insisted that the indigenous people of the region had an "oral culture," dependent on face-to-face communication and human memory, elaborately supported by ritual and custom, to express, circulate, and preserve information.[1] The culture of print outcompeted oral culture thanks to the flexibility of alphabetic literacy and the staying power of the inscribed word.

This story, which in its broad outlines has been dominant for half a century or more, is being challenged. Scholars have demonstrated that for the settlers, eloquence and rumor were as much a source of power as writing. Sounds and gestures were "read" by emigrants with no less interest than they read the Gospel. They sang while they walked and worked. Men and women passed down old stories of the supernatural, of medicine, of family, while God, they thought, filled the natural world with wonders as messages to His people. Our knowledge of indigenous communication has also changed: totemic symbols, wampum, and other physical forms carried messages, even over long distances. Christian converts among the Algonquians, supposedly mired in a culture of sound and memory, quickly learned to read and write, some in English and some in a transliterated dialect. Studies of Canadian First Nations and Amerindian communities of Central and South America suggest that something like multimedia literacy might be a better characterization of American communications norms.[2]

If these new insights hold true, then thinking about early New England in terms of print culture and oral culture may obscure important complexities. Indeed, as we increasingly interact with and through new multimedia technologies in a polyglot, culturally diverse world, what the American Indians and the English were going through in the northeastern woods may seem eerily familiar. This book examines the role of communications systems in the early settlement of New England. Those systems were both occasions for and sites of contest for control over social and economic power because they offered individuals alternative and little-understood ways to gain agency across cultural and linguistic divides. Different as they seemed on the surface, those systems also shared many features. Similarities were as important as differences in the attempt to live together in the challenging landscape of New England. In the years before 1638, when the printing press was introduced to New England, even the task of discerning what was part of the other's system of communication was an inextricable element of the challenge of transmitting and interpreting messages.

The implications of such a shift in perspective are methodological, disciplinary, legal, political, and aesthetic. If Natives and English were both oral and inscribing peoples, then they constituted each others' audiences in ways scholars have only begun to consider. What would count as evidence for a multimedia, continuous topography of communication techniques, and what would a narrative of it look like? What would such a narrative do to our definitions of the boundaries between peoples—even, perhaps, to operating definitions of culture itself? These questions guide *The Networked Wilderness*. To get a sense of the eddies of theoretical and historical interpretation that these questions stir up, it might be best to begin with a pair of stories that suggest how redefining what counts as a communications technology may expand our vision of the information systems of early America and help us begin to ask new questions about colonial cultures.[3]

How to Do Things with Wolf Traps

Shortly after arriving in the New World, during an expedition on Cape Cod, the point men of a Pilgrim exploring party came upon a splendidly crafted deer trap. Perhaps distracted by eagerness to examine its construction, they failed to alert those walking behind them of the trap's presence. The men promptly saw one of their leaders, William Bradford—soon-to-be governor and already an important figure among the emigrants—yanked off his feet by a tree, caught in the trap. The description of the moment (in the 1622 text known colloquially as Mourt's *Relation*) blends humor, ambiguity, and insinuation: Bradford had approached from the rear and "as he went about" the trap "gave a sudden jerk up, and he was caught immediately by the leg." It is not clear whether Bradford set the trap off himself; the narrator offers no more detail about the Puritan leader's predicament but merely remarks, "It was a very pretty device, made with a rope of their own making and having a noose as artificially made as any roper in England can make."[4] As the trap was hidden by the Native hunter, so the means by which Bradford was allowed to step into it and the response to the resulting momentary inversion of authority are hidden by the anonymous narrator. Bradford's impromptu dance, marionetted by a Native American technology, is nested within yet another level of the hidden and the made-legible, for this scene does not appear in Bradford's own account of exploration in his famous history *Of Plymouth Plantation*. Indeed, the *Relation* was published in England without Bradford's consent and, in the opinion of some Plymouth leaders, put the reputation and by extension the credit rating of the venture at risk.

A less-well-known New England history, Thomas Weston's *History of the Town of Middleboro, Massachusetts,* tells a story from later in the settlement era that seems to bookend that of Bradford's embarrassment. English settlers, because they were dependent on livestock, were plagued by wolves. Among other means of reducing the wolf population, the colonists resorted to digging large pits to trap the predators. Inspectors traveled a circuit of traps to release any "innocents" who had found their way into the pits and to kill caught wolves. One day, a Middleboro man checking traps was surprised to find a pit containing a wolf at one end and a Native man at the other. After dispatching the wolf, the inspector detained the Algonquian for interrogation. "He found," Weston reports, "that the Indian was on his way from Nemasket to Plymouth upon legitimate business, so he was released and allowed to continue his journey."[5] Authority seems here to have been reestablished over both nature and the Natives.

A familiar historical interpretation tells how the inevitable triumph of European technologies (imagined as better capable of adaptation than Native American ones) took place hand in hand with the rise of racism—or at least the categorical establishment of difference with Native people. But there is another way of reading such moments. The humor of Bradford's upending and the pathos of the wolf pit conceal the anxious situation of New England's colonists, revealed by Bradford's reticence and the Native man's escape. Bradford found himself caught not merely in a trap intended for an animal—one designed to provide sustenance to Natives—but in the uncertain communications politics of long-distance settler colonialism, as he wrote in *Of Plymouth Plantation,* reflecting on Mourt's *Relation.* Traps are a multipurpose technology; they function simultaneously as defensive or hunting tools and as parts of a communications system. Indiscriminately catching anything that is fooled by it, the trap is a kind of lieutenant (literally, from French, a "place-holder"), telling its setter about local populations or movements otherwise unknown or invisible. It intercepts messages regardless of their origins or intended destinations. Events like Bradford's mishap, the Plymouth settlers would later learn through other encounters with the locals, telegraphed the English presence on the Cape.

The Middleboro case is complicated by Native American systems as well. The captured Native—whose ability to live through the evening with a wolf suggests his survival skills—might well have feigned his communications purpose in order not to suffer the wolf's fate. Whether on legitimate business or not, the Algonquian knew that having a message was how one got out of being accused of trespassing, spying, or skulking on English farmland. Weston's story comes late in the colony's history, after years of mutual adaptation: English were using traps after resisting doing so earlier, and while Natives might not always know where the traps were, at least they knew how to get out of them alive when pitted against either wolves or Englishmen.[6]

By reconceptualizing New England encounters in terms of communications technologies and networks of signification, such moments can be read in ways that reveal how historical interpretation continues to depend on assumptions about the nature of communication. The notion that Native America was doomed by difference is rooted in part in a presumed absence of sophisticated information systems, as compared to those underpinning the English colonial sociopolitical order. But when traps, paths, wampum, monuments, medical rituals, and other messaging systems are taken into account, both cultures appear to have been made from an ongoing exchange of anxieties, imaginations, resources, and performances. In addition, the communications encounters of the early settlement era offer a provocative evidentiary challenge for rethinking theories about the relationships among representation, media, and the social order.

Such a rethinking allows us to see not merely the contours of Puritan and Native culture and politics but those of our disciplinary cultures as well. This is particularly important because the question of Native American sovereignty, and who has authority to construct it, is at issue in any study of historical relationships between settler and indigenous cultures. As Native American scholars have insisted, the discipline of history writing, as a potential source of public authority and a form of investment in intellectual work, matters for thinking about Native self-governance now even when writing about the American past. Scholarly accounts have power everywhere from the public imagination of Indianness and colonial history to courts of law deciding the fate of tribal recognition and land and repatriation claims. The conclusions scholars draw about the events of the Native past during colonization are important—but like all interpretations, they are contestable. Perhaps more important is what analysts take to be evidence for the study of the indigenous past and, by extension, what conceptualizations of culture and social relations scholars make available to lawmakers and to all those engaged in the struggle for survival. Scholars of Native America are debating the concept of sovereignty and its applicability to the situation of North American communities; studies of early colonial interactions inevitably take a part in this debate, but as historical studies, they hitherto have too seldom accepted the task of addressing the living relationship between the past and the present.

The two major fields engaged by this study are the history of the book and Native American studies. These fields have constructed each other, perhaps unintentionally, as incompatible, even in some ways antithetical. For some Native thinkers, the book and its culture are a politically productive barrier when considering the encounter period. Recently at the Newberry Library in Chicago, a group of Blackfoot middle-school students from the Nizipuswahsin (Real Speak) School performed a play they composed about Meriwether Lewis's encounter with their ancestors on the Lewis and Clark voyage. It began in a familiar way, stating that in early Blackfoot life "everything was passed down orally." But in the ensuing scene, a tremendous range of material and performative modes of preserving and transmitting information were detailed, from cooking to the use of sign language, clothing, and crafts. Though it might have been a subversive use of Walter Ong's famous distinction between orality and literacy,[7] this performance used orality to emphasize difference—a trope common in Native heritage politics today.

The acquisition of literacy through specific technologies of representation, such as writing and print, Ong theorized, brought with it changes in the structure of consciousness. By breaking down signification into small phonetic units, alphabetic literacy in particular makes possible conceptual abstractions and comparisons that Ong argued are impossible to maintain in the regime of memory of societies without alphabetic writing. Myth and legend, not theoretical abstraction, establish continuities with the past where written records are unavailable. Literacy, in this theory, though not inevitable, brings a higher consciousness and improves quality of life by enabling other advances and reducing prejudice. It enables the concept of history, as it is understood in the West, by making comparisons both over distance and through time possible. While anthropologists long ago debunked this theory, it has survived in various forms, particularly in the notion that the conceptual realms of those without writing are unreliable, prone to superstition, and situated at an earlier stage in an imagined-to-be-universal developmental process.[8]

For most book historians, the emphasis on textual materiality has seemed to preclude the study of communal, mnemonic, and ritualized information exchange, irrespective of the status of Ong's theory of literacy. "The book historian is grounded in . . . solid materiality," writes Germaine Warkentin, and thus "book history assumes the basic bibliographical requirement of *marks made upon a material base for the purpose of recording, storing, and communicating information.*"[9] Warkentin, in a rich study of northeastern Native uses of wampum for political, spiritual, historical, and economic purposes, points out that indigenous North American recording systems complicate the distinction usually made by historians of writing between semasiographic systems (based on inscription) and phonographic ones that are based on spoken language.

Still, alternative bases for book history might be imagined. When Raymond Williams called for an approach to literary studies that situated texts within their full material contexts of production, he drew on Karl Marx's broader definition of "material," including human labor and the conditions of production. One of the implications of this approach is that it puts bibliography and literary analysis into dialogue as a condition of analyzing meaning. To be persuasive, a close reading must bear the particular edition or state of a text and its cultural-historical context in mind. *The Networked Wilderness* analyzes both the material and what might be called the matériel of representation—from the typography and ornamentation of English printed texts to the qualities of wood and shell on which Algonquian communication relied.[10] These are treated as standing in a mutually constitutive relationship with language, literary history, the immediate conditions of production of a text, and things like ideas, belief, and tradition. The basic unit of analysis here is what I call a publication event, taking "publication" in its broad, seventeenth-century meaning (which included publicly posted or proclaimed information) and insisting on its performative elements. As an embodied act of information exchange, the publication event presumes that its participants are aware that an act of communication is intended (though they may not be aware of the customs and rhetorics shaping it). The event is also constituted by its retransmissions subsequent to the original publication moment, some anticipated by the participants and some beyond their control.

How might the publication event be thought of in relation to seventeenth-century Native Americans? A starting point is Martin Lienhard's conception of multimedia indigenous expression. Lienhard insists that, in the case of indigenous collectivities, the complex narrative and political matrices of literature are located in "expresiones orales o multimediales" (oral or multimedia expressions).[11] The generation, archiving, and transmitting of messages involved language, narrative form, music, rhythm, intonation, gesture, choreography, costume, painting, and a range of inscriptive techniques. Reflexively, each of these modes defined what could count as a message within the protocols of a given society, but they did so only incompletely and only in relation to each other. Each communication was understood as interpretable both at the level of a particular physical instantiation and in terms of its relation to simultaneous and past representations in other media. Like other scholars of Amerindian media, Lienhard recognizes that indigenous expressions became engaged with colonial discourses in a complex interplay involving emulation, appropriation, subversion, signifying, and outright contest. The historically and regionally variable rules of multimedia expression appear in a range of indigenous uses of text; at the same time, texts produced by colonists show the pressure of indigenous audiences.[12] When settlement texts are read with an eye to the serious competition European communications networks faced from indigenous ones, confident narratives of conquest and settlement begin to show anxieties—anxieties that would spawn a long history of worry about how American Indians represent themselves.[13]

But the book, certainly for English colonists, was a multimedia form as well. More, those settlers depended on a metropolitan publishing system to prove the worth of their investors' decisions and to make political claims. Many colonists, particularly those with complaints against the English government, experienced this system as a realm in which signifying was necessary. Here I follow the lead of scholars who have proposed performance, with its attention to space, audience, and the combination of the aural and visual, as a framework for understanding communications systems that will embrace both Native and English practices. Such an enterprise can seem paralyzingly daunting because it necessarily involves adding a wide range of methods to bibliographic and literary ones; in the case of this book alone it calls to the task anthropological, archaeological, medical, theological, and ecological interpretations. In focusing on publication events, the history of the book's ability to sketch the contingencies of a particular moment of communication that will be distributed, retold, and reimagined helps corral these methods. Restricting this study to New England before the arrival of the printing press allows for attention to both the local and the long-distance audience dynamics implicated in publication events. I hope to offer a pathway for approaching settler texts coherent and limited enough to be of interpretive use.

To further that coherence, some of the terms I will use in the following pages beg early definition, since their meanings are contested today. I choose the general word *communication,* not *semiotics* or some other term, because in taking my cue from the history of the book I bring the materials and channels by which messages move into the analysis of meaning-making. Ruth Finnegan's recent definition of "communication," deliberately "fuzzy at the edges," she writes, is compelling for its insistence that communication is a relative and emergent process, a "multidimensional spectrum of acting and experiencing, not a bounded entity." Communication invites definitions. It is an occasion for the masterstroke of modern scholarship, the theoretical or philosophical modeling that is the equivalent of, for example, the unified field theory sought in physics. From the establishment of information theory by Claude Shannon in the wake of the Second World War to Noam Chomsky's grounding of definitions of the human and of history in linguistic communication as an innate and universal biological feature, whole paradigms for thinking about what it means to be human have rested on totalizing conceptions of communication as having a nature. My use of the term attempts to balance historically and culturally specific regimes of interpretation and audience expectation with the more fluid aspects of language and performance. In contact situations, communication was often happening in registers of which interlocutors were not aware, while deception was as often the baseline of decoding as sincerity.[14]

If there is a term more contested than communication, it might be *technology.* In current usage, "technology" usually refers simply to tools, or to a subset of tools that involve digital or electronic components. In what follows, the term often appears in this sense, referring to physical mechanisms of transfer or transformation. But at times it partakes of Michel Foucault's famous use of the term, broader and deliberately fractured, which offers important insights into technology's place in society. Foucault suggests that separating tools from technology too rigidly impoverishes our analysis. Any socially agreed-on mechanism for producing interpretations of the world that can circulate relatively intact is understood to be a technology, including languages, policies, machines, books, wampum, or medical practices. Tools do not interpret themselves; know-how is required to make them function in the ways for which they were designed. Tools are, however, more than means to ends. They may be used in more than one way, may be "repurposed," to use a popular term from the business world. Societies cannot, without oversimplification or even injury, be characterized by their tools. Instead of technology creating a certain kind of consciousness, communications systems shape the imagination of the possibilities of representational politics. Social structures and their material infrastructures must therefore be studied together.[15]

My use of the word *system* is shaped by this notion of technology as a social nexus rather than as a discrete thing that can be thought of as good or bad. By "system" I mean a set of relations among humans and technologies well enough acknowledged by a social group to serve as a locus of struggle for control. These broad definitions of "system," "technology," and "communication," based in cultural studies, help *The Networked Wilderness* to promote an alternative reading practice for approaching colonial culture rather than to offer a theoretical program or another history of New England. Inspired and enabled as my work is by the writings of systems theorists across the disciplines, such as Friedrich Kittler, Niklas Luhmann, or Albert-László Barabási, I do not seek here to create a systematic study of systems. Zones of contact like that of early New England are characterized by heterogeneous networks in which neither the nodes connected nor the means of communicating between them are quite standardized enough by user expectations to be treated as a total system.[16] This is not to deny the temporary or local coherence of communications systems or the attachment of certain rhetorical practices to specific technologies. But by keeping an eye out for both performance and precedent, for the way an audience or an occasion, no less than a code or a medium, can affect communicative acts, we may become more sensitive readers of colonial information worlds.

Writing colonial history, when necessarily approaching Native presence through works written by colonizers, offers a unique epistemological challenge. Stephen Greenblatt once claimed that if you "discard the particular words . . . you discard the particular men" and that early colonial Native representation, being reported by European observers, is thus obscured and unavailable for analysis. Such a declaration, though, suffers from at least two shortcomings. First, Greenblatt's analysis overprivileges "the word" as compared to gestural or visual media. Second, such an attitude evacuates scholarship's responsibility to represent all sides of an academic problem—a real difficulty in the case of Native American studies, in which individual Native informants may offer accounts of history that are unverifiable by Western methodologies, but a difficulty that must be confronted nonetheless. To rely on particular European accounts, even with the rich publication context now recoverable for them, is not enough, as it privileges alphabetic literacy as a mode of representation and a linear notion of causality alien to many indigenous American worldviews. At the same time, the archaeology and the oral history of Native America present a parallel set of challenges given the catastrophic changes wrought by colonization on the human and other-than-human worlds of the Algonquian northeast. Petroglyphs, pottery, wampum, post-hole patterns, and graves and even piles of sticks and rocks left by Native travelers still remain, among many other material evidences of information transmission systems. But they are difficult to interpret—and in order to do so, scholars have relied on the same European-authored texts Greenblatt warns are not particular enough to speculate about Native pasts. Bringing the systematicity of communications cultures into the analysis of the content of those systems allows us to situate acts of communication among several interpretive possibilities. Both native English and Native American audiences mattered in the moments examined in *The Networked Wilderness*. These are "moments in which alternatives exist, when . . . futures are underdetermined and therefore genuinely undetermined," Myra Jehlen writes. In publication events it is not just the outcome but the set of interactions that becomes the focus.[17] The same should be true, I argue, of our stance in studying such events.

This approach to media is informed by work in Native American studies. A contested field—some interlocutors might not even call it a field—scholarly studies of Native America feature a set of debates that I want to engage selectively and always with an eye to the political significance of any study of Native America. On basic issues such as the meaning and uses of "sovereignty" for Native tribes, even the definition of "tribal" identity, scholars of Native America divide over arguments that draw on intellectual traditions that span the globe. In later chapters I will engage the work of such intellectuals as Paula Gunn Allen, Arnold Krupat, Gerald Vizenor, James Clifford, and Paul Chaat Smith on the questions of how to conceptualize tribal or cultural boundaries and on the issue of the forms of power that accompany such divisions. But as a whole this book has been led by work in Native studies that asks readers to be suspicious not just of universalizing rhetoric but even of liberal humanist discourses of understanding. The goal of understanding, some Native Americanists point out, generally redounds to the benefit of the already-dominant. "The concern with getting rid of 'old and isolating world views' and 'unbridgeable chasm[s],'" writes Jace Weaver, "has always been more of a concern for Amer-Europeans than for Natives, who do not view their own cultural responses as 'old and isolating' and who often express scant interest in bridging their worldview with that of the dominant culture."[18] *The Networked Wilderness* suggests that deception and equivocation, seen as inherent potentials in the communicative process, shake the viability of understanding in ways that gave a particular charge of anxiety to moments of encounter in which symbolic capital, actual space or objects, and systemic rules are all at stake.[19] To say that communication happens on a spectrum of media modes is not to say that we are all one people or that we can all understand each other. It is to say that we need to be able to think about representation in ways that acknowledge difference and its effects without insisting that there must be a knowable single source or origin of that difference, and that such knowledge can ground law.[20]

To begin this work of rereading colonial communications requires thinking differently about the periodization of book history in America. Scholars of early America and the history of the book have suggested that to understand the culture of early New England, one must first take into account Puritan leaders' strict control of the circulation of information, both printed and proclaimed. But most histories of the book in early North America begin with the first major threat from *within* the Puritan community to its leadership, the Antinomian crisis of 1637–38, which coincided with the founding of the first English printing press in America. *The Networked Wilderness* examines both the history of the book before the printing press came to New England and the methodological questions raised by studying it. What constitutes evidence in book history, and what would it mean for the stories it tells to account for Native American representational systems? What does it mean for English readers to become audiences for Native American traps—and for Natives to become audiences for English writing, as happened when Thomas Morton posted poetry on a Maypole at his plantation?

In turn, book historical approaches to these questions will have implications for Native studies. The equation of media with cultural boundaries sometimes serves as a tool for recognition based on difference in Native studies. Does arguing for the inherent orality of Native culture in fact speak to the complexities of indigenous communication? Even if such a claim is largely strategic, it may leave in place the basic ideas guiding mainstream attitudes about the hierarchy of cultures. What stories might be told about the stuff of which Native lives and tales were made? How might we use the techniques of the history of the book to look at the social life of Native communication from a systemic standpoint, rather than simply from an intratribal one—and what tradeoffs result? The beginning of *The Networked Wilderness* is shaped to raise these questions and suggest tentative answers. But pursuing these methodological questions raises larger ones germane to indigenous politics today, which I take up in the last two chapters of the book. What insights into the question of the definition of "cultures" do settlement texts have to offer? Might the colonial era's struggles over concepts of sovereignty hold some lessons for today?

Beginning with Bradford dangling from a tree is thus something of a typological gesture; the task of *The Networked Wilderness* is to revisit the major figures and texts of the early settlement, seeing how they were caught up with Native American knowledge production and audiences no less than with English or Puritan ones. Broadening the definition of the "history of the book" will help produce a critical vision for scholars and a reading practice for students less subject to binaries that have often driven North American colonial studies in the past: orality and literacy, objects and subjects, technology and nature. In what follows I propose a theoretical reframing of the question of the production of textuality that addresses how literatures of encounter are analyzed and taught by amplifying the analysis of the material, sonic, and performative contexts of the production of social experience and knowledge in the seventeenth century.

Orality and the History of the Book

The material context of the production of early New England texts, particularly those printed after the establishment of the Cambridge press, has a long historiography. David Hall, whose work anchors the field, has claimed that one of the advantages of studying the northern colonies is that "the whole of New England constituted a reasonably uniform language field, a circumstance that helps us understand how deeply the culture was bound up with print as a medium of communication."[21] But the assumption that there was a common language gives us a key to new ways of approaching the heterogeneity of American information culture. After all, as other scholars of New England communication, such as Sandra Gustafson and David Murray, have observed, we can only agree with this assumption if we forget about the many Algonquian dialects heard and, in the case of discovery and travel narratives, transcribed by early visitors to the region. In the colonies one could hear Dutch, French, even Spanish, linguistic presences that signaled the context of imperial competition within which early New England evolved.

As the history of the book has developed, it has begun to confront over-laps and interactions among uses of sound, manuscript, and print, finding it necessary to describe the complex ways in which these coeval strains of repre-sentation influence or compete with each other.[22] In the case of New England, this has meant beginning to trace the role of nontextual media, from gestures to beadwork to sound, in both European media systems and indigenous sys-tems of communication. But there is an understandable resistance to a too-inclusive definition of what constitutes book history. Robert Darnton, one of the pillars of the field, defines book history in terms that ground it distinctly in printed and bound texts: beginning with "how texts became embedded in paper as typographical signs and transmitted to readers as pages bound in books," book historians study "all aspects in the production and diffusion of the printed word." In his published research Darnton tends in fact to go well beyond this definition.[23] Yet his expression implies a good question: how can extending the history of the book be justified when its definitional restrictions to the world of print culture would seem to be the source of its strength? Even after widening the definition to include predominantly material, inscribed forms, should one not stop there, at the old divide between oral and inscribed, or perhaps the more nuanced distinction between phonographic and semasio-graphic communication?

One of the avatars of the history of the book, the influential bibliographic theorist D. F. McKenzie, answered this question with a fearless "no." Bibliogra-phy, McKenzie argued,

> is the discipline that studies texts as recorded forms, and the processes of their transmission, including their production and reception. . . . What the word "texts" . . . allows . . . is the extension of present practice to include all forms of texts, not merely books or . . . signs on pieces of parchment or paper. . . . Beyond that, it allows us to describe not only the technical but the social processes of their transmission. . . . But such a phrase also accommodates what in recent critical theory is often called text production, and it therefore opens up the application of the discipline to the service of that field too.

For McKenzie, "texts" include "verbal, visual, oral, and numeric data, in the form of maps, prints, and music, of archives of recorded sound, of films, videos, and any computer-stored information, everything in fact from epigra-phy to the latest forms of discography."[24] Only memory itself seems to be left out here—and not definitionally. McKenzie backs up this argument in an important essay that models the study of communication in colonial encoun-ters, "The Sociology of a Text: Oral Culture, Literacy, and Print in Early New Zealand."[25]

While agreeing with McKenzie that it is important to describe "the ways in which the form that transmits a text to its readers or hearers constrains the production of meaning," historian of the book Roger Chartier offers the caveat that the "identification of morphological traits that organize reading practices is . . . necessary but not sufficient to describe cultural differences adequately." Chartier asks us to reconstruct and keep in mind what he describes as "schemes of perception and judgment inherent to each community of readers."[26] Such "inherence" is not available for study in early America. The early settlers and the Algonquians they lived with were communities of readers whose decoding practices were undergoing change. It is impossible to decipher definitively how either of these interpretive communities would read Native signification— indeed, the boundaries of these communities were precisely the subject of the contest. Furthermore, subdivisions within each "community of readers," such as class position, social role, and gender, affect both reading habits and the way in which readerly communities change in response to what is difficult to read. Both within and between representational networks, enunciations from the early settlement period bear witness to morphing literacies—and may call into question the rubric of literacy as such.[27]

McKenzie's influence, like that of Chartier, is pervasive in textual studies, and like Chartier's, his formulations seldom come under serious critique. In part, in McKenzie's case, this is because his radical reconfiguration of bibliography embraces a breathtaking range of analytical ground. This utopian inclusiveness is understandably appealing both to scholars of McKenzie's time who were frustrated with the parochialism of bibliography and to those who, like me, were educated under the (not always compatible) lights of poststructuralism and interdisciplinarity. Like most scholars following in McKenzie's path, I take energy from his insistence on a broad definition of the sociology of the text. But two important weaknesses in his argument reveal the persistence of an ideological blind spot that separates Native American studies and the history of the book. These are McKenzie's approach to the concept of authorial intention and the surprisingly restrictive conclusions he draws from his analysis of indigenous communications spheres.[28] I dwell on these examples because they show the persistence of the oral–literate divide even in methodologies that confront colonial inequalities.

McKenzie offers to help us over an old impasse by suggesting that the idea of authorial intention, rather than being either deified or deprecated, may be used as a "speculative instrument" to reconstruct how authors approached a literary marketplace. We may not be able to know for certain what an author was thinking, but we have a good idea of what she faced in the literary marketplace and what rhetorics were available, safe, or dangerous.[29] But McKenzie's tour de force analyses of William Congreve exemplify one of the shortcomings of his approach. Though usefully modifying the question of authorial intention as one that should serve a more speculative purpose—one of several tools for characterizing the cultural milieu and effects of a given work—McKenzie ultimately recenters the concept, which he sees as proven by the material practices of certain authors. Like Congreve, writers such as William Blake, Walt Whitman, and William Morris micromanaged the production of their texts; as a result, visual details of layout, font selection, choice of materials (paper, ink), and use of illustration can reasonably be attributed as authorial decisions meant to shape the reception of their texts. There is no doubt that extending the concept of authorship into the material construction of the text can produce spectacular interpretive results because it adds new material layers to analyze and because it reassures us that intention matters. But this deprecates, by such a focus on exemplary literary laborers, the majority of printed texts. Most of those emerging from the settlement period treated here, for example, were products of a collaboration among, or at least the aggregate work of, writers, typesetters, booksellers, and others along the way. The same is certainly true of the book you hold right now.

Publication is choral. Regardless of one's understanding of the author function, and no matter how present the author is at the scene of printing, books have always needed a series of producers, each of whose power can predominate over reception or deployment at different moments in the production, circulation, and consumption process.[30] One may certainly speak of the accents of a text, or ask Foucault's question, "What is this speaking doing?" without being required to attribute intention to any particular player in the appearance of that text. I follow the lead of other early Americanists in attempting to trace the multiple channels of contextual signification at work in settlement texts, their involvement in both metaphysical and material politics in the Atlantic world. This is particularly important—and necessarily speculative by the dominant standards of historical evidence—when the collaboration in the production of a text involves Native Americans. Such collaboration is present, and problematic, in a range of forms, from the reproduction (and possibly the ventriloquization) of Native oratory to, in a more complicated way, Native participation in English communications acts. As we will see, Wampanoag sachem Massasoit's illness, Edward Winslow's report of it in *Good Newes from New-England,* Roger Williams's negotiations with the Narragansetts, and his book *A Key into the Language of America* all had audiences that included London powerbrokers who made decisions about charters, boundaries, and investment.[31]

Such a concern for the Native interest in textual studies would seem to be addressed by McKenzie's own famous use of indigenous politics as a test case for his expansion of the definition of bibliography. In "The Sociology of a Text: Oral Culture, Literacy, and Print in Early New Zealand," he analyzed the production of the Treaty of Waitangi, made in 1840 between forty-six Maori leaders from northern New Zealand and the British government.[32] In a powerful reconstruction of the establishment of Western print literacy in New Zealand, this essay demonstrates both the irreconcilable interpretations possible of a document whose main feature is spectacular consent between two cultures and the complexity of the document's interpretation within those cultures.

McKenzie insists that his main story is "the impact of literacy" (meaning nineteenth-century English literacy) on the Maori. The treaty and its afterlife represent "a prime example of European assumptions about the comprehension, status, and binding power of written statements and written consent on the one hand as against the flexible accommodations of oral consensus on the other."[33] With an eye to shaping current debates about Maori sovereignty, McKenzie pursues a line of argument now familiar in many accounts of European colonialism. As with the powerful example of the Spanish *Requerimiento* in the sixteenth century,[34] the fixity of print as a medium of reproducible consent is imagined to be the chief technology of domination, functional not because of the practices that sustain interpretation, but because of the nature of the material medium itself.[35] McKenzie tells us that "manuscript and print, the tools of the Paheka [English], persist, but words which are spoken fade as they fall" (125). To describe oral consent as invariably flexible, like describing cultures as wholly oral or literate, is not only inaccurate, but potentially dangerous. Flexibility and persistence are products of a social relation and its reproduction, not inherent qualities of a technology. The paradox McKenzie enacts here is one that is pervasive in academic analyses of encounter: the oral–literate dichotomy that structures McKenzie's understanding of indigenous performance culture simultaneously functions to evacuate the complexity of indigenous communication and to make a progressive political point about the parameters it will be necessary to place on Westerners' insistence on written performances in negotiations over sovereignty.

McKenzie's lectures on the sociology of text were fueled by his objections to the reorganization of the British Library in the early 1980s. In this context, the tension between oral and written forms highlights a key issue linking bibliographic theory with cultural study more broadly. First, archival preservation requires a physical base, which helps fulfill the ideals of universal access that shape the justification for, if not the reality of, archives. Oral preservation often involves a kind of social authentication in order to get access to information restricted by role, gender, or other factors. This may be particularly pronounced in the postcolonial indigenous situation (about which anthropologists have written extensively), but it is true in Western culture as well.[36] Furthermore, the archive is supported by and answerable to two formations that insist on its materiality: the nation-state (the British Library, Library of Congress, National Endowment for the Humanities [NEH], Social Sciences and Humanities Research Council of Canada [SSHRCC]) and the academy. The space between noninscriptive signification practices and the history of the book opens up at a practical level where it closes at a theoretical one. McKenzie's theory about what should be preserved allows us to understand the preservation of culture in a nonnational, nonmaterial way, but his application of it, based on the great divide of orality and literacy, protects the archive by establishing the irretrievability, the unpreservability of, the oral. Such a theory, however much it may insist on the primacy of oral utterance as a viable form of political representation, keeps in place the idea that such utterance is flexible and thus not legally equivalent to written utterance. As long as presence in an archive qualifies an utterance for verification, reality, and history, what is preserved is not just materials, not only books or treaties, but a way of thinking about consent and about evidence that hampers the establishment of just human relations.[37]

Fascinatingly, the undertheorization of materiality in the history of the book stems in part from a disciplinary gap that began in the same moment of ferment that brought about McKenzie's field-shaping contributions. In the mid-1980s, anthropologists were dismantling the Ongian notion that a culture could be characterized as oral or literate, a dichotomy they termed the "autonomous approach" to literacy. In mounting their attack, scholars such as Brian Street and Ruth Finnegan reframed the terms of inquiry with respect to the physical means and contexts of communication in ways startlingly similar to McKenzie's. Seeking out the ideological contexts of situated literacies, one current practitioner of this approach writes that the

> generalizations that the ideological model of literacy seeks are thus systemic: the model explores how literacy interacts with social categories and communicative processes, and how changes from preliteracy to literacy go hand in hand with changing social dynamics. These generalizations are thus qualitatively different from the universalistic statements that proponents of the autonomous model have traditionally sought.[38]

Substitute "sociology of texts" for the "ideological model of literacy," and swap W. W. Greg–inspired bibliographic approaches for the autonomous model of literacy, and this could be a page from McKenzie. Alongside McKenzie's sociology of the text evolved a parallel anthropology of the text.

There are examples of English uses of inscribed texts from the colonial period that elegantly exemplify the claims of such anthropology. In 1646, passengers en route to England from Massachusetts threw Robert Child's petition to the General Court overboard during bad weather, afraid that the tempest was a sign of God's disfavor for the manuscript. Imagining a particularly tough reviewer, settler Puritans demonstrated in this instance the instability of texts written with alphabetic literacy when faced with a reception field that included at least one supernatural reader.[39] That a printed or written text could be subject to destruction was an option jealously guarded by Englishmen. Books possessed a more animated agency than they generally do today.

In *The Dove and the Serpent* (1614), an English tract that theorizes Christian communication, the author, drawing on a long tradition of distrust of the written word, suggests that spoken transactions might well be better than written ones as a result of these potentially different performances for different audiences:

> To negotiate with men by letters, unless in cases wherein he would advantage himselfe by the reply, is dangerous, uncertaine, and inconvenient. First, because in them he layeth himselfe more open to their Understanding, then in ordanarie Conference, in which his words are altogether Cursorie, and cannot possibly be marked, or considered, but by glimpses, and in passage. Secondly, because they doe oftentimes miscarrie, and by reason of that, may many wayes proove hurtfull and prejudiciall. Lastly, because they are subject to distortions, wrestings, depravations, and inconstructions.[40]

A reader today might add "deconstructions." The metaphors here—sight and movement, "by glimpses, and in passage"—call attention to performative aspects of speech that are useful precisely because of their ambiguity. In everyday speech, it is possible to be ambiguous, and by way of an interlocutor's response, to discern his or her concern or level of familiarity with a topic. More important, this passage suggests, "wrestings" of the meanings of written texts are inevitable: a book is a support inscribed both with a material sign and within a series of situated interpretations.

Anthropologists working on literacy often cannot or do not analyze material textual features that bear crucially on transitions in indigenous uses of sign systems.[41] Furthermore, the insistence that the recognition and unseating of a Western valorization of print literacy "opens the door for the study of hitherto devalued literacy traditions in their own right"—a persistent fantasy of anthropological and historical scholarship—simply reinstates the problem of boundary-driven analyses of cultural literacy.[42] While Stephen Greenblatt may be wrong about the veil that has been drawn over enunciation between the past and the present, he persuasively suggests that the idea of "traditions in their own right" may be the knotty root of the difficulty of giving an account of literacies that enables fusion or tolerance at the junctures of representational fields. In other words, what if, in negotiating for resources with other groups of people, we posit that communication is not to be trusted as transparent, that consent is an ongoing process, and that literacy is not an ideal or an achievement but an evolving, uneven site of struggle for power? Such a framework might displace the ideal of understanding in favor of a more provisional, patient, and humane set of expectations about negotiating.

Media and Colonial Native Studies

Ethnohistorical accounts of the northeastern woodlands provide much of the foundation of the chapters that follow. A series of major rewritings of colonial history were published in the 1980s, including Neal Salisbury's *Manitou and Providence,* James Axtell's collections of essays on east coast Algonquian societies, and James Merrell's *The Indians' New World,* to name just a few. These studies blended anthropological and historical approaches to emphasize the complex social history of indigenous America, and they built on work by Robert Berkhofer, Francis Jennings, Anthony F. C. Wallace, and others in Native history more broadly. More than simply sketching Native cultures with new depth or uncovering lost tribal histories, these works trace the complex ways in which Native, European, and African societies influenced each other during the colonial era. At the same time, ethnohistory challenged boundaries within the academy, blending methods from history, anthropology, and religious studies, and breaking down distinctions between Indian history and colonial history.[43] These works often explicitly or implicitly supported Native groups' efforts toward gaining federal recognition or funding.

Telling a more integrated story of what Axtell termed "the invasion of America" sometimes meant suggesting a complex way of understanding indigenous media systems. Whether in Daniel Richter's accounts of the slow process by which English colonists learned and began to practice the negotiating protocols of the Native northeast, or Richard White's argument for the existence of a middle ground of information sharing in the Great Lakes, ethnohistorians demanded that their readers imagine colonial communications differently. The chapters that follow are inspired by ethnohistorical work on several levels. Axtell's insistence that an anxiety about Indian movements, a desire to control American lands and peoples, shaped English culture in the

New World roots my understanding of the role of communications systems in colonization. Germaine Warkentin's argument that wampum might be studied using the techniques of the history of the book inspires my first chapter, while Colin Calloway's insistence on the compatibility of English and American medical cultures enables the second. David Silverman's complex accounts of the selective adaptation of religious communicative forms by the Wampanoag of Martha's Vineyard enables my argument in the third chapter for a new approach to handling sources like Roger Williams's *A Key into the Language of America*.

Still, *The Networked Wilderness* is not quite an ethnohistory of colonial communication. I focus on questions of deception or epistemological uncertainty in part because I think it is important to extend our knowledge of the layers of deception that shape European narratives but also to acknowledge that Natives can lie and deceive like other humans. Axtell, for example, maintains that Native speakers could not deceive in this way—specifically as a result of cultural difference based on the properties of media. While Natives were "notoriously taciturn among Europeans," he writes, nonetheless "as peoples without writing they believed in the inviolability of the spoken word, particularly in public councils and treaties."[44] The examples of Native deception discussed in the following chapters suggest that, outside councils and treaty negotiations, this is an overstatement—and a potentially dehumanizing one.

Perhaps more important, I want to emphasize the kinds of reading practices we must bring to early American media rather than the delineation of a factual, chronological history. Those practices involve the material instantiation of communication as much as its ethnohistorical context; they also involve thinking transtemporally about media. During the debates about how to build the exhibits at the National Museum of the American Indian (NMAI), curator Paul Chaat Smith (Comanche) pointed out that if it's hard to tell truth from fiction when studying people in the past, it's no less difficult to know it in the present when talking to Indians about their history. "This is the dilemma," he wrote, "We want to tell our stories, but we don't always know our stories."[45] Smith argued that, with this in mind, the NMAI should be as much about what we do not or cannot know, and about how we know what we know, as about a known history of colonial violence. *The Networked Wilderness* is made possible by ethnohistory but takes Smith's suggestion to heart in its narrative. The final chapter in particular tries to bring the realms of deception and simulation from the past into dialogue with those of the present by discussing the connections between colonial documents and a modern tribal museum.

Performance theory is an important methodological tool that historians of the book, particularly Sandra Gustafson and Matthew Brown, have recently brought into dialogue with ethnohistory.[46] Performance theory offers tools for thinking about the new questions we might ask about the book, broadly defined. Judith Butler, following Jacques Derrida, makes an argument that connects the material history of communication to the relations that hold between performance and production. She writes that "performativity cannot be understood outside of a process of iterability, a regularized and constrained repetition of norms. And this repetition is not performed *by* a subject; this repetition is what enables a subject and constitutes the temporal condition for the subject." (An individual, if not a subject per se, does actually perform repetitions of norms in the sense of participating in the convening of the congregation, or treaty body, or jury, that constitutes the spatiotemporal condition of performance. As performers we know what it is like to be in the audience, and we respond accordingly.) "This iterability," Butler extrapolates,

> implies that "performance" is not a singular "act" or event, but a ritualized production, a ritual reiterated under and through constraint, under and through the force of prohibition and taboo, with the threat of ostracism and even death controlling and compelling the shape of the production, but not . . . determining it fully in advance.[47]

Much like a publication sphere, then, seen as a spatial construct, the place of performance constitutes a momentarily stable and readable ground for communication. Henri Lefebvre points out, "Spatial practice ensures continuity and some degree of cohesion. In terms of social space, and of each member of a given society's relationship to that space, this cohesion implies a guaranteed level of *competence* and a specific level of *performance.*"[48] One of the ways out of the orality–literacy labyrinth is by approaching the analysis of moments on a spectrum of publication in space and through performance. The question then becomes how to reconstruct the materiality of oral performance, and following this, to account for the audience as a producer. Then the same terms that may be used to talk about aural authorship as a dynamic of audience and performer may be used to analyze, for example, a circle of manuscript readers, for whom "authorship was a civil or social space whose authority derived from the collective 'poetics of exchange' set up by the circulation of the text in a select social circle," rather than a single, autonomous "author."[49]

The places in which communication happened—whether in the hot, crowded space of a Wampanoag house or around an English Maypole—become a part of the analysis here. Spaces become understood as places through representational contests no less than through violence or formal exchange. How people live in a space, their social experience of it, affects the way they represent that space as a place to others. At the same time, that representation of a person's place is productive—this is most visible today in the case of a place like Orlando, Colonial Williamsburg, or other tourist locales. But it was no less the case in English depictions of Native land as wilderness or of their own American towns as English. The complex relationship between representations and material forces involved in the making and taking of space offers an analytical field in which to explore how "space commands bodies," as Henri Lefebvre writes, "prescribing or proscribing gestures, routes, and distances to be covered."[50] Such a focus brings the analysis of writing systems and other visual codes into a mutually informing relationship not only with ritual expectations, but also with the material limitations of a place, including climate, orientation, difficulty of travel, capacity for human presence, and other physical resources.

Algonquian wampum, for example, when thought about as making meaning within certain performative spaces, could be understood as operating like a book at certain times and between rather than within particular cultures. Wampum's meaning, as a fulcrum of treaty negotiations or intercultural compromise, was generated from cultural contact no less than from the scarcity of the shells of which it was made or the labor of the women who crafted it. Other indigenous North American semiotic systems fit this definition, too: totem poles, ritual tokens, and possibly but not necessarily lithographic inscriptions or paintings.[51]

Native American places, often described as wastelands or ciphers in European narratives, had to be produced as negative or empty space. At other times they are described as transparently communicative spaces, for example, during treaty ceremonies. All of these spaces should be read as part of the communications networks of Native America—but with a grain of salt. Lefebvre warns, "It turns out on close examination . . . spaces made (produced) to be read are the most deceptive and tricked-up imaginable."[52] As Europeans often found out too late, this was as true of certain Native spaces as it was of theirs. There are, of course, spaces in between these poles of negative (hidden) and positive (intended to be read), depending on the competency of the reader—or the reliability of one's guide through a landscape always filled with traps.[53]

Indigenous stories, too, contain representations of real places; they are, among other things, real and continuing claims for power, place, and sovereignty. Michael Elliott elegantly links storytelling to power over territory:

> Ever since Thomas Jefferson in his *Notes on the State of Virginia* quoted Mingo chief Logan's speech lamenting the loss of his family, U.S. writers have frequently positioned American Indians to proudly display a unique, storied

landscape—an affirmation of American exceptionalism that takes little note
of the actual historical claims of Native peoples, claims that could disrupt
the national legitimacy of the United States. It has always been easier for
non-Indians to weep for Logan than to confront the possibility of tribal
sovereignty.[54]

Taking seriously the place from which a certain notion of space is articulated,
then, has ongoing implications for property and sovereignty claims.

Elliott's insight is inspired by a rich and contentious conversation in
Native American scholarship and politics that implicates scholarly method in
cultural sovereignty and revitalization efforts. For some participants in this
conversation, the use of indigenous epistemologies is a key strategy in rebuilding Native communities, irrespective of the political model on which such communities are built. Others go so far as to see it as essential in establishing what
they hope will be Native American sovereignty or nationalism. For still others,
a synthesis of Western and indigenous evidentiary and analytical schemes offers
a powerful position from which to critique the romanticisms and violences
of each.[55] There is little question that, as Elliott suggests, Western ways of
knowing as practiced in the U.S. academy have sometimes helped keep Native
stories outside the pale of sovereignty negotiations. But, especially at a moment
when much of American studies is questioning the idea of the nation, the
question of Native nationalism is a controversial one. The history of Puritan
studies itself, and early American studies more broadly, has been shaped by a
nationalist dynamic. Histories of early America for a long time either sought
the exceptionalism of the United States or contested such a focus. Cultural
nationalism may be a key strategy for Native American decolonization, and its
use by tribal scholars may well be essential.[56]

In studying English and Amerindian contact I am equally interested in the
question of how to contain the potential violences of nationalism. The English
colonists did not lack for cultural nationalism—one they felt necessary to their
survival as an oppressed population living in a wilderness they did not understand—even if they disagreed with the political order ruling that nation at the
time. The role of academics in relation to cultural nationalism is of concern
here, more than the unquestionably salutary programs for spiritual and language revitalization or research and historical preservation in tribal communities. My stress is on method, asking in what ways might early American studies
be pursued that will not simply restate old notions of historical causality and,
by so doing, reinforce racist evidentiary regimes. History must be written using
different evidence and different methods when indigenous North Americans
are part of the story.[57]

The chapters that follow employ a method that may feel odd to some readers, mixing ethnohistorical, bibliographic, and literary-critical strategies. Prioritizing the question of how meaning is made across heterogeneous systems operating within the same space, they ask similar questions about the uses of the literary in gestural human life that they ask about how text inscribed on the page can be considered performative. Might the function of lineation—commonly used to segregate languages in phrase books—be more complex in Williams's *A Key into the Language of America,* given its thematic interest in Native communications technologies? In Morton's *New English Canaan,* how does the use of marginal glosses throughout the text bolster or contend with his arguments about the Puritans' glossing "on a false texte," so crucial to his claims about literacy in that book (see Figures 1 and 2)?

Here the performative elements of the text—not just prefaces, dedications, and appendices, but spatial layout, choice of fonts, and paper size—overlap in provocative ways with the spatial approach to oral performances. Reading the

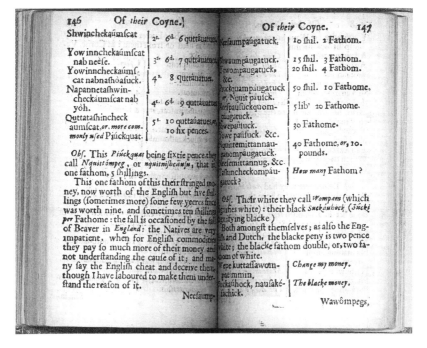

Figure 1. Lineation both separates and links languages. Roger Williams, *A Key into the Language of America,* London, 1643. Photograph courtesy of the Newberry Library, Chicago, Illinois.

negative spaces of meaning-making, even the making of negative space, both in discourse and in physical bodies or places, can bridge the gap in our discussions of material and oral communications techniques and the construction and reproduction of social hierarchies and social justice.[58]

The Networked Wilderness hopes to integrate the study of the physical text with literary analysis and to break down the separation of indigenous studies from the history of the book. To do so means engaging the implications of dissolving orality and literacy into a continuous topography or spectrum rather than thinking of them as a series of overlapping but always distinct cognitive categories or habits. The chapters that follow are just a start, a suggestion for how we might teach and write from a broader conceptualization of the communications technologies, ritual environments, and imaginary audiences through which colonization took, and takes, place.

Networks

The readings that follow move continuously across the fields of the seventeenth-century physical book (typography, paper, morphology, layout) and the material context of communicative performance in northeastern woodlands Native societies (including oratory, dance, animal imitation, path making, and a range

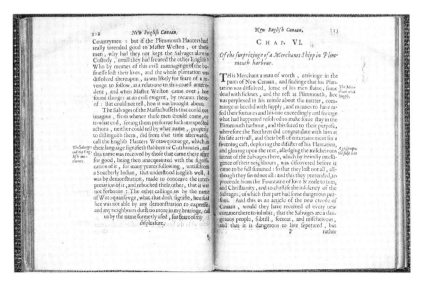

Figure 2. Marginal glosses flock around Thomas Morton's *New English Canaan*, Amsterdam, 1637. Reproduced by permission of The Huntington Library, San Marino, California.

of inscriptive practices). From the Dutch print culture context of Morton's *New English Canaan* to the text layouts of John Underhill's *Newes from America* and Mourt's *Relation,* settler documents raise tensions in English communications culture by bracketing Native voices at the level of content but granting authority to them visually and diacritically. Books, paths, letters, vistas, ceremonial posts, recipes, body decoration, purges, trees, and animals and their sounds all take on new signifying powers as the English negotiate the well-developed informational trails of the Algonquian east coast at the same time they feel the transatlantic pressure of metropolitan informational modes.[59]

The Networked Wilderness peers around in a series of eccentric spaces: the Maypole, the trap, the beach, the bowel, the Wampanoag house, the path, and modern Native American museums. These were spaces in which knowledge and authority were produced and published. I link them to their representation in a range of European settlement documents and to the space of the page: rhetorics of textual matériel, the dance of typography and textual morphology; and the travel stories of the books themselves, as well as those of their producers. In dialogue with such spaces, the physical places of New England and the social order built there by Native people, Europeans, and creoles were given form, reformatted, revalued, and violently contested. Protestant religious dissenters (particularly those of the Plymouth, Massachusetts Bay, and Providence Plantations settlements) are important to my story in part because their self-conscious theorization of communication allows me to construct a dual narrative: one synchronic, about the seventeenth-century nexus of American Indian and English communications systems, and one diachronic, about ongoing cultural investments in a universalist account of human communication. The genealogy of today's theories of communication includes both post-Reformation theology and a citation of indigenous American representational systems in arguments about language and meaning that has been going on since the earliest European accounts of exploration. Because the Puritans and other dissenters who settled in the northeast actively engaged in debates about equivocation, style, and publication, and because they recorded so much of their experience, their social world offers a fertile environment in which to study communications contests.[60]

Long-standing historical questions are my points of departure: Why did the Separatists and Puritans persecute Thomas Morton so violently? Was Roger Williams an avatar of a particularly American notion of democracy? To what can Puritan strategies of preemptive and excessive violence against Native people be ascribed? The four chapters of *The Networked Wilderness* are built around four publication events: Thomas Morton's Maypole party, Wampanoag sachem Massasoit's bout of constipation in the first year of Plymouth's settlement, Roger Williams's life with the Narragansetts as depicted in *A Key into the Language of America,* and the Pequot War. As the book proceeds, it builds an argument for a reading practice centered around contests over communication.

By rethinking Morton's Maypole in terms of its multiple native audiences—from the Algonquian spectators of the ritual itself to the Dutch publishers and English readers of *New English Canaan*—the first chapter argues that Morton's complaint that the Pilgrims were taking advantage of European illiterates to swell their ranks was a trenchant statement about literacy and power. The Maypole was the axis of a transatlantic argument for a kind of public communication that would include Native literacies. Though he had very different theological ideas from Morton, Edward Winslow was equally concerned with the question of information circulation in Indian country. His spectacular curing of Wampanoag chief Massasoit's constipation suggests that, like the Maypole but in different ways, medical treatment, feces, and cooking functioned as capillary mechanisms between Algonquian and English meaning-systems. Chapters 1 and 2 rely on ethnohistorical and archaeological accounts of Native life in southern New England in finding indigenous audiences for European publication events and in reading those publications in light of Native contexts.

Chapter 3 begins to complicate the story told in the first half of *The Networked Wilderness.* As with the Maypole and Massasoit's constipation, reading the material properties of the pages of Williams's *A Key into the Language of America* together with the communications protocols of the Narragansetts he wrote about helps us better appreciate Williams's complex religious and political logic. When we reflect on the fact that Williams's text has served as the evidentiary foundation for accounts of Native life in the early colonial period, we are pushed to expand the parameters of this publication event into the present. Williams's text thematizes Native movement and systems of communication and in doing so calls attention to the standards of evidence by which knowledge of Indians is constructed. It relentlessly suggests that the kind of cultural coherence on which Thomas Morton's appeal rests and the benignity of civility modeled by Winslow's writing are illusions. The flexibility and the ability to manipulate equivocation that Williams found fascinating in Narragansett social systems can help us reassess current approaches to studying the indigenous past.

The final chapter attempts to put that reassessment into practice by examining the relay between the Pequot War and today's controversies over tribal recognition and reservation gaming. The multimedia combat techniques that Algonquians used were bewildering and exhilarating to English opponents.

Such a multimedia onslaught, though difficult to transcribe, offered a chance to show mastery over indigenous systems. Yet such attempts were not always successful; it was hard to tell who was a Pequot and who wasn't, sometimes even who was English and who wasn't. In the recent resurgence of the Mashantucket Pequot tribe, fueled by casino gaming, recognition has become a familiar ground of contest. Current representations of the war by the tribe's Mashantucket Pequot Museum and Research Center reveal a present-day use of multimedia and simulacra of the kind that frightened William Bradford and John Underhill: one that now, as then, unsettles the Pequots' neighbors' ontologies of property, history, and truth. These retellings of contact events as publications help us trace the relationship between sociopolitical belonging and media literacy, offering a reconstruction of the uncertain, negotiated state of delivery mechanisms for social order then and now.

This way of repositioning questions about colonial encounters has important pedagogical and political implications. *The Networked Wilderness* speaks less to what Natives were thinking than to what kinds of information technology might have been recognized as meaningful and how that recognition might have eased or jammed transmission. Considering indigenous representation through the lens of the means of its production—the full range of material and performative means, at each stage of the making of a text, from the ceremony to its reporting in printed texts—gives modern students a chance to use their experience of the density of their own (explicitly networked, multimedia, heterosynchronous) encoding and decoding practices to help read what might have been happening in the southern New England woods and beyond in the early modern era.

Native American and English encounters in American space took place within a continuous informational topography that forced all interlocutors to contemplate communications systems *as* systems. Often parasitically, rather than volitionally, this state of ongoing contamination brought changes to those systems despite their frequent characterization in current scholarship as structurally independent—as oral and literate.[61] Reconceptualizing sonic and inscribed representation as a spectrum, rather than as polar or as modifiers of the term "culture," allows us to bridge the methodological gap between the history of the book and Native American studies. From a historical standpoint, the pre–printing press settlement period can be seen as one of extraordinary fertility for the study of communications systems in America. But to see it as such, at the same time, is to address a set of persistent difficulties in the treatment of Native agency by American literary studies—and by extension to reshape the role of academic authority in speaking about shared American pasts.

One

Native Audiences

Thomas Morton's Maypole, at the plantation he called Ma-re Mount, once served as an axis of revelry and outrage. First Natives and ambitious fur traders danced around it, then angry Puritans circled it, closing in to destroy it. Once it took narrative form in Morton's *New English Canaan* (1637), it began a career as an axis not in space but in time for at least two ongoing stories and their successive tellers. For students of Native American culture, Morton's work is considered one of the most reliable accounts of contact-era northeastern woodlands societies. In this historical ethnography, the Maypole ceremony stands as an unspoken ideal of ethnic harmony and nonviolent, cross-cultural curiosity. For American literary history, Morton's story has been a powerful one, drawn on by writers from Washington Irving to Robert Lowell, Morton's persecution and complaint seeming to voice the struggle of an imaginative writer against a politicized, unironic publishing regime. Morton's invocation as part of a story that authors have told about themselves, fashioning themselves for the literary marketplace, has helped bolster teleological critical readings of the development of American literature. The inevitable theme of American imaginative writing, such readings imply, is an ongoing confrontation between carnivalesque democratic liberalism and prudish aristocratic conservatism.

Morton's appeal changes when it is resituated in the context of the production and reception of *New English Canaan* by three audiences: in England, in the Native American eastern woodlands, and in the Dutch printing world of fugitive English writers.[1] In form, this chapter will join the Maypole dance, taking hold of the ribbons of evidence about each of these three audiences in turn, joining and then backing away from the interpretive carnival Morton's work has generated. Bringing the history of the book to bear on Morton's text, those who teach texts by Morton and his nemesis William Bradford can begin to move beyond Hawthornian comedy-versus-prudery readings of American cultural production. As a result, a different, more sophisticated sense of what colonists felt was at stake when they wrote about themselves and America emerges. Morton's Maypole and his *New English Canaan,* both of which explicitly raised issues of public communication and literacy in the northern settlements, can be used instead to sketch out a conflict over information cultures and social power in early New England.

The tension between Thomas Morton and both the Pilgrims (at Plymouth) and the Puritans (at Massachusetts Bay) has been an enduring, productively controversial episode for cultural historians of New England. What made these religious dissenters pursue Morton so violently? Scholars have pointed to Morton's paganism as a psychological threat and his fur-trading with Natives as an economic one. Yet the dent he made in Plymouth's economic interests was minor, and the psychic problems Morton's merrymaking posed to a supposedly blunt, humorless Pilgrim leadership provoked one of the longest and wittiest sections in William Bradford's *Of Plymouth Plantation.*[2]

This chapter argues that while Morton's poems were important, it was more particularly his mode of presenting them that constituted the core of his challenge to the Pilgrims. Religious leaders tried to exert a stern censorship over communication in all forms in New England, and this conditioned early colonial culture in profound ways.[3] Publishing something in the seventeenth century, we have come to understand, had a meaning broader than its print-bound connotations today—it included posting or proclaiming documents in a public place. This was the method Morton first chose to publicize his densely allusive poetry.

For Bradford and the Puritan settlers' other leaders, a centralized communications structure was the foundation of a sustainable community, but technologies of communication in early New England were diverse. They included posted manuscript messages, letters, oral proclamations (usually from the pulpit), printed texts (usually from Europe), song, and word of mouth (often during commercial transactions). Diaries and journals that might be considered private today were often shared, family Bibles were used to record lineage, and it was not uncommon for worshippers to memorize and transcribe sermons. Settlers invented and adapted a host of methods for communicating with

American Indians, from using translators to drawing pictograms or consulting language guides.[4]

Religious leaders among the settlers, as eager to escape the censorship of England as to establish a community of saintly worship, constantly struggled to keep these technologies under their control. They seldom succeeded thoroughly.[5] Morton's liberties—both in form and content—struck at the heart of this mechanism of social power. What the settlers described as Morton's rebellious immorality was in fact one expression of his self-inscription in international intellectual currents, a priority that would become clear in *New English Canaan*.[6] This account extended the challenge that the Maypole poems began and, within a transatlantic print sphere, dramatized the episode at Morton's Ma-re Mount as a collision of ideas about communication. As my analytical dance around the Maypole hopes to show, the book served as a stage for a contest over communication and colonization that involved at least three systems—English, Native American, and Dutch.

"Their Postures That So Much Bewitch"

The historical outline of Morton's involvement with the Pilgrims and the Puritans is an essential starting ground.[7] Thomas Morton came to New England in 1625 with a man named Captain Wollaston as one of the partners in a private colonizing venture. Morton was a lawyer and no spring chicken; by best estimates he was over forty years old when he first came to America. (Morton's subsequent revels may sound like an early modern version of a fraternity party at first reading, but they were not the product of mere youthful irreverence in a new land.)[8] Not long after establishing their plantation, Wollaston left for Virginia with most of the plantation's men, whose terms of service he sold once they arrived. Together with the remaining men, Morton expelled the lieutenant who had been left to keep order, took over the plantation himself, and renamed it Ma-re Mount.[9] In the course of developing fur trade connections and exploring his land, Morton began carousing with the Native Americans in the vicinity. He revived old English holidays, beginning with the May Day festival. As one historian has observed, this act implicitly associated his plantation with contemporary English state-sponsored strategies of "conservative cultural revival" that attempted to direct nostalgia for the Elizabethan age into popular opposition to the Puritans.[10] Morton, too, was competitive in the fur trade, boldly outmaneuvering the Pilgrims for furs on the Kennebec River.

Arrested by Plymouth authorities in the spring of 1628, Morton was deported to England, under the official charge of selling guns to the natives. He came back about a year later (since the English officials insisted on demonstrable evidence of his crimes, and there was none) and was soon arrested again by the new Massachusetts Bay colony. Once more banished to England, during the next few years Morton wrote and published *New English Canaan,* an account of his travails, the customs of the Natives, and the natural world of New England. The publication of the book was, in part, a political ploy to support another of his activities during this time—an attempt in 1634 to get the royal Privy Council to revoke the patent for the Massachusetts Bay colony by way of a quo warranto suit against the settlers. Morton served both as a witness and as a solicitor in the suit. After more than a decade, spurred to emigrate by the success of the Puritan revolution, he returned to North America. He was taken prisoner yet again after being denounced by John Winthrop and died shortly after his release from jail.[11]

The colonists used extensive legal acrobatics to get Morton repeatedly into custody; "the very savagery of his treatment at the hands of the Pilgrim fathers and the Puritan magistracy," Michael Zuckerman observes, "suggests that they knew all too well that in his freedom there was something extraordinary at stake."[12] The consensus among historians has been that the extraordinary something was Morton's interference with Plymouth's fur trade. Karen Kupperman points out, "Plymouth could not pay off its debts to its English backers without control of the New England fur trade."[13] This explanation has become the dominant one; even literary critics have assumed the underlying economic rationalism of the Puritans, in part because it seems evident that differences over lifestyle choices could not have been severe enough to warrant the exertions required to deport Morton in Plymouth's difficult early days.

Yet this does not explain why Morton continued to appear to be a threat into his dotage (he was about sixty-nine years old when he was released from jail after Winthrop's accusations). Nor does it explain why in at least one document justifying Plymouth's action Bradford does not emphasize the gun trafficking charge as a factor. Economically, Morton was a small competitor among many others and never came close to making a fortune in the New England trade. But when Morton's Maypole and his narrative about the colony are read in the context of the history of European colonial and indigenous American communications networks and their importance to social power, his incursions loom larger. They emerge as a threat more to delicate and experimental political structures than to the momentary economic competitiveness of Plymouth. Morton's opposition defined itself explicitly by its use of print, literacy, and publication to challenge authority structures built on control over those modes of communication.

Let us think of the Maypole as a publishing venue. Morton himself refers to it as a kind of beacon for traders, but if we see it as a sophisticated communications tool, with poems tacked on for communal reading in a public place, it assumes a different significance. Fourteen years before the first printing press was established in Cambridge, Massachusetts Bay, Morton built a tool for distributing information publicly—and for creating a space of authority for oral proclamations as well—that competed with the Pilgrim leaders' control over local oral and written exchanges. It is significant that Morton deliberately includes the detail that the Maypole was erected with the help of Natives, for they emerge as his touchstone in the claim against Puritan authority: "And upon May-day they brought the Maypole to the place appointed . . . and there erected it with the help of Salvages, that came thether of purpose to see the manner of our Revels" (132). In this and the following two sections, I will move through the different performance environments compressed into this comment about the witnessing of "the manner of our Revels" to map how the audiences of English colonials dealing with Morton, his Algonquian trade partners, and the producers and consumers of *New English Canaan* in the Netherlands might have read this scene.

The most renowned content of the Maypole was a series of allegorical poems, presented as riddles or ciphers. It is unfortunate that more is not known about the way these controversial poems were circulated, beyond their posting on the Maypole. We can assume at least that they were in manuscript until transcribed (or recomposed) in *New English Canaan*. English observers on both sides of the incident point to the presence of the poems on the pole during the May Day ceremony and to the Maypole itself as the locus of Morton's power. John Endicott even took extra trouble at a dangerous time of year to cut the pole down before his settlement party made camp at Salem for the winter.[14] From the standpoint of communications technologies, the life cycle of Morton's poems looks something like this: he first published them in manuscript in (and to help create) a makeshift, negotiated public sphere; in all likelihood he established their validity with an oral performance; and finally, after encountering resistance, he upped the ante by releasing them in an established print sphere—Europe.[15]

Past readings of these poems have focused on their content—certainly the dense intermingling, unprioritized and untypological, of classical and biblical references must have infuriated the plain-speaking, iconoclastic Pilgrim leaders.[16] In composing them, Morton used both an ironic narrative voice and a knowledge of his neighbors' rhetoric to attack their authority. As Hall has emphasized, Puritan preachers at this time increasingly borrowed from popular cultural forms, including sensational poetry and stories, to boost the appeal and the accessibility of their spiritual message. Morton's use of poetry reversed this tactic, creating a poetry that was more difficult to understand, favoring the ludic, nimble reading skills of participants in the revels against those of the not-understanding Puritan leaders.[17] By calling attention to the deliberate construction of this comprehension gap, Morton positioned both the form and the content of his poems as being constitutively at odds with Puritan reading practices.

But he implies an even more radical potential for his poetry as published on the Maypole. David Shields observes of riddle-poems, "Because riddles spoke to a wide audience, all who regarded themselves something more than witless, they invoked a general public. They could be considered the citizenship exam for membership in the republic of letters."[18] This understanding of the relationship between form and audience is evocative for Morton's situation: the riddle could be used simultaneously to set boundaries on wit and on citizenship in his ideal plantation. Significantly, in this case those within the boundaries included a good number of Native Americans. Morton takes pains to point out that the residents of his plantation all knew what the poem meant. In making such a claim, Morton moves from a local reading community to an international one, implicitly relating the development of literacy to both university learning and the ideal of civil participation:

> And this the whole company of the Revellers at Ma-reMount, knew to be the true sence and exposition of the riddle: that was fixed to the Maypole, which the Seperatists were at defiance with? some of them affirmed, that the first institution thereof, was in memory of a whore; not knowing that it was a Trophe erected at first, in honor of Maja, the Lady of learning which they despise; vilifying the two universities with uncivile termes; accounting what is there obtained by studdy is but unnecessary learning; not considering that learninge does inable mens mindes to converse with climents of a higher nature then is to be found within the habitation of the Mole. (137)

Morton's publishing tactic restricts proper interpretation to a specific, deviant sector of New England's settlements—anathema to the Pilgrim leaders' sense of community structure and the flow of information controlled by religious leaders. Control of literacy, and by extension the parameters of interpretation ("the true sence and exposition"), was seen as essential to the survival of a dissenting religious group. Whatever the Natives' actual participation in Morton's community, Morton's positioning of the Native Americans against the Pilgrims in the field of English ideas about literacy is a radical juxtaposition.[19]

New English Canaan makes a complex argument for a plural, literate culture of intellectual exchange, and it makes this argument in part by representing Indians as protoliterate by English standards of the time—as already involved in Morton's world of information circulation. By contrast, the Pilgrim leaders are depicted as manipulating a half-literate set of followers, reinforcing their power by restricting interpretation and making, as one of Morton's marginal notes declares, *"Booke learning despised"* (116). This argument begins early in Morton's book. Performing a linguistic analysis on chosen Algonquian words in comparison to Latin and Greek terms, Morton asserts a common theory of the time: that the "originall of the Natives of New England may be well conjectured to be from the scattered Trojans, after such time as Brutus departed from Latium" (22). Evidence from language and speech performances is significant for Morton, who points out that the dynamics of encounter tend to produce creolization: "this is commonly seene where 2. nations traffique together, the one indevouring to understand the others meaning makes them both many times speak a mixed language, as is approved by the Natives of New England, through the covetous desire they have, to commerce with our nation, and wee with them" (20). Sandra Gustafson reminds us of the intellectual context in which Morton was reading and recording his experience with American languages:

> Speech, too, has its technologies, as Renaissance students of rhetoric knew well. Humanists who sought to recuperate the ancient world developed a shared understanding of "the central role of rhetorical skill and achievement in human affairs." . . . To Europeans in the age of humanistic eloquence, oratory was the most recognizable native speech genre as well as the one most crucial for them to interpret.[20]

Morton also claims that "it seemes originally, [they] have had some litterature amongst them, which time hath Cancelled and worne out of use" (19). "Literature" in this context can only mean an oral tradition, but Morton's explanation of its disappearance is phrased elliptically. "Worne out" evokes a sense of physical decay, as of a manuscript, while "use" implies instead a gradual decline in the social need, consistent with the phases of oral transmission. It is as if Morton were uncomfortable with the idea of speech technologies powerful enough to sustain a tradition almost from the time of Ilium, as he proposes.

An often-cited incident, in which Morton teaches a Native how to read, initiates a more direct undermining of nonconformist Protestant concepts of literacy. Morton structures this attack by building a contrast between the

Native capacity for, desire for, and participation in Morton's linguistic sphere and the dissenters' irresponsible use of theirs—both with the Americans and with their own worshippers. The key in this argument is his use of the *Book of Common Prayer,* which the Separatists rejected. As Morton tells the story, he uses the pronoun "we" to reify what he considers the responsible approach to colonizing "them," the Americans—a binary logic that thus shuts out the Separatists entirely:

> And that wee that use the booke of Common prayer, doo it to declare to them, that cannot reade, what Kytan has commaunded us, and that wee doe pray to him with the helpe of that booke; and doe make so much accompt of it, that a Salvage (who had lived in my howse before hee had taken a wife, by whome hee had children) made this request to mee. . . . That I would let his sonne be brought up in my howse, that hee might be taught to reade in that booke: which request of his I granted; and hee was a very joyfull man to thinke, that his sonne should thereby (as hee said) become an Englishman. (50)

This is a fascinating passage in many ways, from Morton's dramatization of the religious lesson (substituting the Algonquian term "Kytan" for God) to his ventriloquization of an Indian in the act of offering that powerful evidence of successful, beneficent English colonization: demonstration of the belief that language acquisition creates a kind of citizenship. In the context of his larger argument, this passage performs the work of showing Native capacity to learn while simultaneously claiming that Morton's paternalistic, text-based method is one that produces Native desire for Englishness.

Morton spins the tangled political web initiated by Native literacy by deprecating the usual apical stage of mastery, writing proficiency. Instead, his narrative valorizes indigenous skills in oral presentation and readiness to learn English as being potentially as powerful as writing—and as racial qualities that must be properly nurtured.[21] However lackadaisical they may have been about it in practice, in theory the settlers did not resist teaching Natives to read and speak English. But the methods Morton chose, and the rewards of literacy he offered, upset the social hierarchies Protestant English literacy was designed to create.

Making more explicit the significance of the opposition of the Separatists to the use of the *Book of Common Prayer,* Morton later takes on their voice sarcastically: "No, no, good sirs I would you were neere us, you might receave comfort by instruction: give me a man hath the guiftes of the spirit, not a booke in hand" (116–17). The result of rejecting this classic text for spreading

Protestant culture to the uneducated, Morton claims, is that "[b]y these insinuations, like the Serpent they did creepe and winde into the good opinion of the illiterate multitude"; he mentions "these illiterate people" again later in reference to Puritan laymen (117, 175). For Morton, the *Book of Common Prayer* conveyed cultural as much as religious power. Insistence on the Bible alone, from this perspective, put those who were not more widely read at the mercy of their leaders' interpretations. His puns about his own use of the book make reference to the larger sphere of English politics. When Morton says, "[M]ine host . . . used it in a laudable manner amongst his family, as a practise of piety," he implies that the Plymouth settlers are impinging on his religious practice (138). At the same time, by alluding to the rigidly anti-Puritan Archbishop William Laud in the pun, he aligns himself with the home powers against which the Pilgrims were struggling.

New English Canaan is a text that demands acrobatic reading practices capable of interpreting the topography of the page together with dense allusive content. At one point, Morton uses a bibliographical metaphor, the textual gloss (interpretive marginal commentary printed or written alongside an interlocutor's text), to make his literacy case in a slightly different way. A merchant comes ashore to find his plantation burned; the Pilgrims did it, but they blame it on Indians, "deploring the disaster of his Plantation and glozing upon the text, alledging the mischeivous intent of the Salvages there" (113). Morton himself is the victim of the next "glosse upon their malice," when he is arrested in chapter 15 (138). This metaphor makes fun of the Separatists' method of interpreting Scripture but becomes, as it recurs throughout the narrative, a more fundamental accusation that English nonconformists are using the technology of the textual gloss irresponsibly. As we will later see, the interpenetration of visual and textual elements on which Morton's text relies does not stop with the use of such metaphors.

To complete his literacy argument, Morton removes himself from the picture momentarily and contrasts the Puritans and the Americans on the grounds of oral expression. In his discussion of the Americans in "Of Theire Subtilety," Morton praises their politics, tactics, and rhetoric (part 1, chapter 14). The centerpiece of "Of a Battle fought at the Massachussets, betweene the English and the Indians" is an example of powerful Native eloquence, quoted as the words of the sachem of the Passonagessit territories, Chickatawbut, following the defacing of the grave of Chickatawbut's mother by the English (part 3, chapter 3). This speech projects a Native communications culture with an inextricable interplay of visual and verbal inscription. It ascribes to Indian political rhetoric a reliance on the diachronic power of monuments that, reassuringly for his European audience, preserves familiar class distinctions:

> [A] spirit cried aloude (behold my sonne) whom I have cherisht, see the papps that gave thee suck, the hands that lappd thee warme and fed thee oft, canst thou forget to take revenge of those uild people, that hath my monument defaced in despitefull manner, disdaining our ancient antiquities, and honourable Customes: See now the Sachems grave lies like unto the common people, of ignoble race defaced: thy mother doth complaine, implores thy aide against this theevish people, new come hether. (107)

This appeal to public memory is underwritten and authorized by a self-deprecatory distancing of the speaker. The first part of Chickatawbut's speech is reported as a message from this female "spirit," while the significance of the declaration is left open to communal designation, "to have your Councell, and your aide likewise" (107). As such the speech evidences a responsible use of power reminiscent, for European readers, of models from classical antiquity. Morton also points out that in the development and differentiation of vocabulary Americans are meticulous: "the Salvages are significant in their denomination of any thing" (82). Building on these assertions of linguistic and rhetorical competence, Morton finds it telling that the local Native word for Englishmen (which he claims originates in interactions with the Plymouth settlers) is "*Wotawquenange,* which in their language signifieth stabbers or Cutthroates" (112).

By contrast, when the colonial leaders speak, Morton argues, they fail to convince without appealing to fear and uncertainty. He insists that the Plymouth settlers—and by extension, nonconformist worshipers elsewhere—are being manipulated by speakers who, to an educated person, are not convincing:

> Socrates sayes, *loquere ut te videam.* If a man observe these people in the exercise of their gifts, hee may thereby discerne the tincture of their proper calling, the asses eares will peepe through the lyons hide. . . . I will deale fairely with them; for I will draw their pictures cap a pe, that you may discerne them plainely from head to foote in their postures that so much bewitch . . . these illiterate people to be so fantasticall, to take Ionas taske upon them without sufficient warrant. (175)[22]

Here Morton offers remediation, in which his writing translates a deceptive orality: he will "draw" for us readers in the correct "tincture" what is obscured by the oral projections of Separatist orators. (He even uncharacteristically rephrases his own foreign phrases in this section, exemplifying the openness he claims the nonconformists lack.) This argument is crucial to Morton's claims that preaching—the chief power mechanism of the Puritan and Separatist leaders—misleads the illiterate, as compared to the text and community-based experience of literacy seen in the examples of the Maypole and the American boy he claims to have taught to read.

Morton dramatizes the failure of the nonconformist leadership's orality with a Native audience in the story of Master Bubble. Making reference to *Don Quixote,* which had recently and quickly risen to the status of a standard text for European intellectuals, Morton shows his awareness of, even as he activates, a transatlantic circuit for cosmopolitan currents of thought. But once again, he does not simply mock the Pilgrims:

> The poore Salvages being in a pittifull perplexity, caused their Countrymen to seeke out for this maz'd man; who being in short time found, was brought to Wessaguscus; where hee made a discourse of his travels, and of the perrillous passages: which did seeme to be no lesse dangerous, then these of that worthy Knight Errant, Don Quixote, and how miraculously hee had bin preserved; and in conclusion, lamented the greate losse of his goods, whereby hee thought himselfe undone. (128)[23]

Here the "Salvages" take the rational position, while the Pilgrims are quixotic—despite their otherworldly rhetoric, in this "discourse" they attach much value to their worldly goods (which it turned out had not even been harmed by the Natives). Even when restored to safety by the Americans, they are still "maz'd" men, unable to find their way in the physical world, much less the spiritual. Morton concludes the story by saying that when the Indians were exonerated, "the whole Company made themselves merry at his discourse of all his perrillous adventures," suggesting that Master Bubble's speech was laughed "at" rather than "with." As told by Morton, Bubble does things like taking off his pants and putting them on his head to protect himself from arrows—the reader has been laughing at the story all along. The conclusion thus puts readers in sympathy with the Natives, humanizing them, while uncivilizing the Puritans, referring to them as Master Bubble's "tribe" (128).[24]

While the tiny circulation of *New English Canaan* prevented any studied response among the settlers to Morton's claims about Native literacy, the Puritan leaders' reactions to the Maypole and the poems show an awareness of its potential as an alternative publishing space. In a private letter to Sir Ferdinando Gorges justifying their arrest of Morton, for example, Bradford did not stress the official charge of gun trading:

> That which further presseth us to send this party, is the fear we have of the growing of him and his consorts to that strength and height, by the access of

loose persons, his house be a receptacle for such, as we should not be able to restrain his inordinariness when we would, they living without all fear of God or common honesty, some of them abusing the Indian women most filthily, as it is notorious.[25]

Bradford's diction here is in some ways deliberately deceptive. The pronoun "we," as it did in Morton's narrative, establishes a communal norm that is threatened. But Morton ("his") increases to "they" when "loose persons" are added, performing grammatically the population growth Bradford fears at Ma-re Mount. "Loose" here signifies settlers unassociated with any particular plantation and possibly Americans as well, but could also have implied immorality, wantonness.[26] Bradford thus allows the mission to take on moral and political importance without saying so explicitly until the issue of the presence of indigenous women at the plantation is raised. Accusations of interracial sexuality and the presumption that Plymouth should be able to "restrain" Morton ("to restrain his inordinariness when we would") run together in the same sentence. That the activities of Ma-re Mount could be "notorious" was fundamental to the problem. Morton's publishing tactics were working to produce a rumored "inordinariness," the exact nature of which had to be left vague, as a potential, in order to justify taking him by force.

Of Plymouth Plantation, while more witty, exhibits the same semantic struggles to reshape Morton's challenge in moral terms. In his famous description of the Maypole, Bradford moves from drinking to dancing to interracial "frisking," then adds a sentence fragment in an attempt to get at the delusionary quality of this carnival:

> They also set up a maypole, drinking and dancing about it many days together, inviting the Indian women for their consorts, dancing and frisking together like so many fairies, or furies, rather; and worse practices. As if they had anew revived and celebrated the feasts of the Roman goddess Flora, or the beastly practices of the mad Bacchanalians.[27]

Bradford here parries the implied ironic hysteria of the scene he is describing with his own accusatory pun—"fairies" becoming "furies"—but loses control of his pronouns, allowing the Indians to become in readers' imaginations part of the "they" that "had anew revived" heathen celebrations. While Bradford's text parries Morton's accusations both of Pilgrim dullness and ignorance of classical tradition, it dangerously (by its own standards) permits Native Americans to participate in Englishness (however reprehensible) and borders on prurience in its obsession with "riotous prodigality and profuse excess."[28] The threat of Morton's publishing venue called forth a risky response as leaders like Bradford tried to make themselves appear to be more responsible administrators of American systems.

American Audiences

But how much were American Indians participating in Englishness in Morton's revels? And perhaps more important, what would it mean to consider not just the "native" audience of Englishmen to which Morton was writing, but the Native Americans he and the Pilgrims depended on for both food and financial gain as an audience for his Maypole writings? One of the paradoxes of the study of print culture in early New England is that not many people at the time read the texts that have become central to the study of the northeastern contact zone. Morton's work, which was printed in Amsterdam, was not read widely because many copies of the book were confiscated at the docks as a result of English strictures on foreign-printed books in English. Certainly few copies made it to America.[29] It is possible that Morton's American audience for the Maypole festival was larger than the audience in his native England for *New English Canaan.* A consideration of these questions adds another layer to the implications of the Maypole episode and accounts of it, prompting a methodological shift in my argument.

On one level, Morton's inclusion of Natives was at least as much a rhetorical device as it was a recording of a fact, when it came to English literacy. There is unfortunately no known evidence other than Morton's account and panicked reactions from the Pilgrims to suggest the specific ways in which Natives were involved in Morton's literary circle. Morton, according to recent scholars, appears to have had an admirable command of the language of the Algonquians he encountered.[30] It is entirely possible, as he suggests in *New English Canaan,* that Morton delivered orally some version of the poems during the May Day festivities. By his own account quoted above, at one point he shepherded a Native to literacy in English, at least to speaking and reading. (Certainly later it was not uncommon for Native youths to be raised as servants in white households partly for this purpose.) And Jack Dempsey has pointed out that Morton's poems hail a Native audience by including American events such as the devastating sickness brought on by European contact in 1616–19.[31] But as Kupperman observes in *Indians and English,* New World narratives from the exploration and settlement era made a series of conventional arguments that had to balance claims that American Indians were allies and assets with legitimate accounts of the problems they posed. The colonists knew that if they made the Americans out to be completely savage, it "would imply a devastating comment on the American environment and its capability of sustaining complex cultures. . . . The American natives in these early works were ready to be taught, and ripe for study."[32]

One might augment this suspicion about the textual record using Stephen Greenblatt's argument about New World indigeneity, discussed in the Introduction: there is a veil over seventeenth-century indigenous American discourse and identity that should not be lifted; "discard the particular words and you have discarded the particular men." Yet to dismiss the question of the Native audience for lack of evidence would be to repeat a procedure all too common in the history of colonization. Vine Deloria Jr. reminds us that "easy knowledge about Indians is a historical tradition."[33] If the traditional experiential accounts by whites of Native essence are too easy, it is also too easy, and perhaps dangerous, to shut down our critical inquiry at the point Greenblatt and others ask us to, however self-consciously. For all the textual and architectural evidence, the minds of the Puritan settlers are just as closed to us as are those of the Native Americans. As scholars from Perry Miller to Matthew Brown have pointed out, Puritan discourse itself "foregrounds the intangible interaction of readers and texts" and is thus "a project particularly suited to the excessive semiotic energy of New Englanders living in a world of portents and wonders, but one that resists empiricist legitimation."[34]

Restricting an inquiry into indigenous audiences to empiricist standards does justice neither to the political situation of the student of early America nor to the potential of the history of the book to contribute to debates about colonialism. Several recent accounts of early America have offered ways of opening up the dilemma of our dependence on shifty early colonial European descriptions of Indianness. Daniel K. Richter's *Facing East from Indian Country,* for example, uses deconstructive and comparative literary analysis, anthropology, archaeology, and outright fictionalization to capture "stories of North America during the period of European colonization rather than of the European colonization of North America."[35] Joyce Chaplin's *Subject Matter,* a study of technology and the body in early America, offers an analysis of the "invisible bullets" episode in Thomas Hariot's *Briefe and True Report* that is a long-needed counter to Greenblatt's influential reading of the same scene.[36] By noting how Europeans recorded so-called knowledge about American Indians that went beyond, put pressure on, or was uncontainable within European intellectual currents, Chaplin offers an alternative reading practice. Colonial debates over technology and the body are considered as negotiations, rather than simple conquests, triangulating settlers, European scientific discourse, and Native American social systems.

Another approach would take into account the effect of telling Native histories at the present moment from the academic publishing realm. To make methodologies speak to the range of representational possibilities and conceptions of social being, time, and space in the different cultures under study, we can attempt to think and argue from "hybrid conceptual frameworks and spaces in between," as Walter Mignolo puts it.[37] This means not dismissing the debate over Native representation in early seventeenth-century New England as an unresolvable methodological choice between unethical projection and fictionalization in the interests of contemporary politics. Instead, the same attention to performative context must be brought to our own act of analysis that we bring to the study of seventeenth-century contact stories. Rather than attempting to valorize one set of descriptions over another, ranking them by always controversial categories, we might instead privilege how a description functions rather than how accurate it is. Assuming that there is no subjective or objective position with regard to one's culture or another's, the moment and performance of an interpretation of a culture become the important analytical objects.

As Deloria and others insist, the position of academic authority with regard to Native land and cultural property claims is significant because it serves as an authentication mechanism and as a policy resource—not simply as an ambient shaper of culture by way of our teaching or our more popular publications. Academics must ask what was Native enunciation doing, what was European enunciation doing, and what is current scholarly enunciation doing? Such an approach necessarily entails thinking about the production circuit of texts both from the past and in the present: methodologically, it is dependent on the history of the book. Instead of taking as a goal the unspecifiable content of "a more careful attempt to understand the histories, literatures, and perspectives of indigenous Americans," we can start a reformulation of the question of understanding Native American cultures by beginning not with the content of claims about Native life but the techniques of signification that Natives employed.[38] Pursuing the question of Algonquian readings of publication events argues their historical, and by extension legal, equivalence with other forms of knowledge in the North American record.

In the case of the Maypole, the notion of the homograph can serve as a way of beginning to address the question of the links between English and Native American audiences. Literally, a "homograph" is a "word of the same written form as another but of a different origin and meaning," such as "red," which indicates a color in English but a net in Spanish.[39] In what follows, the sense of what "word" means in this definition is broadened but still applies to either a material object (such as a Maypole) or an aggregation of gestures that require such a material context (the Maypole ritual, the ceremonial reading of poems from a sheet of paper). Such objects or gestures must also be recognized as the center of temporary apparent agreement about "meaning," regardless of the actual diversity of interpretations among observers. "Homograph," because it is a term grounded in the materiality of gesture or inscription, is more precise than "homolog," which could still suggest unanswerable metaphysical questions, leaving the problematic critical desire for understanding in place. Homo*graph* insists on the coincidence of inscribed or performed structures (which could conceivably be extended to homo*aurality,* difficult to recover though that would be), against the presumed logical or intellectual isomorphism of the homolog. This concept has potential for structuring the analysis of moments in colonial situations in which communication was clearly happening independent of the assumption of understanding. The homograph as a communicative possibility haunts the belief that a common humanness or, even at its most equivocal, a meaningful connection of some kind that makes rationality imaginable neces-sarily underwrites communication.[40]

What might Morton's Native audience have been? It was presumably a group of Massachusett people, but possibly included travelers, traders, or wan-derers from other eastern woodlands societies—and probably women as well as men. Several scholars have suggested that the Maypole ceremony might have made a certain kind of sense to the Native Americans Morton claims helped him and his men put up the Maypole. What is hazarded here is based on linguistic, anthropological, and historical work on southeastern New England societies of the early seventeenth century (work that is examined in more depth in chapter 3). An obvious initial condition is the recognition that Morton was a comparatively astute European observer of Native culture; it is therefore entirely possible that he was using the May Day event to do pur-poseful culture brokering. Having told us about Native ceremonies that he had witnessed earlier in *New English Canaan,* Morton opens the possibility that, deliberately or not, with the Maypole and other more performative parts of the Maypole ceremony he created the kind of visual and aural affinity that might be called an intercultural homograph. The village-central poles that appear in many east coast Native archaeological sites and in some other European reports form the most obvious homograph with the Maypole (see Figures 3 and 4).

These poles had military, gaming, and other uses associated with assem-bly, always intertwined with spiritual implications. Their specific symbolic capital is difficult to reconstruct, but Kathleen Bragdon points out:

Figure 3. Theodore DeBry's engraving of a Roanoake village depicts ritual posts (B and C). Note the specially shaped listening hut in cornfield (F), designed both to shelter a guard and to gather and focus (or project) sounds. Photograph courtesy of the John Carter Brown Library at Brown University, Providence, Rhode Island.

Many Algonquian-speaking people believe that the Cosmic Axis, located at the center of the world, serves as a pathway through the openings in the layers of the universe. The Axis, like the World Cedar Tree, which emerges through this same pathway, connects the levels of the cosmos. In many recorded rituals, circular pits, lodges, or other ceremonial structures, placed at the point of intersection between earth and sky, and earth and underworld, represent a symbolic entrance to both worlds.

Morton's ceremony, anchored by a pole and occurring on a prominence, may have borne enough similarities to eastern Native social rituals to present itself as this kind of liminal or connecting ritual space.[41]

The buck horns that Morton reports were placed at the top of the Maypole might have evoked Manitou, the Algonquian concept of spirit-power, by way of totemic signification, a system that associated animal names, and sometimes complete transformation into such animals, with particular kinship or social groups within a society. This affinity would have been sophisticated, involving a number of possible metonymies. In terms of gender and sexuality, the buck horns, when combined with the Maypole, form a phenomenological common

Figure 4. Diorama of Cofitachequi, Wateree Valley, as it might have appeared in 1540, featuring village-central poles. Courtesy of the South Carolina State Museum, Columbia, South Carolina. Photograph by Susan Dugan.

ground. The specific totem, the buck, would have carried both sexual or repro-
ductive connotations and gender-role denotations based on food-gathering and
maturity ritual patterns. Morton, whose plantation was engaged in fur trading,
not agriculture, might have been read as attempting to signal his ability to provide for his companions within the bounds of a culture that identified hunting
and trapping with masculinity at all levels of the social hierarchy. Archaeological evidence from a Mohegan site in Connecticut "suggests that deer provided
close to 90 percent of the edible mammal meat in early contact times" in southern New England.[42] Totemic signification here might have been functioning
alongside, rather than overwriting, an economic or material meaning.

This association with providership points to an important potential significance for the Mayday ritual for local Native readings of Morton's claims
to power. It is crucial to remember that Morton's interactions with the Massachusett and other American societies were, according to all observers, keyed
to establishing or defending trade relations. The societies of southeastern New
England kept up a wide-ranging trade and communications network that famil-
iarized them with other, often quite distant communities and their practices.[43]
This network included trading arrangements and sessions with other societies and with Europeans, and it would have been predominantly within that
context that a feast at Ma-re Mount would have been interpreted by Native
participants. Morton and his men would probably also have been dealing with
a subset of Native people with respect to the social roles historical ethnographers have described in eastern Algonquian communities. Since Morton mentions no leaders, it is unlikely that, for example, men and women of the high
social standing of Chickatawbut, the sachem discussed earlier, were present. It
is more likely that Morton attracted some subalterns within Native society in
this area. Bragdon concludes that the "hierarchical nature of Native society,
commented on by many observers, was marked in clearly differentiated status
attributed to different classes and in the presence of a permanent class of servants or slaves."[44]

Morton might have been interested in legitimizing his plantation less with
(or against) Plymouth than with the local Native population. Lacking an explicit kinship connection, it is possible that Morton was positioning himself
within a sachemship mode that, while he may have only imperfectly understood its dynamics, made sense to him as a display of certain linked modes of
power—distributive and ritualistic (in the form of the Maypole party), but also
demanding and trade-oriented, in the case of his aggressive fur trading. The
sachem often played a crucial role in organizing and regulating trading sessions. Hosting and gift giving showed a sachem's commitment to and prowess

within the community; channeling wealth proved one's ability to command tribute, to provide protection, and to serve as an ambassador in the difficult cultural encounters required to establish good trading relationships. "The notion of the sachemship served to articulate and reconcile communities with conflicting interests," Bragdon observes, "to 'naturalize' the increasingly unequal interpersonal relationships." Certainly this was one of Morton's important sources of power: he offered a way around established systems for Native Americans as well as for servant-class English settlers. Morton's style of leadership—personal, unmediated (he may have been the only person on his plantation with a half-decent grasp of Algonquian), and if we take him at his word, generous—may have promised Native Americans a more familiar market relationship than that offered by Plymouth and the other unallied plantations.[45]

How the Maypole ceremony was enacted, then, would have been significant to American Indian observers. Morton's former life at the Inns of Court, the surviving contemporary accounts of his character, and his use of elements from English performance culture in *New English Canaan* suggest that he had a flair for the dramatic. As a sachem figure, Morton would have been expected to lead the ceremonies, to hail his audience, and to solicit its responses as well.[46] Perhaps Morton's holding forth, with a mixture of levity and gravity, looked familiar; and in particular, his inclusion of everyone—the specific mentioning of Natives at various points in his poems and songs—might have persuaded a Native audience that Morton respected the rhetorical norms of Indian country.

Lest this sound too utopian, too much like the culture-crossing hybrid manqué of Morton's story popular from U.S. fiction, it is useful to underscore that in this interpretation, Morton's homographesis was in the service of asymmetries of power. He advertised a domination-based relationship with the Natives that would be effected by learning, mastering, and putting to English use the extant communications techniques and material culture of the Natives. He would not have wanted the authority of either the *pawwaw* or the warrior (unlike, perhaps, Edward Winslow or John Underhill, as we will see in later chapters), but that of a sachem. This inverts our received interpretation of Morton's May Day event: the quality of misrule that *New English Canaan* attributes, tongue in cheek, to the festival may in fact have been only a print performance for the native English audience. For Morton's American audience, far from misrule, the manipulation of material and performative elements of public ritual, totemic signification, and sachemship would have constituted a claim to the establishment of order.

Finally, there is the question of what the presumably handwritten poems would have stood for, from the standpoint of Native American audiences.

Germaine Warkentin, along with Peter Wogan, claims, against James Axtell and others, that "the importance of literacy to the ideology of European culture . . . has obscured for us evidence suggesting that Native peoples took writing in their stride."[47] Warkentin's work on the ritual place of wampum as a sign-carrying mechanism—one that necessitated an accompanying performance in order to be decoded—suggests parallels with Morton's use of poetry and the Maypole. If the account in *New English Canaan* is roughly accurate, the poems were probably read out loud, oralized along with the songs Morton mentions, and then tacked in written form to the ceremonial post. Morton's public performance of the text, combined with its symbolic display on the pole and with the presumed generosity of the May Day feast, would have marked Morton as someone trying to command authority. Deliberately, accidentally, or something in between, Morton may have exploited "what Native signification systems seem to exploit with real cultural flair," in Warkentin's estimation, "the performative element that establishes a narrator, orator, or shaman as a privileged reader charged with communicating the textual artifact's meaning."[48]

Still, it seems that Morton did not garner enough authority with the region's Natives to earn him powerful allies against Plymouth. As we will see in the next chapter, he was, for one thing, competing with savvy Separatist negotiators. He was also not collaborating with the powerful Narragansetts or the rising star Massasoit of the Wampanoag. But Native polities, too, might have had as many fears as Plymouth did about Morton's attempts to become a communications node in the area. For very different reasons, those fears might equally have been rooted in the uses of the Maypole. But before returning to the question of Morton's fate and the communications system that brought him to his end under the power of John Winthrop, I consider a final set of performances connected to the publication event of the Maypole. Here Morton's agency as an author, as the principal performer of the event, is less important than the book itself—the physical embodiment, *New English Canaan*. As printed, published, distributed, and possibly read, this book was another space of performance, one with different but structurally similar homographs, gestures, and relationships among author, audience, and material medium when read in the transatlantic print world. It was here that the potential audiences for the Maypole converged, with what were for some readers troubling implications.

The Space of the Page

While much scholarly attention has been paid to *New English Canaan,* little of it has examined the visual qualities of the book. This is surprising, given the playfulness of the narrative, Morton's thematic attention to spatiality and textuality in general, and the presence and influence of a large body of scholarship that has recently animated our sense of early modern material culture. Having considered Morton's Native American audience, we can bring similar questions to Morton's book in its "native" printing and reception context—that of Jan Fredericksz Stam's printing work in Amsterdam and English print publication more generally. How did these contexts of circulation relate to the establishment of the performative publication space of the Maypole, and why might they too have been seen as a threat to the New England social order?

New English Canaan, like Morton himself, ran into trouble with authorities more than once. Registered with the Stationers' Company in 1633, evidence suggests that an early version of Morton's book began to be printed—where exactly is not known—in late 1633 (which would have included the first months of 1634 by today's calendar). Charles Greene, the English bookseller who registered Morton's title, complained in late 1637 that "when some fewe sheets of the said booke were printed, it was stayed and those sheetes taken away by the meanes and procurement of some of the Agents for those of Newe-England." It is possible that Greene, who made his petition to Archbishop Laud, was using the dissenters' agents as a scapegoat for some other cause of delay in the book's production. (Greene added that he was "a young man and but a smale time tradeing for himselfe," confessing a possible lack of competence and soliciting pity for a beginner.)[49] Equally possible is that, true or not, he included this accusation in order to get Laud's men to look past the title page, since they would find in the book's contents a message that harmonized with the archbishop's. If it is true that agents from one of the New England ventures were keeping tabs on Morton, the confiscation provides a vivid example of the connections between media production in New England and the metropole. It is more definitely known, though, that as a result of the Star Chamber decree of 1637 concerning printing, which prohibited the importation of books printed in English in foreign places, many copies of *New English Canaan* were confiscated, and few, if any, made it to America. Despite the controversy he provoked then and since, Morton's work was not read widely in the seventeenth century. Still, the visual architecture of the book can add much to our sense of its potential meanings. *New English Canaan* was not made by Thomas Morton alone; it was significantly coproduced by his printer, Stam.

It is evident that *New English Canaan* in its full form was printed at Amsterdam, whatever the untrustworthiness of its title page and variants, because of typographical evidence that also suggests why Morton might have preferred to have it printed there. Morton's book uses the same illuminated initials and ornaments found in a range of books printed by Stam at about the same time, from James Prempart's *A Historicall Relation of the famous Siege of the Citie called the Bvsse* (1630, with editions in both English and Dutch) to unapproved editions of the Bible in English.[50] Paul R. Sternberg has suggested that Morton used the Amsterdam publishing house in part because he thought it might help him reach a Puritan audience, since "by 1637, Holland (and especially Amsterdam) had become the haven for the printing of seditious and schismatical books directed against the English Crown and the Established Church."[51] Certainly Stam printed many books and pamphlets by controversial Puritan authors, including William Prynne, Henry Burton, and Alexander Leighton, who were seeking to publish and distribute works critical of Laud's regime. In the same year that Morton's text was printed, Stam printed Bastwick's *A briefe relation of certain passages in the Starre-Chamber* and Prynne's *A Breviate of the Prelates* and *XVI New Quaeres. New English Canaan*, if it reached the same audiences as these other books, would have raised godly tempers. But it seems equally possible that Morton had his book printed on the Continent, and with a Puritan-friendly press, to keep his text off the radar of agents of the New England Company, who might have assumed it was yet another nonconformist-friendly work.

What then might it mean, for reading and teaching *New English Canaan,* that it was printed in Amsterdam? The publishing worlds of Holland and England were, by the late 1630s, closely intertwined. While government control of distribution and censorship of content were provided for by law (through the Star Chamber and the Stationers' Company in England and the series of *plakkats* issued in the United Provinces), it is clear from contemporary accounts and print histories that national boundaries were porous—sometimes deliberately so. By some estimates, half the printed books extant in Europe during the seventeenth century were made in Holland. It was, significantly for empire builders, the leading producer of maps and navigational charts, and the first English newspapers, the *corantos,* were produced there. The market for Bibles was so lucrative in England (and the practice of smuggling so reliable) that Stam printed thousands of fraudulent copies of Christopher Barker's Bible in violation of the Royal patent. Through legislation, diplomacy, and espionage, Laud attempted to exert control over Dutch printing and to get local *plakkats* enforced, prohibiting anonymous printing or authorship. Laud's efforts, parts of a larger attempt to control English church forms in foreign countries, stemmed partly from, as he wrote later when on trial, "a great and just fear conceived, that by little and little, printing would quite be carried out of the kingdom."[52] His rationale, however, may have had much to do with the fact that Dutch printing was constitutively antihegemonic and so was employed by dissenters and radical theorists from across the Continent. It was one of Laud's transnational efforts to crush this Dutch reputation that ended the brief career of William Brewster's Pilgrim Press in Leiden in 1619.

Such attempts to suppress dissent across the channel were only irregularly successful (in part due to government resistance in Holland). They never halted the appearance of unauthorized Dutch-printed texts in England and Scotland.[53] Without considerable international political pressure, local regulations were unlikely to be enforced in what were decentralized, provincial publishing spheres. Contests for control of English expression in Amsterdam and elsewhere, though, gave weight to those texts that made it to the island. Morton was less interested in making a profit than in having an effect on the Privy Council's deliberations about the Charter. The fact that the exile presses of the time were in Amsterdam and Leiden, and that his use of one put his work in the way of the law, gave Morton a dissenting vibe even though he was a Laudian. At a broad level, then, the publishing history of Morton's text throws into relief the parameters of law and dissent within which book production across the English Channel operated. English writers imagined their publishing options (as well as their readerships) in a nonnational way. Nor was economics in any immediate sense what was important to Morton. For him, no less than for Prynne and Bastwick, it was political results that mattered in this medium, and Dutch publishing and smuggling were the pathway.

There were, of course, meanings local to Amsterdam and Leiden that Morton's text evoked. Concentric potential decoding realms attached to each text printed in English in Amsterdam. The nonconformist English community there, which used Stam's press, would have been as interested in the first two books of *New English Canaan* (about Native cultures and potential commodities) as it would have been angered by the last—a reaction Morton would have relished. But for several reasons a broader audience for *New English Canaan* in Holland would have been more likely. First, John Robinson's church, which had been the community center for the Separatist émigrés in Leiden, had declined considerably since Robinson's death in 1625, and nonconformist churches in Amsterdam were also struggling. Second, Stam and his wife, with whom he ran the business, had Arminian sympathies;[54] to local consumers, it would have come as no surprise that Stam was producing texts on both sides of a controversy. But Stam was also a printer of other exploration books and books of military history, and in that context a book like Morton's would have been appealing. As Benjamin Schmidt has shown, Dutch interest in New World narratives of all kinds was longstanding and by the 1630s had become integral to Dutch national iconography.[55]

Since there is no known evidence of Dutch sales or response to *New English Canaan,* however, the morphology of Morton's text may be a more fruitful source. In it, Dutch meanings resonated, but early modern English genres mixed potently as well. To see the text this way means looking at typography, images, and text layout—more broadly, it involves thinking of the page in visual terms, bringing things that we now ignore as negative space into focus. As one critic puts it, "The space surrounding print is not a vacuum but a plenum," and in the seventeenth century, readers expected to be engaged in that space.[56] Marginalia, for example, frequent in *New English Canaan,* could be used for emphasis, notation of memorable passages (known as *sententiae*), collation of places or important textual moments, and preempting readers' own handwritten marginalia. These uses in the aggregate established the space of the page as a highly political zone in which readers expected to find evidence of a writer's opinions. Despite the seductiveness of the term *marginalia* as a metaphor for a center-periphery hierarchy of textual power relations, the margins were not marginal in this sense in early modern texts. They were temporal zones as much as spatial ones because they forced readers to interrupt their reading of the body text. They were often (as in theological polemics) where the substance of a text was located. Given this crucial element of how texts from the period worked, this shifting spatial locus of the text's bottom line, or main argument, it is worth paying close attention to the visual dynamics of *New English Canaan*'s pages.[57]

The layout of *New English Canaan* was likely beyond Morton's control. But the material choices Stam's shop made in setting up the book created an important set of potential interpretations. The Amsterdam title page of *New English Canaan* seems reasonably plain (see Figure 5). It describes the contents of the three books and declares Morton's source of authority to be his "tenne yeares knowledge and experiment of the Country."[58] The language of the page is dominated by natural metaphors, as befits the allegorical framework of its title. Yet it is also shot through with a recognition of the technology required to make nature bountiful. Terms like "tractable," "planted," and "commodities" hint at human effort. Even the form of the page is "cultured" in a way that associates the labor of printing with equally famous Dutch gardening: well-organized type becomes like the flower—perhaps a tulip—whose throat and stem are formed by the tailpiece and publishing data. (Amsterdam's balcony flower gardens and tiny urban plots were internationally renowned; the book was printed at the height of the tulip mania that swept the United Provinces in the 1630s.) Such visual and textual suggestions guide the reader into the book's contents, which promote Morton's understanding of colonization as a matter of first

NEW ENGLISH CANAAN
OR
NEW CANAAN.

Containing an Abſtract of New England,

Compoſed in three Bookes.

The firſt Booke ſetting forth the originall of the Natives, their Manners and Cuſtomes, together with their tractable Nature and Love towards the Engliſh.

The ſecond Booke ſetting forth the naturall Indowments of the Country, and what ſtaple Commodities it yealdeth.

The third Booke ſetting forth, what people are planted there, their proſperity, what remarkable accidents have happened ſince the firſt planting of it, together with their Tenents and practiſe of their Church.

Written by Thomas Morton of Cliffords Inne gent, *upon tenne yeares knowledge and experiment of the Country.*

Printed at AMSTERDAM,
By JACOB FREDERICK STAM.
In the Yeare 1 6 3 7.

Figure 5. The Amsterdam title page of *New English Canaan* features a simple but cultured layout. Reproduced by permission of The Huntington Library, San Marino, California.

shaping the external, natural world before turning to his combat with his neighbors' inward struggle for grace.

Each of the Adam-and-Eve-like grotesques in the title-page tailpiece grasps a fruit-bearing plant of some kind, and each has a naked anthropomorphic torso, coded male or female, with a flowery head and a scaly, serpentine body. (Sensibly, in the false English title page the flower-and-vine motif is preserved but the shape has changed to a rectangular, less organic one, reinforced by horizontal bars delineating the attribution of authorship and the medallion. In it, actual serpents have replaced the anthropomorphic figures and the crown figures conspicuously.)

The twinned structure of these figures dominates all of the images in the text, underlining the allusions to Proteus that Morton weaves throughout the third book. At the same time, these twinnings call attention to the symmetry and asymmetry of the page, and by extension to at least two paired sets of relationships: that of Old England to New England, and that of the typological Canaan to this (typographical) New Canaan. In the address to the king, for example, the letter *T* design contains a pair of lion-like creatures emerging out of plant structures. At one level this image offers symmetry, but disentangling its design reveals categorical disruptions, fusions of plant and animal more characteristic of old world fantasies about monsters of the terra incognita than the eyewitness accounting of Morton's narrative (see Figure 6).

Most of the illuminated initials used in the text feature the grotesque creatures frequently seen in books from this period. These perhaps harmonize better with Morton's classicized irony than they do with the nonconformist iconoclasm of Henry Burton's *A divine tragedie lately acted* (1636), in which the same initial appears (228; see Figure 7).[59]

By the time readers arrive at the "The Authors Prologue," they have been well prepared for the fertility metaphor introduced there to explain why New England needs to be exploited. The labor required to do so is figured explicitly as sexual:

> If art & industry should doe as much
> As Nature hath for Canaan, not such
> Another place, for benefit and rest,
> In all the universe can be possest,
> The more we proove it by discovery,
> The more delight each object to the eye
> Procures, as if the elements had here
> Bin reconcil'd, and pleas'd it should appeare,
> Like a faire virgin, longing to be sped,
> And meete her lover in a Nuptiall bed. (10)

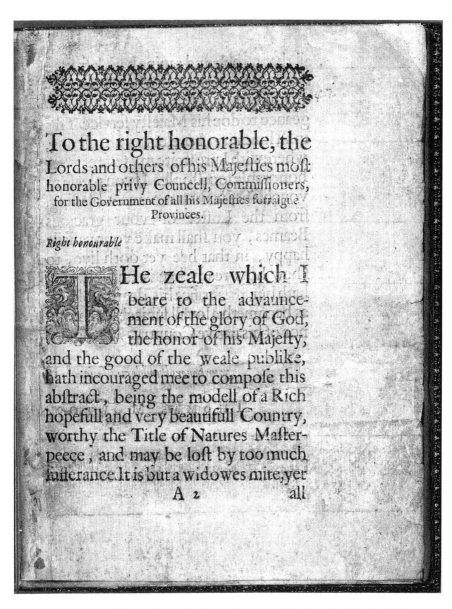

To the right honorable, the Lords and others of his Majesties most honorable privy Councell, Commissioners, for the Government of all his Majesties forraigne Provinces.

Right honourable

He zeale which I beare to the advauncement of the glory of God, the honor of his Majesty, and the good of the weale publike, hath incouraged mee to compose this abstract, being the modell of a Rich hopefull and very beautifull Country, worthy the Title of Natures Masterpeece, and may be lost by too much insterance. It is but a widowes mite, yet

A 2   all

Figure 6. Fusions of plant and animal characterize many of the illuminated capitals of *New English Canaan*. Reproduced by permission of The Huntington Library, San Marino, California.

Examples of Gods judgments

VPON

SABBATH-BREAKERS.

Hefe Examples of Gods judgements hereunder fet downe, have fallen out within the fpace of leffe then two yeares laft paft, even fince the Declaration for fports (tolerated on the Lords day) was publifhed , and read by many Minifters in their congregations ; for hereupon ill difpofed people (being as dry fewell , to which fire being put , quickly flameth forth ; or as waters , pent up and reftrained being let loofe, breake forth more furiouſly) were fo incouraged , if not inraged , as taking liberty difpenfed, thereby fo provoked God , that his wrath in fundry places, hath broken out to the deftruction of many , would to God to the inftruction of any. And the judgements are fo much the more remarkable , that ſo many in number, as here are obferved , (befides many more , no doubt which have not come to our eares) fhould fall within fo narrow a compaffe of time, fo thick, and that in fo many places : as we read not of fuch a number

Figure 7. The same set of illuminated initials used to print Morton's text were used in Henry Burton, *A Divine Tragedy Lately Acted . . .* , Amsterdam, 1636. Reproduced by permission of The Huntington Library, San Marino, California.

The illuminated initial *I* features the royal rose and thistle of England and Scotland intertwined. In the light of the poem's allegory—about having sex with New England in order to make it produce commodities—the illumination contributes to a hybridization metaphor that puts the text at odds with discourses of sexual purity from the very beginning. Though the separate but intertwined metaphorics of English-Scottish political relations might be a background for this work, *New English Canaan* is filled with far more explicit (re)productive interminglings that gesture toward hybrids. Visually, these include the Edenic tailpiece image on the title page and its tulip thematics; historically, its publishing history (an English text about America published in Holland); and textually, the narratives of both the "Authors Prologue" and the famous *"Lasses in beaver coats come away"* plea from the Maypole episode (135). Thus far, it would seem that the visual qualities of Morton's text celebrated the taint of friskiness that so worried William Bradford.

But the typographical choices do not simply promote unbridled priapism leading to uncontrolled hybridity. The letter *I* used to initiate "The Epistle to the Reader" contains images taken from a widespread image of Dutch industry (see Figure 8). Again, there are two figures here, in chiral symmetry, both gardeners. The gardeners are pulling on vines, presumably to keep them away from the flowers in pots below. The gardeners seem to be in pots themselves, though the structures they appear to be stuck into might be balconies. The presence of four kinds of flowers in the pots, with tulips featured prominently,

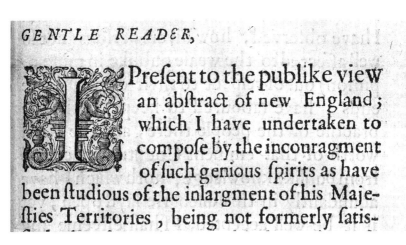

Figure 8. Gardening in the capitals of *New English Canaan* resonates with the book's thematics of cultivation. Reproduced by permission of The Huntington Library, San Marino, California.

reminds us of the local environment in which this book was produced, even as we read in it an "abstract of new England." The tulip was known in England as a marvel of hybridity produced by meticulous cultivation. Thomas Fuller, in *The History of the Worthies of England,* observed, "As Jacob used an ingenious invention to make Laban's cattle speckled or ring-straked, so much the skill in making Tulips feathered and vereigated, with stripes or divers colours."[60] The appearance of horticulture icons in Morton's text, together with its Dutch printing, situates *New English Canaan* in an international interpretive realm that celebrates the skills of cultivation and combination.

Such skills were the explicit topos of the popular genre of the gardening book. Given the narrative and visual thematics of cultivation, particularly in the front matter and the first two books of *New English Canaan,* Morton's book might well have resonated with that genre for some readers. Rebecca Bushnell has argued that early modern English gardening books participated in social and intellectual debates from arguments about scientific experimentation to anxieties about class mobility. Her genealogy of gardening books situates them in relation to developing notions of science, the self, and social authority. Gardening books confirmed residual Aristotelian notions of the order of nature, but they were just as much about exploiting nature for new and profitable ends—and possibly, as a result, for social betterment. "It was," Bushnell reminds us, "a world in which the organic was subdued at every level by the knife and the surveyor's rod, and the books both directed and advertised this subjection."[61] This was as true of North American settlements as it was of English gardens.

But the obstacles were considerably different in America, and nature in the colonies was not as tractable as that of the household garden. Morton's paradise was one in which man could intervene substantially. Such an intervention had much to do with social rank, something Morton could well have expected to be on the minds of readers with interests in colonial investment or emigration.[62] Though Morton includes pages of descriptions of New World plant and animal life, including methods of agriculture used by the Americans, he would not have wanted readers to imagine him doing the work of cultivation personally. Despite the do-it-yourself tone of many gardening books, well-to-do gardeners were imagined not as performing labor but as politicizing leisure. Morton presents himself as a gentleman, carefully balancing his claims of being involved in the laborious foundation of the colony with a characterization of that labor in vague or managerial terms. *New English Canaan* itself, readers are to conclude, is Morton's labor; it is not a consumable product of the colony but a tool for the establishment and perpetuation of legitimate, responsible governance there. The utility of the tulip layout of the title page and the carefully staked-out textual zones indicated by marginal glosses are to be found in their establishment of a visual analog for Morton's textual skills: promoting colonization and lobbying the Privy Council.

The marginalia, too, trim the text, hinting at Morton's skillful managing of history. In at least one instance, such cultivation of the narrative resonates powerfully with the ways Native Americans managed their own histories. Recounting local Native military practices (an account structured in part by European conceptions of honorable warfare), Morton includes a discussion of personal duels (see Figure 9):

> I have bin shewed the places, where such duels have bin performed, and have fuond the trees marked for a memoriall of the Combat, where that champion hath stood, that had the hap to be slaine in the duell? and they count it the greatest honor that can be, to the serviving Cumbatant to shew the scares of the wounds, received in this kinde of Conflict, and if it happen to be on the arme as those parts are most in danger in these cases, they will alwayes weare a bracelet upon that place of the arme, as a trophy of honor to their dying day. (37)

Next to this passage there is a marginal gloss:

> *Trees mar_*
> *ked where*
> *they performe*
> *a duell.*

Morton's page is marked, much as the tree is marked, in a place where a duel happens. Generic mixing, typographical manipulation, and use of marginalia all contribute to an interpretive latitude more like that of the Maypole ritual or European–Native encounter than that of what we usually think of as a book. Morton's book is in this moment a production of and within performative space that, if not influenced by Native communications systems, makes its readers dependent on them momentarily, vertiginously.

We know that Algonquians marked trees, but we also know that Morton put his mark on the Maypole, a famous inscription on a tree, the evidence of which is only preserved in *New English Canaan,* since the tree that was the site of his duel with the Pilgrims has been removed by them. The typography of *New English Canaan* bears witness as a bracelet on the arm to the disfigurement Morton describes himself to have received. If the text on the Maypole was "those parts . . . most in danger" in Morton's case, then this account in print, with its telegraphic marginal reminders, is meant in part to function as a trophy of honor.

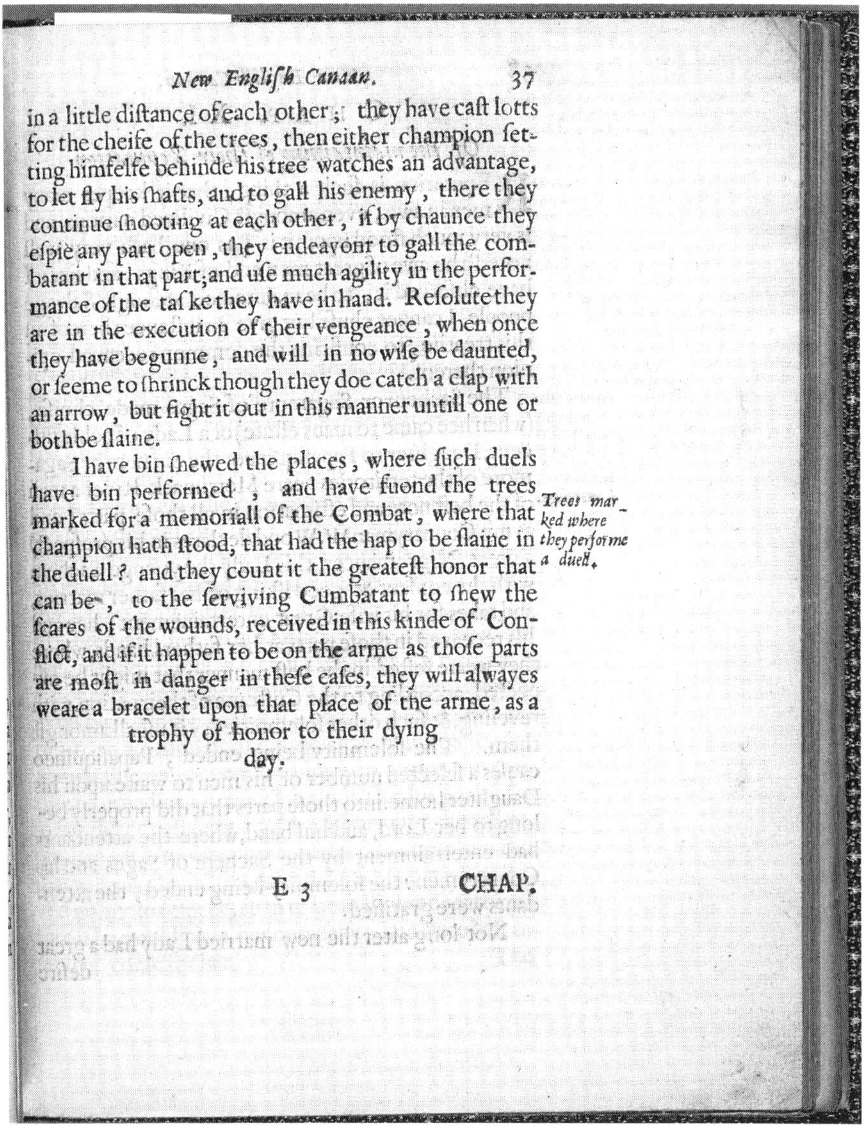

in a little diftance of each other; they have caft lotts
for the cheife of the trees, then either champion fet-
ting himfelfe behinde his tree watches an advantage,
to let fly his fhafts, and to gall his enemy, there they
continue fhooting at each other, if by chaunce they
efpie any part open, they endeavour to gall the com-
batant in that part; and ufe much agility in the performance of the tafke they have in hand. Refolute they
are in the execution of their vengeance, when once
they have begunne, and will in no wife be daunted,
or feeme to fhrinck though they doe catch a clap with
an arrow, but fight it out in this manner untill one or
both be flaine.

I have bin fhewed the places, where fuch duels
have bin performed, and have fuond the trees *Trees mar-*
marked for a memoriall of the Combat, where that *ked where*
champion hath ftood, that had the hap to be flaine in *they performe*
the duell? and they count it the greateft honor that *a duell.*
can be, to the ferviving Cumbatant to fhew the
fcares of the wounds, received in this kinde of Conflict, and if it happen to be on the arme as thofe parts
are moft in danger in thefe cafes, they will alwayes
weare a bracelet upon that place of the arme, as a
      trophy of honor to their dying
           day.

E 3   CHAP.

Figure 9. Morton's margin is marked, much as he describes Natives marking trees,
where important events happen. Reproduced by permission of The Huntington Library,
San Marino, California.

The Letter Killeth

For Morton, it was important to argue that the Pilgrims' inability to bring international standards of intellectual endeavor to their enterprise would spell their doom. The blending of Dutch printing expertise with a demonstration of his knowledge of Native American systems implicitly argued this point. But more explicitly, Morton's final incantation in the persona of Jonas protests:

> And in that posture hee greeted them by letters retorned into new Canaan; and ever (as opportunity was fitted for the purpose) he was both heard & seene in the posture of Ionas against them crying repent you cruel Seperatists, repent. . . . The Charter and the Kingdome of the Seperatists will fall a sunder: Repent you cruell Schismaticks repent; If you will heare any more of this proclamation meete him at the next markettowne, for *Cynthius aurem vellet.* (198–99)

Ending with a conventional but obscure Latin phrase referring to the summoning of a witness to testify, Morton both alludes to the legal maneuvers he assisted against the Massachusetts charter and a tradition of erudition that, through invocation, the cosmopolite reader can imagine he shares with the narrator.[63] But this closing sentence, referring to the practice of public proclamation, the power of the audible word ("heard & seene"), and "letters" back to America, also directs our attention to the role of oral and private communication in the early American information sphere. As it turned out, if the Maypole as publishing mechanism began Morton's career as a danger to the communications channels of Separatist and Puritan authorities, and his engagement with Atlantic print culture furthered it, the letter and oral challenges ended it.

Thinking his efforts to revoke the Massachusetts Bay patent had succeeded, Morton wrote to William Jeffreys, a planter in New England, bragging about his work. It is likely that Morton, who salutes Jeffreys as "My Very Good Gossip," expected his crowing to be talked about among the powers-that-were. (The letter is provocatively dated May 1, 1634.) After Jeffreys read the letter, he took it to Winthrop, who alerted the colony's magistrates about Morton's "railing speeches and threats against this plantation, and Mr. Winthrop in particular." In this letter, Morton persists in his arguments against Puritan literacy practices— predicting that when the patent is revoked, the Puritans will "find, and will yet more to their shame, that they abused the word and are to blame to presume so much,—that they are but a word and a blow to them that are without."[64] Morton was, once again, challenging the basis of New England authority structures.

Winthrop's counterstrategy was, in a sense, to vocalize this private written communication, arguing to the magistrates that it was, functionally, *oral* criticisms Morton was making—"railing speeches and threats." "It was with more than moral outrage," writes Daniel B. Shea, "that John Winthrop could speak of Morton as 'our professed old adversary,' identifying Morton's threat as a literary one, 'who had set forth a book against us and written reproachful and menacing letters to some of us.'"[65] Winthrop's use of the word "professed" here both suggests the public nature of Morton's challenge and perhaps mocks Morton's attempts to pose as a scholarly authority. Winthrop preserved the letter (it is transcribed in his journal; the original is missing), knowing that it would be essential in prosecuting Morton should he return to Massachusetts. Ten years later, he did, and the letter got him jailed.

In effect, Puritan leaders used the private world of information circulation to counter Morton's scheme—forcing it into the public world and thus making it actionable. Puritan retribution against Morton's plantation was deliberately carried out in front of a Native audience, in part to counteract Morton's attempts to include them in his sphere. As Morton put it, "This they knew (in the eye of the Salvages) would add to their glory" (143). Despite the formal accusations, Morton had something potentially far more powerful than weapons to offer the Natives of Passonagessit—an integral place in the construction of New English cultural life. Both the Maypole and *New English Canaan* were premised on an English model of print circulation that, while taking advantage of the power of subversive publication to spread knowledge as fast as more official publication, vaunted a world of open, if hierarchical, exchange of ideas and traditions.[66] In Morton's world, masques performed at the Inns of Court and royal proclamations had equal status as legitimate public communications. Both were part of a spectrum of intellectual and political activity that could not be considered centralized.[67] Morton, it seems, was aware of the power of private communication but did not take seriously enough his own account of the Puritans' ability to rationalize legal action on the basis of a religious ideology that superseded English law.

Morton was throwing a wrench into delicate social machinery. "The transformative impulse within Puritanism," writes Sandra Gustafson, "had its clearest manifestation in the pulpit, for the printed Word erupted through the existing social order only when given voice by Puritan ministers."[68] Morton claims in *New English Canaan* that the means of control of information practiced by his contemporaries at Plymouth was not a viable one for an English colonial project that wished to exploit American resources. By imposing a stranglehold on the exchange of cultural and linguistic information, Morton argued, the Pilgrims were making it impossible to do the work of enlightening the Natives.

From a twenty-first-century perspective, *New English Canaan* can seem progressive, given its focus on indigenous language and culture. But it also helped forge foundational imperial technologies—the hierarchies of literacy over orality and of English as center and Native as subordinate periphery. What Bradford saw as the dangerous hybridity enabled by the Maypole, its "frisking" interracial bodies and its communicational "inordinariness," seems to position Morton as a cultural critic able to see the connections among sexuality, communications technology, and social power in English colonization. But Morton's use of hybridity sought to bring Native Americans under English "cultivation" and political rule, not to establish a conscious program of negotiated cultural exchange that might preserve indigenous self-determination.

Still, Morton's famous Maypole was more than a pagan symbol or beacon for degenerate fur smugglers. It exemplifies the interpenetration of media in the communications networks that shaped power in the northern colonies. The poems written at Morton's tiny plantation served a local purpose. When published on the Maypole, however, they offered a more general challenge to the representational hegemony of the Pilgrim leaders. Back in England, Morton took his argument to another level, portraying the Puritan leaders as naïve pedagogues exploiting illiterates—showing to advantage his own high ironic style but always taking into account the power of literacy to organize culture and create access to that culture for individuals. Morton, years before the Antinomian controversy, critiqued the nascent Puritan matrix of communication and authority, proposing an alternative public sphere. In this argument perhaps his own intellectual touchstone, but certainly his rhetorical fulcrum, was the relationship of Native Americans to the different mechanisms of communication they encountered. They reveled and traded openly with Morton, while inventing new words for untrustworthiness as a result of interacting with the Pilgrims. His complaint that the Pilgrims were taking advantage of illiterates should be seen as a basic statement about power in society. The Maypole was an attempt to act on that episteme, bringing a different brand of public communication to New England.

Two

Good Noise from New England

Massasoit, also known as Ousemaquin, sachem of the Wampanoag people, could with justice be considered the most important figure in the settlement of early New England. It was he who sent English-speaking Samoset to make contact with the Pilgrims at Plymouth—prior encounters, as we will see in chapter 4, were not encouraging to either the Americans or the newcomers. From a pivotal position geographically, at Sowams (near present-day Barrington, Rhode Island), and politically, at the nexus of the Narragansetts, Pequots, and English, Massasoit facilitated mutually beneficial agreements and prevented conflicts that might have terminated English colonial endeavors. In his community, he was a remarkable force: he survived two plagues and fended off incursions, sometimes violent, from the French, the Dutch, the English, and Native groups from the north and west.[1]

Because Massasoit held influence with the region's kinship networks—the crucial political and economic context into which the settlers had to fit—the Plymouth settlers invested substantial time trying to interpret and accommodate him. In turn, he used the English presence to increase his share of power against the dominant Narragansetts. Massasoit's son, who would become known as King Philip, inherited his father's commitment to Wampanoag society but, as the English would discover in 1675, not his comparatively peaceful approach to politics. It is perhaps telling that so significant a figure in American history has never elicited a full-length scholarly biography. Massasoit's presence permeates the literature of settlement and subsequent histories.[2]

Like Thomas Morton, Massasoit garnered his social authority through communications networks and performances, mastering the representational properties of available media technologies and their socially constructed rhetorics. This chapter examines a moment at which those networks and rhetorics were activated and struggled over by Massasoit and the masterful Pilgrim negotiator Edward Winslow. Considered here as a publication event, it is one of the most famous scenes in settlement history and one of the many times when Massasoit was key to the persistence of the colonial project. In March 1622, Winslow cured Massasoit of what the Wampanoag community feared was a mortal illness. In thanks, so the story goes, the leader told Winslow of a growing plot to eliminate the English and suggested a means of undermining the plan. Winslow, who like Massasoit receives little discrete attention in the writing and teaching of early American culture, performed the cure again not long afterward. This time, though, it was in written form, for an English audience, in a book devoutly titled *Good Newes from New-England*.[3]

It has seemed reasonable to regard this episode as exemplary of English advantages over indigenous American cultures: science and alphabetic literacy, hand in hand, inevitably worked a transfer of power even when war and plague failed. This chapter tries to understand the curing episode in light of the interconnectedness of the communications systems and medical cultures of the Wampanoag and the settlers rather than understanding those categories as sites of difference that outline cultures. It explores how Winslow's cure activated both Native and English communications channels through the medium of Massasoit's body and the cultural conventions associated in Wampanoag and English society with such bodies. Sickness and other processes of the body were profoundly meaningful for both the English and the Wampanoag. What went in and what came out and at what rate held sexual, spiritual, and political meanings for both peoples; for both, such meanings were crosscut by considerations of gender and rank.

This episode can help us rethink notions of technology—here medical technology—to emphasize its collaborative and communicative aspects rather than to argue for its inevitable, self-interpreting power. Today, many people are persuaded that the geography of guns, germs, and steel determined the outcomes of conquest. Certainly diseases introduced by Europeans contributed significantly to the decline of Native populations and to cultural fragmentation. But Massasoit did not succumb to disease, or to guns. His case is a provocative counter to the sense that collapse was always or inevitably the outcome of colonial medical encounters. Stories and the control of their movement in space and time, no less than kingly wisdom and supernatural approval, were essential. To see the significance of Winslow's cure of Massasoit in its broader dimensions, this chapter begins with a sketch of the events leading up to the cure, focusing on the cultural and communicational terrain of Wampanoag territory. It then turns to the little-discussed core of this political drama—constipation—and how it linked Algonquian and English conceptions of media circulation in a way that suggests the interdependence of parasite and host rather than a hierarchical domination.[4]

Native Networks

On the chilly March day that the residents of the struggling Plymouth colony heard news that their ally the sachem Massasoit was sick, their political and military viability in America was still very much in doubt. They had lost one of their most helpful translators, Tisquantum, to sickness the previous autumn. Plymouth's palisade and combination fort and meetinghouse were virtually complete, but the winter had been hard on their occupants. Rumors of attack by the powerful Narragansetts, or even by a combination of local nations, were constantly in the air. What would happen if Massasoit passed was unclear, but a disturbing object—a large snake's skin wrapped around a bundle of arrows— delivered the year before by a messenger from the rival Narragansett sachem, Canonicus, intimated a shift of power that would hardly benefit Plymouth.[5]

By this time, however, the settlers knew many of the indigenous customs, and they knew that when a Wampanoag leader died, his or her friends and tributaries were customarily present. Such a gathering indicated respect but was also an opportunity to reconfigure the economic and political order. Succession was a complicated, not necessarily genetic matter in American societies. Wampanoag sachems, Neal Salisbury observes,

> "ruled" only by satisfying their "subjects." Massasoit's regional esteem derived from his having established a successful alliance among a group of neighboring bands. But the members of these kin-based, face-to-face communities were under no obligation to "obey" him or to assume that any agreement he made with an outside party bound them, especially if they doubted the wisdom of the agreement.[6]

This system of social regulation entailed a communications system with complex protocols: kinship rules; histories of tribute, gifting, and military prowess; oratorical powers; and demonstrable support by other-than-human or spirit powers would play into any shuffling of power among the families that made up the Wampanoag. Under the circumstances, the scene at Sowams was likely to be an intimidating one and especially so for outsiders. Being there, however, would give Plymouth an unparalleled opportunity to show its potential to participate in the Wampanoag world. Plymouth chose to send Edward Winslow as its envoy, along with Wampanoag translator Hobomok and a visitor from London, John Hamden.

Winslow had been to Sowams before and knew Massasoit better than most newcomers. With a reasonable command of the Wampanoag dialect of Algonquian, he had become a skilled negotiator in both trade and politics. He would eventually be one of the most solicited international negotiators in New England, settling claims in the Anglo-Dutch war, negotiating boundary issues between Algonquians and English, and dying in 1655 on shipboard while serving as civil adviser to the English military expedition to capture Jamaica and Hispaniola. Winslow's unique sense of diplomacy was in part a result of his travels as a young man in Europe—travels that culminated in Leiden, among the Separatists, with his conversion by John Robinson. Trained at a preparatory school as a young man, he probably had been instructed in languages, most likely Latin and Greek. The printing apprenticeship that he had left behind in England to go on his continental travels no doubt contributed to his negotiating skills as well. It had acquainted him with a variety of books and pamphlets, many of them in popular genres, which gave him the ability to converse knowledgably with a wide range of people.

Whatever the reasons, Winslow had a preternatural sensitivity to the representational conditions in Indian country, where, as far as the English were concerned, information traveled in confusing ways. References to such anxieties can be found throughout settlement literature, but Winslow's account of the events leading up to the healing at Sowams offers a particularly telling example. What perplexed the English was the untraceability of information, the difficulty in authenticating it, and the rate at which it traveled.

First were the rumors. From the first sentence of *Good Newes from New-England,* the omnipresence of "common talk" and rumors, unattached to a known person or authority, haunts Pilgrim life in America. With the happy arrival of new residents in November 1621, Winslow writes, came the unwelcome fact that "the Great people of *Nanohigganset,* which are reported to be many thousands strong, began to breath forth many threats against vs" (Br). The ambiguities here are telling, for as a writer, Winslow was usually quick to specify his sources and fastidious about making distinctions between things he witnessed and things reported by others. The vagueness introduced by the numbers of the Narragansetts being only reported is amplified by the metaphorics of the threats, "breath[ed] forth" in a natural exhalation of malicious spirit, the more frightful because untraceable.[7]

No less disturbing than untraceable information was the problem of authentication. The messenger who left the snake's skin and arrows, for example, seemed all too eager to leave. When questioned by the settlers, who hoped "now to know some certaintie of that we so often hearde," Canonicus's messenger refused to give a definite interpretation of the object. Worse, the story he chose to tell subtly emphasized the uncertainty inherent in any sending of a message, calling attention to the way in which message and messenger could be interrelated. Winslow records,

> At first feare so possest him, that he could scarce say any thing: but in the end became more familiar, and told vs that the messenger which his Master sent in Summer to treat of peace, at his returne perswaded him rather to warre; and . . . de[t]ained many of the things were sent him by our Gouernour . . . ; so that he much blamed the former Messenger.[8]

In frustration, unable to discipline the messenger ("it being as well against the Law of Armes amongst them as vs in *Europe*"), the Plymouth leaders acted on Tisquantum's interpretation that the snakeskin message was a threat (3). They sent the skin back to Canonicus stuffed with powder and shot. The Pilgrims soon realized that Tisquantum's interpretation may well have been more self-serving than accurate.

The struggle a few months later over Tisquantum's translating services exemplifies the attempts by both English and Native communities to control information circulation. Tisquantum delivered a series of interpretations that turned out to be false, perhaps to garner influence or perhaps to ameliorate the developing tensions in the region.[9] Massasoit requested that he be delivered up to the Wampanoag for execution. The demand to surrender Tisquantum was a message to Massasoit's followers about how the network should function. But it also carried a message for Plymouth—which badly needed Tisquantum as a translator—about the filial nature of Wampanoag communications culture. Adherence both to the proper means of communication and to the message a community's leaders agreed to send was required of everyone in the chain of transmission. Performance of such adherence was one delineator of the boundaries of a Native group. As would be the case later with Massasoit's illness, medical information was the catalyst for this reprimand. Tisquantum had been claiming that the English "kept the plague buried in the ground, and could send it amongst whom they would, which did much terrify the Indians and made them depend more on him, and seek more to him, than to Massasoit."[10]

The Pilgrims in turn resolved the problem of Indian truth telling by taking advantage of Tisquantum's falling-out with Massasoit. The other crucial translator was Hobomok, who was resolutely faithful to Massasoit. Using a divide-and-conquer communications strategy, the Pilgrims wielded Hobomok and Tisquantum against each other to produce referential integrity. "They made good use of the emulation that grew between Hobomok and him," Bradford tells us, "which made them carry more squarely. And the Governor seemed to countenance the one, and the Captain the other, by which they had better intelligence, and made them both more diligent" (99). When Bradford writes that the Governor "seemed" to take Tisquantum more seriously than Hobomok, the principles espoused in Tuvill's *The Dove and the Serpent* (as we saw in the Introduction) appear to be at work: when tapping into Native networks, pretending to prefer a source of information that might normally be seen as tainted Machiavellianism was acceptable strategy. It was, of course, a tactic that the Wampanoag and the Narragansetts understood—after all, they were doing the same thing.[11] What Winslow metaphorizes as "squarely" communicating was in fact happening in something more like a circle.

If the difficulty of tracing information and establishing its reliability posed epistemological challenges for the English attempting to tap in to Native networks, the speed at which such information traveled was perhaps a greater threat. Given that the Natives had no writing, no horses, and no English roads, these potentially unhealthy messages traveled through what Williams termed "all the body and bowels of the Countrey" at a pace that was unnerving.[12] Early on the Plymouthites had a vivid lesson in this when, Winslow reported, "a town under MASSASOYT: and conceived by us to be very near, because the Indians flocked so thick, upon every slight occasion, amongst us," was found instead "to be some fifteen English miles."[13] Natives seemed to compress space and time with their speedy travel and their quick apprehension of what made for an English occasion.

The urgency with which Massasoit's illness and the heading off of the conspiracy is reported by Winslow in *Good Newes from New-England* offers another telling example, as does Winslow's attention to the frequency with which the news was updated. Having heard that Massasoit was sick and that, at the same time, a Dutch ship was beached near Sowams, the English made haste to send their envoys the same day; the party got as far as Nemasket by nightfall. They set out early the next morning and by midday had reached a ferry in the country of Wampanoag tributary sachem Corbitant (a Pocasset, who was something of a rival for Massasoit's power, operating between the Narragansett and the Wampanoag). There they were told that Massasoit was dead. "This news struck us blanke," writes Winslow, "but especially *Hobbamock,* who desired we might return with all speed" (25). It was a difficult moment, because if the news were true, "*Conbatant* was the most like to succeed him, and . . . we were not above three miles from *Mattapuyst* his dwelling place" (25). They chose to take this detour, and found that Corbitant was not at home but already at Sowams—precious time had been lost. What was more, Corbitant's wife informed them that in fact there was no certainty that Massasoit was dead. Winslow employed one of Corbitant's community to "goe with all expedition to *Puckanokick,* that we might know the certainty thereof, and withall to acquaint *Conbatant* with our there being" (27).

The inconsistency of the news reported from Sowams might represent simple misunderstandings. But if we take Native communication to be more deliberately constructed than some histories have, then Winslow appears to have been outmaneuvered by Corbitant—and he likely suspected it.[14] "About halfe an houre before Sunne-setting," Winslow records, "the messenger returned, and told vs that he was not yet dead, though there was no hope we should find him liuing" (27–28). Though not explicitly claiming that the misinformation offered at the ferry was in fact disinformation, Winslow made unusual haste to reach Sowams, despite the lateness of the day and the assurance of the messenger that there was no chance they would arrive in time. The envoys "set forward with all speed, though it was late within night ere we got thither" (28). Both the urgency with which Winslow acted in this instance and the comparative speed with which the English and the Natives traveled were significant. The runner had made it to Sowams and back, approximately an eleven-mile round-trip, and acquired the news in a few hours. The English party could not have moved quickly at night without danger and difficulty, yet they went to the trouble, knowing that by this time the whole of Massasoit's tributary community, despite the large territory from which it was drawn, was likely already there. And indeed, when they arrived, though the news had just come to Plymouth the day before, and though Massasoit had been seriously ill for only about three days, the leader's large winter house was at full capacity.[15]

How did the Americans do it? As some English settlers would learn, and as Roger Williams detailed in *A Key into the Language of America,* Native communications involved a sophisticated widespread network composed of and maintained by exceptional pathfinding knowledges, physical strength and speed, swimming skills (when boats capsized, as they often did), and, crucially, the sharing of news when individuals' paths crossed. When "meeting of any in travell," Williams reports, Algonquians would "strike fire either with stones or sticks, to take Tobacco, and discourse a little together" (73). By this means, each exchange between messengers became a node in a web of news sharing that could, with even a small number of "discourses," swiftly distribute news over a widespread area and, in many cases, across political boundaries. Williams notes that the Narragansetts seldom traveled alone, which increased the likelihood both of the message's transmission (in the event of attack or accident) and, under normal circumstances, of its fidelity. Not all news was intended for public broadcast; Bradford and Winslow both report of "secret" communications frustrating their search for political agreements with local leaders. Such transmissions were governed by a different set of protocols.[16]

Settlers who, like Morton, Williams, and Winslow, attempted to learn some Algonquian and participated in the rituals of Native networks could find themselves in the loop to a much greater extent than their compatriots. But they then had to acquire a higher order of skills—to discern layers of meaning and potential deceptions within Native messages and to learn indigenous audience dynamics. Winslow and Hobomok (Native-style, Winslow never traveled alone) found themselves in just this position when they came to the first node in their voyage to Sowams. There they had been delayed by Corbitant in one of a series of the sachem's attempts to garner power and, simultaneously, to preserve the indigenous regional system for doing so by containing the English. Still, communications were so fast, and Winslow and Hobomok so savvy, that they, with John Hamden in tow, managed to reach Sowams in time.

Once they arrived, another contest for communications mastery began. Natives had been healed before by the settlers' medicine; surgeon Samuel Fuller had treated a man and a woman (probably Wampanoags) injured in a conflict with Corbitant in 1621. But the Separatists had been at fault for the wounds that time, and with treatment happening in the confines of Plymouth it had been a different situation both performatively and politically.[17] Knowing the speed and geographic reach of the informational channels that converged at Sowams and knowing that the Native men and women present were atop the hierarchical order, Plymouth could, with a successful intervention by Winslow, expand its access to Wampanoag networks. On the other hand, if Massasoit died following English treatment, there was the potential for war.

The Body and Bowels of the Country

"When we came thither," Winslow reports, "we found the house so full of men that we could scarce get in" (28). Beginning with a picture of Hobomok and himself shouldering their way among the powerful bodies of the gathered Wampanoag men, Winslow sets the tone for the threatening, intimate scene to follow. He also maps out the audience in the medical theater: first, the Wampanoag kinship leaders; then the *pawwaws,* "in the middest of their charms for him"; next, the "six or eight women" attending the sachem; and finally Massasoit himself (28). This was no cold, isolated, confidential space. Winslow's diagnosis and cure would happen in a warm, smoky place with an attentive, critical, deeply interested audience encompassing a broad range of Wampanoag social ranks. The Dutch had already left the area—oddly, earlier that day, although they must have been aware of the crisis at Sowams.

When Winslow and Hobomok arrived at his side, Massasoit was alert and apparently not feverish (a diagnostic key Winslow would likely have mentioned), but "his sight was wholly gone." His mouth and tongue were swollen, "exceedingly furred," and it was difficult for him to speak; he did so "very inwardly" (28). Winslow offered "a confection of many comfortable conserves, &c." to the leader, which he accepted. Massasoit's mouth was so swollen that, in a description taken in subsequent scholarship as emblematic of the double-edged "gifts" of colonization, Winslow had to administer the conserves "on the point of my knife . . . which I could scarce get through his teeth" (28). After cleansing the Wampanoag leader's mouth of "abundance of corruption," Winslow gave him more of the "confection" mixed with water (29). "Within half an hour," he reported, "this wrought a great alteration in him . . . presently after, his sight began to come to him" (29). At this point Winslow asked the two cardinal questions of European medical practice of the day: "how he slept, and when he went to the stool?" It had been two days since he had slept, and five since his last excretion. Winslow immediately prescribed a chicken broth, and since fowl could not be quickly had, gathered the ingredients for and prepared, with the help of Wampanoag women, a vegetable and herb soup. "After this, his sight mended more and more: also," Winslow emphasized, "he had three moderate stools, and took some rest" (30). Winslow had cured Massasoit of constipation.

This incident has been, with good reason, interpreted by historians as a crucial moment both in the political history of New England colonization and in the cultural history of indigenous spirituality.[18] Events like this were, for Winslow and others concerned about Native conversion to Christianity, essential to the work of shifting Native faith from *pawwaws* to the Gospel. As the Puritan missionary John Eliot would later write to Winslow, "They have no meanes of Physick at all, onely make use of *Pawwawes* when they be sick, which makes them loath to give it over: But I finde, by Gods blessing, in some meanes used in Physick and Chyrurgery, they are already convinced of the folly of *Pawwawing* . . . but I much want some wholsome cordialls, and such other medicines."[19] When one operated on the body, one operated on the soul. At the same time, without question, Winslow's long subsequent career as a diplomat to the Native people and the comparative peace he helped effect had their origins in part from this moment. For Winslow the endeavors of diplomacy, medicine, and spirituality were part and parcel of each other.

But considered in light of its English and its American Indian audiences, this scene appears to be animated by more than an English desire for Indian souls. The context of anxiety over American Indian communications practices is more than mere foreground to this story, and Winslow's ability to cure Massasoit's constipation was based on more than luck. Rereading Massasoit's constipation in the context of the Galenic theories of the body Winslow employed to cure him, and Winslow's account of it within its London print culture context, offers a richer understanding of the role this incident played in New England's history. Massasoit's body, as many English would have seen it, was that of a king. The treatment of a leader's body always implicated the body politic at large. Winslow's performance of the cure and his framing of that performance in *Good Newes from New-England* placed him at the nexus of English and Wampanoag communications realms. It did not, however, confer unambiguous authority, because Massasoit's was not the only body that mattered. Medical treatments in these two cultures were administered to and by gendered bodies, and the rules by which behaviors were attached to genders were different in Native American and settler societies. Curing the sachem, and telling the story of that cure, required Winslow to transgress boundaries of gender that were considered fundamental both to the social order and to medicine— by both English and Wampanoag.

The ability of Winslow's publication event to assuage worries over both Native information systems and the uncertainties of communication with England rested on an uneasy movement across gendered popular literary genres in England and across gendered practices in America. To see the constipation cure in larger context will require first thinking about the disease itself, about the demands it places on narrative, and about the conceptions of the body in seventeenth-century Algonquian and English societies. Given these conceptions, what might Winslow's account have been designed to evoke for its London audiences in the 1620s, and what might the theater of the cure of Massasoit have signaled for the region's Native American audiences?

Massasoit's illness happened in March, a difficult time for digestion in New England. From October through late March, when planting would begin again, "villages broke into small family bands that subsisted on beaver, caribou, moose, deer, and bear," William Cronon observes. "Northern Indians accepted as a matter of course that the months of February and March, when the animals they hunted were lean and relatively scarce, would be times of little food"— and not particularly tasty food, at that.[20] It was also, like several other times of year, a time of transition from one set of dietary staples to another, as fowl decreased and planting began. In the vicinity of Massasoit's home at Sowams, scarcity and a lack of gastronomic diversity were less extreme than in other regions of southeastern New England. Still, as Winslow reported, for fresh herbs and vegetables only strawberry leaves and a little sassafras root could be found when he was at Sowams, while Massasoit insisted that Winslow prepare the kind of heavy chicken soup he had once eaten at New Plymouth. March was a prime trading period and consequently a time when cross-cultural eating was at its height, as Natives had furs to exchange and trading in food supplies was in high demand. The stranding of the Dutch ship in early March might have resulted in some interesting dietary additions for Sowams's residents. If the Dutch had food to share, they would have done so first with the sachem at his home; the resulting departure from the usual Wampanoag winter diet, independent of the amount of food consumed, might have induced constipation.

Still, Winslow's description of Massasoit's sickness contains a number of details that suggest that Massasoit had food poisoning. Possibly, it was a mild case of botulism, the only digestive disorder known to feature the range of symptoms he appears to have exhibited: loss or blurring of sight, dry mouth, loss of appetite, dehydration, and constipation. Botulism is also widely endemic.[21] Given the speed with which it can manifest, usually anywhere from a few hours to a few days, and given that he is the only one mentioned as suffering the full range of symptoms (though Winslow reports other people requesting that he administer his broth to them, perhaps in sympathy), it seems possible that Massasoit contracted it from food the Dutch shared with him during their unplanned visit to the village. The method Winslow used—beginning with a sugary and probably fruit-based concoction, followed by the same mixture blended with water, then a vegetable broth, and finally a fowl broth—would be referred to today as a "stepped-care" approach to "simple" constipation.[22] By treating Massasoit's dehydration and his constipation, Winslow speeded the recovery process and may well have saved the leader's life.[23]

One of the suggestive aspects of this disease, when it is considered as a historical and theoretical phenomenon, is that it leaves no archaeological, forensic trace. Because in its food-borne form it is the neurotoxins, rather than the bacillum *(Clostridium botulinum)*, that cause the disease, testing for it is difficult. In its aftermath, nothing is left in human remains that would allow for historical reconstruction after a long period of time.[24] In the case of gastrointestinal diseases this is common, and it characterizes diagnosis as well: "The key to accurate diagnosis and effective management of gastrointestinal problems," as one textbook puts it, "is flawless history-taking. Since up to 50% of gastrointestinal disorders are associated with no anatomical change, no physical findings and no positive test result, diagnosis and therapy must often be based on the medical interview."[25] In the absence of material signs, treatment of digestive disorders demands close attention to the patient's story and a willingness to bring the flexibility and contextual understanding of an approach not based on hard evidence. Narrative, then, is key in a more basic way to the diagnosis, past or present, of such disorders than some others.

Early modern English notions of the body and disease, which focused on humoral balance and the regulation of flows in and out of the body, were unusually sensitive to such stories of the body, as Michael Schoenfeldt and Gail Kern Paster have shown. In certain cases, medical practice based on such theories could be just as effective as that of the twenty-first century. Because the gastrointestinal tract, with its resident processes of digestion, nutrition, and evacuation, was the core of early modern theorizations of health, English people had a number of precocious treatments for such ailments as nausea, vomiting, and constipation.[26]

Humor theory was based on the physiological studies of Galen (Claudius Galenus of Pergamum). Galen elaborated and rationalized Hippocrates' ideas (from his *Airs, Waters, Places*), putting the digestive system at the center of health and profoundly linking the body with environmental influences. The four elements—earth, air, fire, and water—embodied four characteristics: coldness, dryness, hotness, and wetness, respectively. Four "humors" circulated within the body: phlegm, blood, and yellow and black bile. Food was converted into humors by a process called "concoction," which was hampered by uncooked or large items. The humors circulated throughout the body and generated waste in the form of excrement, nails, hair, and sweat. The aggregate balance of humors and characteristics resulting from this process made up a person's "complexion" or temperament. A person who was melancholic was cold and dry; a person who was sanguine was hot and wet; and so on. These innate complexions could be altered by travel to a different environment and through the excitation of humoral fluid production by what were known as the nonnaturals, or shifting influences: rest, food, exercise, passions, excretion.

In the absence of a widely accepted germ theory of disease, Joyce Chaplin explains, "most commentators remained satisfied with the concept of diseases as manifest symptoms of imbalance or disfunction, and they explained contagion without the need for germs or seeds—disease could spread simply through the general quality of the air or water" or by how much sun or shade the place one dwelled received.[27] There was no simple prescription for combining elements, characteristics, or humors, because each person was born with a different initial blend of these (women, for example, were imagined to be more cold and wet; men, more hot and dry) and groups of people lived in different environments. (National temperament, a notion still alive today, was rooted in the humors in the seventeenth century.) Achieving healthy balance meant paying close attention to the processes within one's body and to those in the environment as well.[28]

A story of flow was the logical beginning of diagnosis. When Winslow asked about the state of Massasoit's nonnaturals—his sleep and his excretions—he was beginning with questions fundamental to medical practice at the time. Both of these questions are designed to generate a history of flow because influxes and effluxes maintained or disturbed humoral balance. When flows stopped or accelerated—with lethargy or sleeplessness, with flux (diarrhea) or blockage (constipation)—a variety of dangers began to fester within the digestive system. Most medical treatises of the sixteenth and seventeenth centuries, as a result, focus on the digestive system, and constipation was a major impetus for remedy development.[29]

For Winslow's readers back in England, the use of Galenic medicine in this scene would have pointed to the larger question of the nature of the body being cured—Massasoit's—and the governance of the colony.[30] So powerful was the Galenic conception in English culture that it served as an analogy for a range of social practices. Two particular effects of humor theory on the imagination are significant here because they are conjoined in the retelling of Massasoit's illness: somatic flows as a synecdoche for the body politic as a whole and for the communications systems that knit that body together.[31] For English readers, each body was a small but integral part of the state. Individual bodily flows and humors were described by writers as isomorphic to the flows and balance of information, people, goods, lands, and other assets of the English nation, and this was particularly resonant when the body concerned was that of a leader. Puritan settlement narratives encouraging English emigration to America drew on the anxiety of imbalance at the demographic level, for example. They cited damages to the flow of goods and information within the island consequent upon overcrowding, imagining the "unoccupied" American land as a zone of relief that could therapeutically restore balance to the English body demographic.[32]

Given the colony's ambiguous status with relation both to local Native societies and to England, Winslow's famous treatment of Massasoit and the metaphorics of bodily flow he employed attempted to establish *Good Newes from New-England* as an authoritative but not entirely comforting account of the flow of power in New England.[33] "Their *Sachims* cannot be all called Kings," Winslow is careful to point out, "but only some few of them, whom the rest resort for protection, and pay homage unto them." Never completely leaving behind the projection of European understandings of hierarchical rule, Winslow insists, "Of this sort [of king] is *Massasowat* our friend, and *Conanacus* of *Nanohigganset* our supposed enemy" (55). The body on which Winslow was operating, from the standpoint of his native English audience, was that of a king. Any treatment of the body of a monarch in early modern Europe could also be thought of as a treatment of the body politic. The humoral body and the social order could serve as figures for each other; as Schoenfeldt summarizes, in "hierarchical readings of bodily organs . . . the belly is normally linked to the lower classes, while the upper classes are aligned with the heart or brain."[34] The lower parts, when constipated, threatened to infect (that is, to rebel against) their noble superior organs—an analogy for social disorder that would have had important portents in the case of Massasoit's struggle to evacuate. Too rapid voiding was equally dangerous, because the steady but nutritive process of concoction was not allowed to take place. The fast and untraceable flow of Native messages discussed above, then, in the imagination of English bodily metaphorics, threatened the dignity and sensibleness of government. Puritan chewing, or improvement, of messages (taking time to relate God's providence, man's weakness, and the community's interests all to each other before deciding on an action) was interrupted by the rapid, unpredictable circulation of information in Algonquian territory.

A metaphorics of consumption, blockage, and elimination pervades Winslow's text as a whole, insinuating to the early modern English reader a sense of speedy, dangerous flux in American Indian communication and slow, frustrating constipation in transatlantic messaging. This metaphorics is amplified by the formal role that the cure of Massasoit plays in the course of *Good Newes from New-England*'s narrative. In it, Winslow positions himself as a doctor simultaneously of communications, of the body, and of the social order. *Good Newes from New-England* itself was a product of a circulation of manuscripts and print documents spectacularly subject to chance, yet on whose functioning the governance and reputation of the colonies depended.

Certainly in an everyday material sense, if Native American communication seemed eerily speedy, transatlantic messaging was unpredictable, laborious, and slow at best. William Bradford perhaps exaggerated for spiritual effect when he wrote that "the mighty ocean which they had passed . . . was now as a main bar and gulf to separate them from all the civil parts of the world."[35] Still, as David Cressy has shown, although every ship carried letters, correspondence nonetheless

> was generally slow and erratic. Passages from west to east were faster ("downhill" as the sailors put it), so in principle news could travel more quickly from Massachusetts to old England. But in practice all hinged on the chance of shipping and the vagaries of the winds. . . . Often, for safety's sake, a writer made duplicates of letters and dispatched them on different ships, by different routes.[36]

Such redundant practices were an attempt to maintain the pace of communication, an adaptation to an unreliable system. Letters could take from six weeks to a year to arrive, averaged about two months in transit, and could arrive out of order. Communication was always less frequent in winter as shipping lulled. Pirates, privateers, political interception or censorship, shipwreck, and war were obstacles that could terminate a transmission, whether oral or written. Threats from imperial enemies were so pervasive that bags of correspondence were weighted for quick disposal at sea in case of capture.[37]

Cressy notes that though they often expressed anxiety or frustration with the pace and certainty of any particular communication, in general "early migrants in fact had little difficulty exchanging messages with family and friends in England," even if messaging was expensive and infrequent.[38] The actual loss of letters was less common than long delays, which could make correspondence related to diplomacy, economics, or publishing frustrating. Particularly in the early settlement days, the temporal gap was a new everyday experience for recent migrants, and the instability of and lack of a model for political communication with London increased anxieties about the integrity and predictability of information exchange. As the century went on, frequency of communication increased by virtue of the expansion of trade and migration, even if the speed of delivery of a message or its chances of arriving (which always fluctuated with political and climactic change) did not.[39]

Sometimes the metaphors that people in England and America used to describe the effects of correspondence from across the Atlantic emphasized the somatic, using terms that echoed the Galenic concern with flow or the kinds of folk remedies found in recipe books. A Scituate, Massachusetts, writer claimed that letters from home added "quickening life and edge into my affections," while an English woman said of a letter from New England that it "lay by me as a cordial which I often refresh myself with."[40] "Miscarriage," a term particularly closely associated with seafaring and written messages, was a metaphor frequently used in reference to the interruption of communication.[41] Winslow, in *The Glorious Progress of the Gospel,* uses this metaphor in a way that, unusually for him, makes no reference to God's providential power. "In the year 1648," he records, "our Letters miscarried many of them, in that the Ship that brought them was taken by the Prince of *Wales,* to the Countries great prejudice, as well as many other Vessels and their lading formerly; by which miscarriage I was wholly hindred from giving any further account till this instant, 1649" (B1v).[42]

As its double-meaning title declares, *Good Newes from New-England,* as both physical object and narrative, presumably embodied successful transatlantic information exchange. Yet Winslow's somatic metaphors emphasize rawness, blockage, and difficulty of transmission. Leading up to the scene of Massasoit's cure, blockage has served *Good Newes* as a trope relating the Natives and the English. In his dedicatory epistle, Winslow complains of the "stumbling blocke" bad Christian behavior puts in the way of Native salvation (A2). Although this phrase emphasizes its biblical resonances (Ezekiel 3:20), the figure next appears in a more directly political context. Tisquantum, Winslow argues, spread rumors of Wampanoag hostility in an attempt to unseat Massasoit, "hoping whilest things were hot in the heat of bloud, to prouoke vs to march into his Country against him, whereby he hoped to kindle such a flame as would not easily be quenched, and hoping if that blocke were once remoued, there were no other betweene him and honour" (8). Tisquantum's attempt to increase the settlers' "heat of bloud" by circulating unhealthy information would lead, ideally, to the removal of the "blocke"—literally, of Massasoit himself—precipitating Tisquantum's too-swift rise to power.

The section of the text that tells about the cure at Sowams initiates an odd diegetic shift that doubles *Good Newes from New-England*'s tropic blockage at the level of narrative, bolstering humoral metaphorics with a break in the account's flow. Winslow's story of the envoy to Massasoit is an analeptic one: it interrupts the story he has been telling about Myles Standish's visit to Manomet. Attempting both to trade and to probe the rumors about an anti-Plymouth conspiracy, Standish undergoes a number of threats to his life in this scene. (At one point his inability to sleep—another salvific humoral interruption—prevents him from being assassinated.) Having raised the military tension to a narrative climax, Winslow, in a formal sense, constipates his own narrative. Interrupting the story of Standish's return with his news of Native antipathy, Winslow steps back in time and takes almost five pages of a sixty-six-page text to tell the story of Massasoit's cure. At the end of it, Winslow acknowledges to the reader that he has gone on too long and that he could have gone on longer: "Diuers other things were worthy the noting, but I feare I haue beene too tedious" (32). Standish's delivery of the news is in diegetic limbo, heating up in the narrative appendix the text has placed it in momentarily. Blocking and then releasing his story at almost exactly its middle point, Winslow appeals to an English reader's sense of proper narrative balance, naturalizing the sanguinary scene that follows: the massacre of Wituwamat and his alleged coconspirators by Standish and his men.

Winslow's "preservation" of Massasoit by what he perhaps punningly refers to as "raw" means, nested inside a moment of narrative congestion, argues its writer's ability to maintain the proper flows of power in America through the logics that make possible his skilled restoration of proper bodily balance. Symbolically uniting transatlantic audiences by demonstrating a knowledge both of Native American linguistic vernacular (displayed conspicuously throughout the text) and English medical practices, Winslow balances the flux of indigenous communications practices with the constipation of Anglo-American ones. As Winslow reminds his readers, explicitly and through his narrative's form, more than metaphors are at stake. The flow of text and the flow of food between England and the colonies are interdependent. Thomas Morton, as we have seen, made a similar argument about his competence as a colonizer, but his narrative approach was to divide his readership along intellectual and religious lines.

In concluding *Good Newes from New-England,* Winslow binds his readers once again. This time, he leaves the maintenance of proper flow at least partly in their hands. The beginnings of the plantation, he reminds his audience, were "raw, small, and difficult," and while he has "seene [English] men stagger by reason of faintenesse for want of foode," at any moment these same men might be "swallowed" up by the Natives (64, 52). Rawness begins as a metaphor, but its connotations of digestive risk resonate when actual starvation is described. Winslow insists that the loss of balance has in part been caused by exaggerated published textual accounts of the settlement. Emigrants left England thinking to find America a land of plenty, but, "their foolish imagination made voyde"—at one level of meaning, turned to shit—they then despaired of survival. Winslow's concern is with the difficulty of the flow of transatlantic information and goods as he reminds us of the frequent "repulses" captains offered to settler requests for food and of the wrecks of supply ships. But he is equally concerned with the authority wielded in the print marketplace by accounts that did make it back to England. Mourt's *Relation,* for example, "came to the Presse against my will and knowledge" containing too-exuberant praise of American natural bounty by Winslow himself (52). Such an incontinent print sphere, combined with a constipated Atlantic, made for a shortage of literal digestible matter in the colonies.

Cooking and Colony Building

For London print audiences, Winslow's depiction of his management of information and bodily flows would have demonstrated his mastery of important
aspects of Englishness and natural philosophy. The diplomat here makes an
argument for the competence of Separatist colonization by using discourses
with which the Separatists were not always in accord. (Humor theory and its
relationship to providential authority, as well as the value of traditional or folk
knowledge that sometimes could seem like witchcraft, were contested subjects.)
As in Morton's *New English Canaan,* the native English audience is invited to
imagine indigenous people as part of the public and as potential audiences for
colonial communications. The complex dynamic of distancing and bringing
together that characterizes Morton's text is at work in Winslow's, too. Native
literacy, for Morton, both brought Indians into English debates and could serve
as a tool for their economic subjection; in *Good Newes from New-England,*
Indians join English audiences as readers of Winslow's actions, but English
readers are enjoined to re-create distance between themselves and the Natives
by becoming actors, performing civility.[43]

Winslow is concerned with the American Indian audience from the beginning of *Good Newes from New-England.* The colony is not yet an English audi-
ential space, he emphasizes in the dedicatory epistle; one cannot act there
as one acts back home. Even though it is a working, residential space that is
increasingly "English," it is one that requires qualifications. People who would
live there must be reasonably godly, for example, before they arrive, rather than
counting on the fact that in New England "the Church of God" is "feared in
sincerity" and thus can correct bad characters (A2r). Winslow asks readers to
keep in mind that Plymouth has an indigenous American audience that must
be maintained *as* an audience, "with astonishment and feare of vs" (A2v). If
not, the Galenic flows may be reversed, fulfilling Winslow's fears of the English
being "swallowed . . . up" (A2v) by them. The "Doctrine of manners," Winslow
writes, "ought first to bee Preached by giuing good example to the poore Savage Heathens amongst whom they liue." Winslow's audiences are joined, articulated, by his grammar: literally, the "vpright life and conversation" (speaking
properly will prevent its opposite oral action, "swallowing" by the Indians) performed for the Native Americans will help make more Englishmen use good
manners (A3v).

Assuming that the details of Winslow's account of his own behavior at
Sowams are reasonably accurate, what might the reception of his performance
in the theater of Massasoit's house have been? Winslow's successes in defending

the colonies' political status in England and his widespread fame as a negotiator suggest that his native audience believed him to be a good systems administrator. (Roger Williams, for example, went up against him in England while defending the charter for Providence Plantations, but never ceased to praise "that great and pious Soule, Mr Winslow," for his astuteness and honesty.)[44] But thinking about Winslow's American Indian reception suggests that gender and rank, as partially but not completely intercultural categories, played fundamental roles in the publication event that was Massasoit's cure.

What is known of Wampanoag theories of the body and of its reciprocity with nature suggests that, in the light of humor theory's interweaving of environment and person, those ideas shared many concepts with English ones. Human bodies were understood as malleable, capable of morphing into other-than-human forms such as animals. Manipulation of the body to produce effects on the mind or personality were customary, as for example in the use of emetics during adolescent manhood rituals to induce spiritual visions. Sexual difference underwrote social roles and demanded different health practices for men and women, although the particular elements of these, such as seclusion during menstruation, differed notably from English traditions. As was the case with the English, supernatural interference was considered to be a frequent first cause of illness. But also as with the English, some diseases had well-known treatments, from vegetable-matter plasters that fought topical infection to medicines for stomach pain.[45] In a world shaped by reciprocity among men, gods, and the other-than-human, the flow of commitment and responsibility, like the flow of seasons and of the body, were of central concern. The Wampanoag were not reported to possess a reliable treatment for constipation; Winslow benefited in this case from his culture's obsession with digestion and, perhaps, from its peculiar dietary features.[46]

Certainly, given that the set of symptoms from which Massasoit suffered required *pawwaw* treatment, Winslow's success in curing Massasoit must have conferred tremendous respect. *Pawwaws* were predominantly men, they often had a streak of the renegade, and they had to be conversant with all forms of power, whether creative, destructive, or trick playing. Occupying this role, Kathleen Bragdon writes, "were adepts whose knowledge of medicines and treatments was enlightened by their unique relationships with supernatural forces or beings, and whose own actions might affect the health of individuals or groups." Treatment was directed not so much at an individual as *through* her to the larger system. As was the case for the English, for Algonquian society "the health of the individual was often understood to be a mirror of community well-being." Ritual gift-distribution ceremonies and harvest celebrations were occasions that made explicit the interdependencies both among humans (economic, familial, or intimate) and between humans and the other-than-human (health, fortune in war or play, spiritual revelation through dreams). The same could be said of healing rituals.[47]

What Winslow was doing in treating Massasoit probably seemed from the Wampanoag perspective to be an odd mix of medical and domestic work. The forms of authority, political and medical, that he garnered in treating Massasoit cut across the gendered practices imagined to attach to those forms. The Wampanoag had four leadership ranks: sachem, *pawwaw, pniese* (an exceptionally skilled military and political adviser), and a role whose label was unreported, occupied by warriors thought to be invincible. Textual and archaeological sources suggest that while sachems and *pawwaws* were occasionally women, warriors and *pnieses* were not. Winslow was clearly neither a sachem nor primarily a military man. He had been sent by a superior on more than one occasion to negotiate with Massasoit, and Myles Standish was unambiguously the military leader. But unlike a *pawwaw*'s cures, Winslow's did not involve the kinds of manipulation of insects, colors, fire, or language familiar to the Wampanoag.[48] Instead, his methods involved cooking and herb gathering in partnership with one of the women of Massasoit's house. Winslow reports this in a passage worth quoting at length because it is crucial for interarticulating Wampanoag and English interpretations of the cure:

> After his stomach coming to him, I must needs make him some [soup] without Fowl before I went abroad, which much troubled me, being unaccustomed and unacquainted in such business, especially having nothing to make it comfortable, my Consort being as ignorant as my self. But, being we must do somewhat, I caused a woman to bruise some corn and take the flour from it, and set over the grut or broken corn in a pipkin. . . . When the day broke, we went out (it being now March) to seek herbs, but could not find any but strawberry leaves, of which I gathered a handful and put it into the same. And because I had nothing to relish it, I went forth again and pulled up a Saxafras root, and sliced a piece thereof and boiled it till it had a good relish, and then took it out again. The broth being boiled, I strained it through my handkerchief, and gave him at least a pint, which he drank and liked it very well. (28–29)

This treatment producing the desired defecation, Winslow praises God "for giving his blessing to such raw and ignorant means" (29). But though the result—and Winslow's shooting a duck later that day—marked the Separatist as a healer and a man, his picking herbs and roots and preparing and serving the vegetable soup associated him with women's work in the Wampanoag view.

This womanly gesture, whose interpretation was likely apparent to Winslow, kept him an enigmatic entity. Such a technique, garnering authority by deftly navigating rather than overpowering a system, worked in English culture as well. If Winslow deliberately introduced systemic noise by mixing gendered activities in the Wampanoag presence, he repeated the procedure in the form of *Good-Newes from New England*. The passage quoted above reads even today like a recipe: the goal of the recipe, the ingredients, the technique of preparation, the mode of serving, and even the pleased reaction of the eater are offered in sequence. Despite the explicitness of the recipe, Winslow emphasizes that both he and his "Consort" John Hamden are "ignorant" about the work required to prepare and administer a cure for constipation—work at this time explicitly associated with "huswifery" and the domestic "oeconomy" over which women, it was argued, naturally ruled.

The disavowal of gendered knowledge Winslow exhibits was not uncommon in printed accounts of domesticity authored by men. As Wendy Wall shows in her study of the popular household advice genre of early modern England, the domestic was imagined through paradoxical and competing notions of gendered duties and class desires. The household was, in the early modern era, the principal site of a family's economic production. It was also a site of ideological reproduction, and gendered divisions of labor were a part of educating individuals to a proper understanding of social hierarchies (including gender and rank). The realms of medicine and food preparation had not yet separated into professional and domestic disciplines; household guides contained recipes for and gave women dominion over both, commingling remedies from folk wisdom with those guided by Galenic thinking. A common fantasy of fatherly or masculine rule over the household stood in tension with one of female control over the realm of preservation—of food, of the family economy, and of the social order. A Puritan-authored domestic manual of the time insisted that there should be matters in which a husband "giveth over his right unto his wife: as to rule and governe her maidens: to see to those things that belong unto the kitchin, and to huswiferie, and to their household stuffe; other mean things."[49] As feminist historians have demonstrated, women's control over movable property—signaled in this quotation's reference to "household stuffe"—was less "mean" than previously thought because in practice it often balanced their comparative lack of control over real property. It has become clear that there was, in Natasha Korda's words, "a marked disparity between the patriarchal theory and the quotidian practice of oeconomy."[50]

It is no surprise, then, that domestic manuals of the time, often written by men, sometimes feature clumsy disavowals of female knowledge like Winslow's.

Nor is it surprising that Winslow did in fact know a cure for constipation or that he considered it likely that administering a sugary preserve—thought to assist digestion—would help ease Massasoit's discomfort.[51] Winslow's recipe, in fact, is strikingly similar to printed constipation remedies of the time, such as this one from Thomas Dawson's *The good hvswifes Iewell:*

> To make Pottage to loose the body. Take a chicken. Seeth it in running water, then take two handfuls of [V?]iolet leaues, and a good pretty sorte of raysins of the Sunne, picke out the stones, and seethe them with the chickins.and when it is well sodden, season it with a little salte, Straine it and so serue it.[52]

In assigning and preparing his cure, Winslow found himself in the difficult position of having to apologize for lacking both Samuel Fuller's more formal medical knowledge and women's authority over cures.

Another disavowal, though, is at work here. Winslow was very likely one of the printers of Gervase Markham's *The English Huswife,* produced at John Beale's shop while Winslow was an apprentice there in 1615.[53] This popular compendium of household advice and instruction was part of an active public contest over models of domesticity. As Wall shows, books like Hugh Plat's *Delightes for Ladies* (London, 1602) appealed to a desire to display refinement among social-climbing urbanites and country gentry. Consequently, its recipes focus on spectacular effect, trompe l'oeil confectionery, and unusual dishes. In contrast, the book Winslow probably helped print argued for an efficient, morality-conscious home economy based, as Markham's title signals, on traditions imagined as distinctly English. *The English Huswife* describes a remarkable range of procedures for home production and medical treatment. "Markham makes the productive household the place in which the middling sort could rescue the national rhythms of days past," Wall writes, while Plat "places the household at the forefront of a malleable social order dependent on innovation and the market."[54]

That Winslow claims to be ignorant of such things, despite having printed a home economy book, paradoxically helps align *Good Newes from New-England* with Markham's argument about domesticity. Concealing his role in the commercialization of traditional knowledge allows Winslow to act as the male bringer of "newes," while womanly knowledge, pervasive but not explicitly attached to Winslow's body or text, stays healthily old. That Winslow finds the cure is a result of the cure's emergence from his traditions, from an unnamable but English sense of what would make a good constipation cure.[55] The rhetorical tactic doesn't eradicate tension though. While changing both cultures was, at least in part, what Winslow was attempting to do, playing woman between two cultures ran risks with both. For a Separatist and cosmopolite like Winslow, such a vertigo was fundamentally prescribed by God's command to members of the true church to be spiritual pilgrims and to question the connections between nation and religion. But in depicting Massasoit's illness, Winslow extended the common humanity posited by Galenic theory and by Separatist theology to Native American bodies in a way that many English would have seen as threatening. The ambivalence of gendered domains, first in gesture and then in genre, makes possible the approach of Wampanoagness and Englishness through Winslow and Massasoit, while the notion of a natively English cure retreats from such a conjunction.

The printing and distribution of *Good Newes from New-England* in London was not the end of this publication event. The last seventeenth-century word on this incident might well have come from Massasoit, who commemorated the cure over a decade later by playing a practical joke on Plymouth. John Winthrop recorded what he called this "pleasant passage . . . acted by the Indians" in his journal for 1634. As Winslow was returning from a trip to Connecticut,

> intendinge to returne by land, he went to Osamekin the Sagamore his olde Allye, who offered to conducte him home to Plim: but before they tooke their iornye Osamekin sent one of his men to Plim: to tell them that mr winslowe was dead, & directed him to shewe how & where he was killed: wherevpon there was muche feare & sorrowe at Plim; the next daye when Osamekin brought him home, they asked him why he sent such worde, &c: he answeared, that it was their maner to doe so, that they might be more wellcome when they came home.[56]

As Mark Twain might point out, premature reporting of mortality is one of the oldest ones in the book. But this deliberate deception has a complex relation to the past. Reversing the roles of the crisis at Sowams eleven years earlier, Massasoit sends deliberate misinformation to the Plymouth colony. The news of his own death having been exaggerated, he reenacts and reverses the confusion of Winslow's midnight trip through the woods. He then augments the misinformation in answer to the naïve question about his motives. Massasoit mocks the English notion of culture itself—a warning that still resonates as we try to read this incident today—by claiming that such deliberate misinformation is a Wampanoag trait or ritual. It is a many-edged joke, even leaving aside the amusement the recorder Winthrop clearly enjoys (partly at the expense of his competitors at Plymouth and partly at the verification it seems to offer that God intended some to be leaders and others to be followers). Where would the colony be without Winslow? asks Massasoit implicitly, suggesting his ambassadorship to Native America might be underrated by the other-worldly Separatists. Though presumably the jest offers an occasion for reminding everyone that discerning the truth in messages is a problem shared by all, it hints that uncertainty and ambiguity are conditions of being an audience. It reminds the English that though they have escaped death, they have not yet mastered local information systems and that a Native audience is aware that its "maner" is being observed.

The digestive system still offers suggestive homologies. Filled with bacteria that assist digestion, outcompete pathogens, and stimulate the immune system, our colons and small intestines are dens of parasites. The increase in marketing and research of probiotic and prebiotic foods attests to a larger rethinking of our relationship to the idea of the parasite.[57] Michel Serres observes that parasitology teaches us that "what is essential is neither the image nor the deep meaning, neither the representation nor its hall of mirrored reflections, but the system of relations."[58] For Edward Winslow, authority stemmed from his recognition of and ability to use systems of relations; as a result, his texts demonstrate what appears in retrospect to be an unusual sympathy for Native American cultures. But what they exhibit might be more usefully thought of as an unusual sensitivity to, and rhetorical performance of mastery over, systems of communication themselves.[59]

Winslow was adept at occupying multiple systems simultaneously. In this sense, he might be thought of as a parasite—but perhaps, learning from the biologics of the digestive tract, without exclusively negative connotations. There is no system without its parasite, after all, and it could be argued that the parasitical is the basic relation of humans to their environment—and to each other. We are all parasites, whether of food or other resources or of ideas, and we are all hosts in turn. For the Native people of the northeast, this was a truth with spiritual consequences. Reciprocity countered or tempered parasitical tendencies, and it demanded the care of ritual as well as of the self in order to maintain communal balance. One took from nature, tricking its systems into giving up resources. One also helped restore those resources by, for example, giving away things or shifting hunting areas, planting plots, and town sites. Not all Natives, of course, maintained such attention, and certainly most English thought of systems as porous, but not ideally so. The Galenic body itself, with its flows and precarious balances, was an imperfect system for a fallen world.

The settlers as a group constituted a parasite in many senses. They were a "para-site," another England, with respect to property and, to some extent, laws and customs. The Separatist congregants served as another "para-site" in the sense that they hoped to become a non-place-specific "garden" shut off from the world in fulfillment of biblical commands. For writers like Bradford, Plymouth Plantation was a "*pere*-site" (from the French for "father") in the sense that this biblical command also made them fathers of the subsequent generation of the saved. Finally, they were literal parasites in an ecosystem that, as Cronon has shown, the English altered so substantially as to empty the land of countless animal and plant species, almost to empty it of multiple human cultures, even to change the shape of the coastline and river lands.[60]

Winslow himself was a parasite in the literal sense—in the sense of living in proximity to another and in dependence on that other—and in a meta-phorical way. His ability to move among the signifying systems (including the languages, bureaucracies, and protocols) of the Algonquian, English, and Dutch societies made him at once important and risky, as those groups invented new relationships and ways of interacting in New England. If Native people respected Winslow's abilities, it was in part because he, like they, recognized the ambiguities that attended negotiation in any language. Winslow's accounts of his conversations with Native leaders capture this mutual recognition with a double gesture. They convey to English readers his own political savvy while suggesting that Native conversational practice acknowledged and exploited the noise, the interruptions and divergences of meaning that both infest and give meaning to communication.

As Winslow depicted himself mediating between the Wampanoag nation and the English settlers, he grappled with the problem of how to portray the relationship between information—medical, or more broadly domestic in this case—and a social order. Noise from New England, was, seemingly paradoxi-cally, a good thing, because it kept the colonists in the public eye and because it gave men like Winslow an opportunity to model the right way of walking, and talking, among those they were trying to colonize. "The body cannot be thought separately from the social formation, the symbolic topography, and the constitution of the subject," write Peter Stallybrass and Allon White, because the body is neither simply metaphorical nor natural but "is a privileged oper-ator for the transcoding of these other areas."[61] Winslow and Massasoit knew that the body was also a crucial site for thought and contest over flows—of power and commerce to be sure, but more basically of information. The flows of the body, particularly those of digestion, trouble the distinction between the somatic and the environmental, or the body as such and the body as property, or the body as bounded by a culture. They can come to model the means by which symbols or materials get around. Even in this the body troubles such distinctions because in circulating symbols and materials, the body transforms them. What goes in does not quite equal what comes out—unless something goes wrong. And if nothing at all comes out, both symbolic economies and material ones are in crisis no less than the particular body (individual, social, political, religious) concerned.[62]

Paster reminds us that "humoral theory was instrumental in the production and maintenance of gender and class difference." The inability to master the body and its boundaries, leaky or potentially blocked, was a source of fear. Galenic discourses, for all their radical confusion of inside and outside, put women, rustics, and others in a position of visible inferiority. The lack of control over the informational boundaries of new settlements far from the physical centers of power raised such anxieties to the scale of the colonial Atlantic. Narratives like Winslow's were shaped by a desire to demonstrate mastery at the level of the body social and politic. It was not the question of information not getting out or in, of insularity, that grounded these publication events, but the problem of establishing proper regulation, a balance of both the rate and content of information coming and going.[63]

New systems are born out of parasitical relationships, but parasites can also exploit commonalities between systems, shared structures that users of different systems are unaware they cohabit. In Thomas Morton's case, the homograph that the Maypole represented was perhaps an unwitting instance of such exploitation. In Winslow's case, the introduction of gendered elements that should have been threatening to his authority might have been intentional, an attempt to make the manly mastery of *Good Newes from New-England* counter the loss of control displayed in the exuberant and dangerous praise of American plenty in the earlier, unauthorized Mourt's *Relation*. But in both Winslow's and Morton's publishing events, it was the need to acknowledge and to link native English and Native American audiences that helped shape the narration of settlement. In curing Massasoit in print, Winslow was instructing Englishmen how to act for American Indian audiences.

Winslow, like Thomas Morton, offers a radical position for Native Americans as audiences (if predominantly through the body of an elite) and an unusually sensitive portrayal of an indigenous American society. But as in the case of Morton, we cannot forget that Winslow's account of this publication event was a power play. Displacing simultaneously the gendered authority of the home remedy and the spiritual rule of the *pawwaws,* Winslow's *Good Newes from New-England* adapts both of these to promote the "peaceable enlarging of his Maiesties Dominions."[64] He was both a settler and an investor (first in the amount of sixty pounds and later more as he became one of the undertakers of Plymouth's debt). Peaceful negotiator that he was most of the time, he ordered

Wituwamat's head displayed in Plymouth as part of the effort to strike terror in Native people that John Robinson famously criticized as unchristian. "How happy a thing had it been," the minister wrote from Leiden, "if you had converted some, before you had killed any."[65] Winslow would later argue against the role Samuel Gorton attempted to give Narragansett sachems in London politics through print publication, and he was integral in most of Plymouth's efforts to establish colonial outposts throughout New England. If his turn to the body opened up possibilities, induced noise in the colonial system, it did so nonetheless in the service of ways of thinking about spreading both the gospel and English territorial power that competed with Native sovereignty. And as the next chapter will show, there were alternative ways of looking at Native bodies and of thinking about proselytizing and power.

Three

Forests of Gestures

Figures are the acts of stylistic metamorphosis of space. . . . *Forests of gestures* are manifest in the streets. (Michel de Certeau, *The Practice of Everyday Life*)

[T]he Priest . . . spends himselfe in strange Antick Gestures, and actions even unto fainting. . . . I confesse to have most of these their customes by their owne Relation, for after once being in their Houses and beholding what their Worship was, I durst never be an eye witnesse, Spectator, or looker on. (Roger Williams, *A Key into the Language of America*)

It was to Massasoit's village that Roger Williams fled in the winter of 1635 when he was exiled from Massachusetts Bay for his dangerous political and religious opinions. Not long after, Edward Winslow made a present of a gold coin to Williams's wife Mary to help them make it through a difficult economic time. Like Thomas Morton, Williams was a trader, a dissident, and a friend to many Natives in southern New England. Despite Williams's risky ideas, exiled status, and lack of wealth, he was valued by leaders like Massasoit, Winslow, and even Williams's apparent antagonist John Winthrop for some of the same reasons they persecuted Thomas Morton. Williams was a network builder who operated across the signaling systems of English and indigenous polities. His printed works, produced in London, were still considered dangerous, but one of them is perhaps the best-known study of early colonial Native society and language, *A Key into the Language of America,* published in 1643.[1]

This little book seemed to offer a solution to the mysteries of Indian communication that made Winslow's readers uncomfortable. It was a phrase book, organized topically, with convenient illustrative passages offering insights into indigenous culture in the region of Williams's Providence Plantations (now Rhode Island). There was, of course, a catch. To use *A Key into the Language of America* to tap into the informational worlds of the Native northeast, one also had to attend to Williams's exhortations to godly behavior that were woven throughout the book and condensed into short, barbed poems at the end of each topic. The heathen Natives, he insisted, were by nature no worse than Englishmen who ignored their own souls.

So far we have looked at poles, medicines and healing practices, books and letters, and networked Native news systems for insights into contests for control of communication in the early settlement of New England. This chapter turns to another colony, another theology, and another set of communications devices. Here the practices associated with Native speech itself become the focus, inseparable from the broader, and to English eyes troubling, issue of Native movements. In the epigraph to this chapter taken from his influential study *The Practice of Everyday Life,* Michel de Certeau celebrates such troubling movements. Certeau was interested in how inhabitants of modern cities remake the functionalist, limiting landscapes within which they live—built by governments and industries that hope to limit human resistance—by literally moving where they aren't supposed to go, against the grain of urban architecture and law. But his phrase "forests of gestures" is no less suggestive for the seventeenth-century northeast coast. To English settlers, movements like the "Antick Gestures" Williams saw in Narragansett rituals were frightening. And as we saw in Winslow's case, Indian walking and running obeyed an unfamiliar set of rules. The forests, seen by Williams's Puritan and Separatist neighbors to the north as "wilderness" or "desert," antagonistic and unregenerate, were animated by gestures both Indian and other-than-human that only the Natives seemed to understand—no doubt with the help of the devil.

Still, for all his Protestant queasiness about Native spirituality, Williams seems to have been unusually open to intercultural dialogue, even to defending Native territorial and political autonomy. In Williams's rendering, knowledge of American Indian paths offers little comfort because it is used to illustrate English shortcomings. It is true that the tracing of communication in the woods of America, here as in the texts of Winslow or Morton, carries the weight of arguing for a model of English social organization; if Morton used *New English Canaan* to assault his settler nonconformist enemies, Williams wrote *A Key into the Language of America* as part of a larger critique of the entire organization of English government and society. Yet *A Key* has had a long-lasting impact on Native political power; to this day it serves as the evidentiary basis for much scholarly understanding of the region's Native ways in the early seventeenth century. Less an attempt to understand the Narragansett than a theorization of the relationship between communication and governance, Williams's text demanded close attention to Narragansett understandings of these systems and has served ever since as a ground for contests over their relationship.

In other words, *A Key into the Language of America* seems to offer the same promise of being a cultural go-between, historiographically, that Williams himself offered strategically to the leaders of powerful New England polities in the early seventeenth century. Generically, it sells itself as a lens for seeing from one language into another. But functionally, it is a kind of prism in which the subject of language is refracted into a range of concerns: translation, conversion, Indianness.[2] Williams's attention to Native life was guided by an obsession with how words got around, an obsession rooted in his theories of proper governance. This meant that when he depicted the Narragansetts, he attended both to how they moved through the forests and to the practices they used to convey, remember, and parse information. That attention, as in the case of Morton's *New English Canaan,* had effects even in the appearance of Williams's text on the page.

This chapter examines *A Key into the Language of America*'s fusion of politics and theology by viewing it in terms of communications systems. Instead of taking one publication event as its focus, it considers two: the depictions of Narragansett messaging practices within *A Key,* and *A Key* as a publication with a long afterlife. When it comes to the question of Native audiences, Williams presents a crucial problem, requiring me to introduce a methodological wrinkle into the story of communications systems and social power that I have been telling. That wrinkle is, in a sense, a wrinkle in time, a beginning of a suggestion that I will pursue more extensively in chapter 4: that attention to colonial media is a transhistorical enterprise.

Since the nineteenth century, as Perry Miller observed with exasperation long ago, Williams's works have been taken as points of origin for the separation of church and state in the United States.[3] His founding of Rhode Island as a community that tolerated religious diversity is considered by many the beginning of a particularly American tradition of liberty of conscience and tolerant, consensual governance. While recent analyses of Williams's work problematize that story, instead seeing him as difficult to categorize and even something of a deconstructionist, in other fields Williams remains an originary force.[4] In particular, *A Key into the Language of America* is a pillar of the ethnohistorical, anthropological, and archaeological analysis of seventeenth-century Native American cultures of the northeast.[5] To argue that Williams's vision of American Indian society both shaped and was shaped by his understanding of the way in which God's communications systems should be of primary consideration in the design of man's law is to argue that what scholars know about New England indigenous society has itself been profoundly shaped by a selective vision.

More important, that selective vision idealized certain aspects of what Williams perceived to be Native political organization and communicational behaviors—basic structures the character of which anthropologists and ethnohistorians have been arguing about for decades. That *A Key into the Language of America* is the evidentiary basis of what has been argued as the anthropological reality of seventeenth-century southeastern New England indigenous life is problematic, but it can also be instructive. Williams's willingness to think systemically and spiritually, but also politically, as he looked at Native culture offers ways of rethinking the goals of studying the Native American past.[6]

Williams's own movements offer an entry into the complex political context of his work. After examining his political theology, this chapter will turn to an examination of those beliefs' role in *A Key into the Language of America*'s focus on communications systems. *A Key* was itself a communications device: an examination of its own gestural qualities, its material presence in the act of reading, leads to a reevaluation of the role its Native American audience has played both in the seventeenth century and in current scholarship.

Roger Williams, Parasite

Williams was exiled in 1635 because he proclaimed four positions that colonial religious leaders considered dangerous to the polity. Williams insisted that any minister professing the true church must make a public declaration of separation from the Church of England. By the same logic, his second and third positions were that oaths in the name of God could not be demanded for civic purposes and that civil government could not be called on to judge people's violations of the First Table (the first four commandments). If this rigorous claim about the separate foundations for and conducts of civic and religious authority were not enough to frighten the New Israelites, his fourth claim pulled the last bit of rug from under the political logic of the settlements. The true owners of the land on which the colonies were built, Williams insisted, were the Natives: royal charters guaranteed no title.

Well before his exile was pronounced, Williams had begun to establish himself in Narragansett territory using Native and English trade and political contacts he had forged at Plymouth. His journey during the winter of 1635–36 to what would become Rhode Island may or may not have been in reality as arduous as he described it (and as retold in many accounts of his life), but Williams had a place to go and a society ready—if cautiously so—to accept him. His trading post at Cocumscussoc functioned as a nexus of Native-English interactions. It was a zone in which Williams could observe the Narragansett closely and a conversational space where he could practice his peculiarly hands-off version of Christian teaching. The establishment by English law of the larger Providence Plantations and eventually of Rhode Island, as the communities Williams and his partners negotiated with the Narragansetts were known, was not an easy process. Most of Williams's published works were issued while he was on diplomatic missions in London either to establish or to defend the autonomy of Providence Plantations as a chartered colony.

His belief that such a colony must exist both under sanction from England and in friendly, ongoing exchange with the Narragansetts put Williams in difficult positions during the Pequot War and, later, King Philip's War. His ability to speak Narragansett (along with English, French, and Dutch) made Williams a frequent go-between at the request of both English and American Indians. He was a complicated and sometimes contradictory mixture of translator, free agent, and double operative. Williams used his authority to carve out space for Providence Plantations, but he was used in turn by his English and Native friends to keep track of and to manipulate each other. Particularly in legal and quasi-legal documents—affidavits, official letters, formal complaints, treaties— Williams can appear contradictory, accusing Natives of being natural drunkards or double-crossers and advocating English dominance (to the point of selling Native prisoners into what was effectively slavery in the wake of King Philip's War) in language much stronger than would appear in the books and pamphlets he published in England.

But Williams's manipulation of the circumstances of production and circulation of different kinds of English documents suggests, at the same time, his unusual sensitivity to the sophisticated communications sphere around him. This does not absolve him of responsibility for his role in English expansion or indigenous slavery, but his relationship to communications systems throws light on some apparent contradictions. Why was Williams, a more virulent theological threat than most, allowed to thrive by both Massachusetts Bay and by the Narragansetts? How can—or should—the sensitive, influential portrait of southeastern American Indian life in *A Key into the Language of America* be reconciled with his criticism of Natives elsewhere? And finally, how did Williams's contact with Natives relate to and qualify his nationalism; that is, what relation might there be between Williams's life with Natives and his political ideas?[7]

Like Morton, Williams challenged the sovereignty of Massachusetts Bay and criticized its leaders' version of Puritanism and its relation to civil law. "Williams's argument," Neal Salisbury observes, "not only struck at the ideological heart of the colony's purpose and existence but implied that Christians and heathen were alike in all matters non-spiritual, including politics, economics, and culture." This protouniversalism caused tensions between Williams and colonial authorities when it came to Native America: for Williams, any nation that allocated territory for the use of individuals could claim sovereignty, "since the *Soveraigne power* of all *Civill Authority* is founded in the *consent* of the People."[8]

But unlike Morton, whose publishing site threatened Puritan control by advocating an alternative social order, Williams had something to offer John Winthrop that made a sustained relationship with him profitable. As Salisbury insists, Winthrop's reaction to Williams showed a greater strategic awareness of his potential to enhance Massachusetts Bay's control over both communicative and economic networks. At the least, "having a colony under Williams's leadership on Narragansett Bay was far more valuable than sending Williams to England, where he could only draw unwanted attention to New England."[9]

While Winthrop may have thought of him as a lieutenant, Williams seems to have functioned more like a parasite, or perhaps a ghost in the machine. His theological ideas were both products of and a revolt against an important boundary-defining discourse, that of evangelical nationalism. His ability to express and propagate those ideas using the law and the London publication sphere was a function of the system for educating potential leaders (in places like Cambridge) in a country whose governance fused religion and politics. Yet such a combination made him uncontrollable. Radical arguments for purification of the church and a cosmopolitan mysticism that prioritized the regenerate community of the "body of Christ" freed him from being invested in extant churches and particular nations.

Williams hoped for a revitalization of English faith and wrote many books toward that end. But his attempts to reform English governance did not seem to the Narragansetts to extend to their polity. The southern Natives, Salisbury argues, were probably worried mostly about their access to trade. The control of information was crucial here, too—and Williams's linguistic abilities and political connections favored him. The Narragansetts realized, as soon as he had been expelled from the colonies, that as a free agent Williams could bolster their territorial domination. Since his plantation firmed up English settlements by bridging the bay area colonies and the Connecticut River, and since Williams was not in complete agreement with any of the other English colonies, from the Narragansett standpoint "Williams's arrival appeared to ensure their continued hegemony on Narragansett Bay as the English supplanted the Dutch there."[10] It was in this context that Williams wrote *A Key into the Language of America.*

Williams, then, can be understood as a node, an informational juncture. As a result, he was something of a publication event in his own right—and he seems to have known it. No doubt, as in the case of Thomas Morton, much of his attention to information flows had its origins in economic interest. A smart merchant knew that maintaining leverage was a matter not just of tracking English movements, both intellectual and physical, but of knowing where indigenous feet and politics were headed as well. But for Williams, influence and economic interest did not determine his attitude toward publication. Williams, after all, could have been a successful trader almost anywhere. Before turning to *A Key into the Language of America* and its depictions of Native communication, we must appreciate Williams's religious understanding of communication.

If They Come to Catch: Transmission Theology

For Williams, perhaps even more than for Winslow or Bradford, how messages got around, who heard them, and where they came from were subjects of intense contemplation and rigorous theological justification. The results of this hybridized information theory—intermingling legal, political, theological, and social influences—are nowhere clearer than in his arguments about how religious truth should be spread, the publishing of the gospel.

Fortunately, Williams's unusual theology has already been studied at stupendous length by historians, specialists in religious studies, and biographers. In general Williams agreed with the Puritans with respect to iconoclasm, the evils of popery, the necessity of personal regeneration, and the need to return to the primitive model of the church. The departure from this orthodoxy that resulted in his exile from Massachusetts Bay and Plymouth hinged on a difference with most nonconformists about the use of typology to understand history and man's place in it.[11] The notion of the type and the antitype was a powerful way of establishing the relationship between the Old and New Testaments, with their apparently substantial differences. "The beauty of the method," writes Richard Reinitz, "lies in the way in which it makes it possible to find Christian meaning in Jewish history and ritual and at the same time to establish the fundamental differences between Judaism and Christianity." Unique to this method of reading, as opposed to the Thomistic fourfold approach or other canonical methods, was an appreciation of tension, of a multidirectional gospel and a multilayered experience of history: "the typological relationship indicated not only continuity or discontinuity, but both at once."[12]

For many Puritans, the Bible was the type and Christian history (of which they were a living part) was the antitype, or spiritual enactment, of the material events told in Scripture. For Williams, the Old Testament was the type—a material example, God in the history of the world—while the New Testament was the antitype, a spiritual interpretation of that history, whose example humans should follow in pursuit of grace. The coming of the Catholic Church, for Williams, had irrevocably changed history. The miracles of the Bible were things of the past until the Antichrist of the Roman Catholic church was expunged. Williams's interpretation of the place of the written word of God, following Paul's example in Corinthians, emphasized "Spirit" over the letter; a skepticism about written authority haunts his every turn of phrase.

The implications of Williams's typological interpretation for spreading the gospel were legion and are difficult to characterize for a modern reader. The conversion of Native Americans to Protestant Christianity was one of the stated objectives of colonial settlement and was considered important proof of its success. The methods by which such conversions would take place were controversial, as we saw in the case of Thomas Morton's defense of using the Book of Common Prayer to that end. Williams certainly opposed syncretism and conversion by force of arms, which he identified with Catholic practices in the Spanish settlements. But among the other extraordinary gifts of God that the Catholic church interrupted was the apostolic succession. The ministerial spirit of the early apostles no longer had a sanctified genealogy that would license new missionaries to confront those unfamiliar with the gospel. Williams believed that the first task was to fight the Antichrist and its followers, after which it might again be possible aggressively to proselytize as of old.[13]

How did Williams think salvation could be communicated to American Indians? In a diatribe against the ministerial activities and organization of the English church, Williams outlined his views on conversion and the proper role of preachers. Williams critiqued Anglican preaching on the grounds that it was performed not by a called ministry but by an evangelistic, proselytizing group. Such preachers were a hired cadre, employed by a corrupt church:

> English preachers are, not Pastors, Teachers . . . , but preachers of glad news (Evangelists) men sent to convert and gather Churches (Apostles) embassadors, trumpeters with Proclamation from the King of Kings, to convert, subdue, bring in rebellious unconverted, unbeleeving, unchristian soules to the obedience and subjection of the Lord Jesus. I readily confesse that at the

Pastors (or Shepheards) feeding of his flock, and the Prophets prohecying in the Church, an unbeleever coming in is convinced, falls on his face and acknowledgeth God to be there: yet this is accidentall that any unbeleever should come in; and the Pastors worke is to feed his Flock, *Acts* 20. and prophecie is not for unbeevers, but for them that beleeve, to edefie, exhort and comfort the Church.[14]

True Christians, Williams and other Protestant dissenters argued, had to rely on the kind of passive, environmental, or infectious conversion described by Paul in 1 Corinthians. "If any come in" to a meeting of the regenerate, Williams wrote, "yea if they come to *catch, God* will graciously more or lesse vouchsafe to *catch* them if he intends to save them."[15]

"This is accidentall that any unbeleever should come in": the church and its performances of prophesy should lie in wait of wandering souls. Once again, we have returned to the trap, the wolf, and the shivering Native. But in this case, at least as Williams would have it, the technology of the church meeting does not actively snare but rather makes possible clear evidence of God's will in the "catching" of any particular convert. The onus fell on professors of Christianity to act and speak from the well of their own faith rather than to regale others. Aggregate performances of personal faith would inevitably draw those who sought righteousness to the fold—their commitment recognizable by a spectacular gesture of submission (falling face forward).

This passive model of conversion implies a complex theory of communication. For Williams no less than for other Puritans, how one walked, how one moved and carried oneself in space, was fundamental to the creation of both civil and religious society. "Walking" was more than a trope for kink words and good behavior toward neighbors. It also meant avoiding making the sign of the cross, superficial gestures of politeness such as taking off one's hat at the mention of Jesus's name, or other ritualized physical gestures. Since Williams considered conversion to be a more passive, negative activity than did most English, the movements of humans in space glowed unusually bright with significance for the possibility of a truly Christian social order. The way one moved and how one articulated material space indexed one's relationship to God. Those who were prepared to receive Christ's gift but not yet regenerate had a certain sense of space and of movement within it while those, like Williams, who considered themselves partakers of God's grace, had another.

The English term often used to describe this sense of space and the proper movements within it was "civility." Scholars have suggested that *A Key into the Language of America* posed a basic challenge to the concept of English civility itself. This made Williams unlike Puritan missionaries such as John Eliot, who insisted to Edward Winslow that it was important to teach Natives civility first, then the gospel. J. Patrick Cesarini writes, "What makes the *Key* truly critical is . . . its reconfiguration of some of the basic *categories* of English—and especially English Calvinist—thought."[16] Williams, Cesarini argues, saw English audiences' understanding of "civility" as a work. That is, civility was considered an unrevokable status, almost a sacrament, in the fallen world. As such, civility itself was to be treated with suspicion by good Calvinists, lest they implicitly promote a doctrine of works. A doctrine that put civility first was a doctrine of works, for Williams. But criticism of such categories was only part of his argument; the process by which Christians interrogated the church was just as important.

Willliams often tried to model such processes in his writing. In many of his works Williams admits that his points were what he termed "controversiall," by which he meant that they were being debated widely in public, often in writing. Certainly in the openings and closings of his texts Williams could be a flowery flatterer and humble servant even to the ungodly. But this was less disingenuous self-deprecation than the demonstration of a willingness to commit to a particular structure of godly public conversation. For Williams, as for many radicals, spiritual truth, far from being a completed canon, was still being generated. For believers such as John Robinson, there was "more Truth yet to break forth" in the world, and only a sustained Christian debate was likely to produce it.[17] In Williams's work, as in John Milton's, this necessity is wedded to an analysis of the political systems necessary to protect not just the possibility of unretributive Christian disputation but the constant circulation of prophesy and interpretation in all media. The separation of church and state was designed, Williams insisted, to promote the publication of the Spirit, which was the only reliable counter to the Antichrist: "The first grand *Design* of *Christ Jesus* is, to destroy and consume his *Mortal enemy Antichrist*," he wrote, which "must be done by the *breath* of his *Mouth* in his *Prophets* and *Witnesses*: Now the *Nations* of the *World,* have impiously *stopt* this heavenly *breath*."[18] For Williams, even the rebuking of Peter by Paul (for having used the same approach to convert the Gentiles as had been established for Jews) modeled a contentious, agonistic, conversational Christianity.

These considerations of right walking and right speaking, the gestures and processes of godly comportment, informed the way nonconformists like Williams looked at American Indians. In *A Key into the Language of America,* references to Native American mobility or spatial concepts are not determined solely by politics. Nor are they determined by anthropological vision, a presumably naturalistic report of what Williams was seeing in Narragansett society. Instead, discussions of movement and space link politics (both local, performative politics and transatlantic print politics), Narragansett practices, and Williams's radical political theology. The movement of bodies and information was of chief concern—more than race, rank, or even trade—in the shaping of a polity. What, then, did Roger Williams make of the Natives whose movements, as the Pilgrims had found, were so difficult to track or understand? How could their "Antick Gestures" and other obscure signaling habits contribute to debates about good governance or church order?

Moving Indians

Williams's texts are vertiginous with motion, both his and the Natives'. *A Key into the Language of America* details the difficulties of getting around in the American woods, the movements (not nomadic but cued by the flux of food availability, disease, and trade) through the landscape by Narragansett families and towns, and Williams's experiences traveling with them. Williams's "wilderness" is no desert; it is striated by paths and trade networks and filled with people.[19] "In the Narigánset Countrey," he writes, "a man shall come to many townes, some bigger, some lesser, it may be a dozen in 20. miles Travell" (3). At one level, such specification was an important generic element of New World narratives. European settlement's success relied on both the physical paths made by Native people and by those peoples' web of social and economic relations. Williams's account of these relations and his rich depiction of Narragansett life made him a transatlantic authority on American political economy.[20]

To become such an authority, Williams frequently relied on Natives as messengers. They had the advantage of not being able to read his communications, and often his instructions to the recipient included advice about how to handle the desires of the messenger. But there were disadvantages, too—that speedy information system that Winslow used in his cure of Massasoit didn't always work when an English message was put into it. "Tis true I may hire an Indian: yet not alwayes, nor sure," Williams wrote in 1638, "for these 2 things I have found in them: Sometimes long keeping of a letter: 2ndly if a feare take them that the letter concernes themselves they Suppresse it, as they did with one of speciall Informacion wch I sent to Mr Vane."[21]

Native communications webs offered other dangers; they were risky to activate or even to parasite. In addition to physical risks, there were political and religious ones. Safely walking American paths meant learning some of the rich history of affiliation and conflict among its societies and knowing their current relationships with other European powers. That knowledge could be polluting in turn; as James Axtell has shown, many settlers were drawn to leave European settlements in favor of an indigenous community. There were risks entailed in simply representing these networks. English readers might not have felt certain they knew how best to exploit the New World, and they certainly disagreed about the best religious policy there, but they more or less agreed on the superiority of English communications technologies and social order. Williams's text confrontationally suggests that the Indians need neither in order to be masters of their terrain.[22]

"Machípscat | *A stone path.* | *Obs.* It is admirable to see, what paths their naked hardned feet have made in the wildernesse in most stony and rockie places" (68). To a seventeenth-century English reader, the admirableness of what appears today to be a purely anthropological observation might have been rooted not in scientific observation but in its resonance with biblical precedents. Yet Williams represents American Indians as "admirable" in the act of making the very paths that, only a few years before in the Pequot War, conducted them to war on English towns. Pulling the frame back, looking at *A Key into the Language of America* in the context of Williams's writings as a whole, reveals another twist: the one most often depicted as traveling through difficult places, making literal and spiritual paths in the wilderness, is Roger Williams himself. These hard, naked feet are the Narragansetts', but they are at the same time Williams's own. These paths are information networks for Native people, but they are at the same time potential channels for godly communication.

Michel de Certeau observes that enough walking eventually makes a path, but walking is also inherently errant: as a series of individual steps, its trajectory is unpredictable and fragmented. Walking has such power and such fascination because in an instant one can utterly change direction. "Walking affirms," Certeau writes, but it also "suspects, tries out, transgresses, respects, etc., the trajectories it 'speaks.'"[23] It was a truth American Indians knew and exploited: Williams makes no effort to shield the reader from the ways in which paths do not constrain Native movement. "They are so exquisitely skilled in all the body and bowels of the Countrey (by reason of their huntings)," he insists, "that I have often been guided twentie, thirtie, sometimes fortie miles through the woods, a streight course out of any path" (71).[24]

For English readers, Williams's dramatization of this unpredictable but expert movement had disconcerting implications. The trade and political communication made possible by Native paths was already haunted (in the wake of the Pequot War) by the possibility of the use of such paths for military ends. But if Algonquians could find their way even without the path, then there had to be ad hoc networks, invisible to the settlers, available to Natives as well.

When Williams goes off-road, on land or at sea, he specifies that he relies on Native guides, invoking biblical parallels once again to suggest that God works through the American Indians: "I having been necessitated to passe waters diverse times with them, it hath pleased God to make them many times the instruments of my preservation: and when sometimes in great danger I have questioned safety, they have said to me: Feare not, if we be overset I will carry you safe to Land" (109). In moments like this, Williams implies that political mastery of the Natives is, if not unnecessary, secondary to Christian salvation. Expecting to find the customary message that the paths of the Indians will help bring the voice of Christ to the wilderness, readers find that voice ("Feare not . . . ") already there. Instead of staging the mastery of systems Morton and Winslow perform in their publications, Williams's reliance on guides and his confessions of wonder at Narragansett pathways open the possibility that those same paths, and paths unknown, can bring violence to the settlers. Physical control of such conduits is not possible, Williams implies—safety must be sought by other means.

The fact that paths do not index indigenous movement might have been troubling enough, but Williams informs his readers that dwellings and whole towns move: within a few hours, a house he has slept in and hopes to stay at again disappears completely, as its owners move to their next group site. When his guides conduct him through seemingly unmarked wilderness, such detachment from space, customarily so antagonistic to European property concepts, comforts Williams. In one of the poems that conclude each chapter of *A Key into the Language of America,* he writes:

> *Yet I have found lesse noyse, more peace*
> > *In wilde America,*
> *Where women quickly build the house,*
> > *And quickly move away.*
> English *and* Indians *busie are,*
> > *In parts of their abode:*
> *Yet both stand* idle, *till God's call*
> > *Set them to worke for God.* Mat. 20.7. (48)

In *A Key,* the concepts of mobility and stasis themselves are always kept moving. No proper meaning or value can safely be assigned either to human movement or to fixity in space. Why does Williams deprive himself of one of the key rhetorics of colonization, the notion that the colonizer has the monopoly of proper meanings?[25]

The beginnings of an answer can be found in his frequent depiction of his own movement, by which Williams marks himself as a spiritual cosmopolite.

Williams, too, deviated from both physical and social paths: first from those of the state church and the university system that supplied its ministers, then from the space of England itself, and finally from the established colonies. He recites these movements in space and politics everywhere in his writings, both published and unpublished. Customarily he does so as an initiating gesture. "*I know what it is to* Study, *to* Preach, *to be an* Elder, *to be applauded,*" Williams claims in the preface to one tract, "*and yet also what it is also to tug at the* Oar, *to dig with the* Spade, *and* Plow, *and to labour and travel day and night amongst* English, *amongst* Barbarians!"[26] Emphatically echoing Paul's lamentations, Williams draws himself constantly in exile, caught between what were for radical nonconformists utterly divided realms: the spiritual and the material, God's law and man's.

His understanding of such exile made him critical of nationalistic religion, since the spatial logics of man's law—with its arbitrary (and interested) geographical or racial boundaries—were corrupt. Williams's depictions of his mobility and of the Natives' merged most powerfully in his arguments against state-mandated religion and, by extension, against the belief that England was the new Israel, the chosen nation of God. For him, the historical fracture caused by the advent of Jesus Christ rendered the salvation of the Nation of Israel a "nonesuch," a historical event with no antitype; rules for relating church and nation from the Old Testament were forthwith to be considered "*shadowish* and *figurative*."[27] It also seemed materially impossible that a large polity could be made up exclusively of true people of God. To call any nation "Christian," as many English habitually did, was to equate "christening" with "Christianity" and hence to emphasize ceremony instead of internal struggle, appearance instead of belief. To use such a nominalization to justify violence or land appropriation, moreover, was to risk one's soul.[28]

For Williams, then, the rationale for limiting claims to national Christianity—a component of European claims to Native land—and the rationale for restricting proselytization had the same root. In *The hireling ministry none of Christs,* Williams argued that to resist the proselytizing urge was to resist the church-state fusion that he saw as an impediment to rebuilding the true church. Williams uses the occasion of the debate over the civil employment of ministers to detail the logic of the separation of church and civic government. Space and mobility, both material and metaphorical, were fundamental concepts in his rationale: "Blessed be the *Father* of *Lights,*" he wrote, "who hath shewne his people of late times, the great difference between the *stated* and setled *Nationall Church,* the *Ministry,* and *maintenance* thereof, and the (ordinary) afflicted, moving, flying, state of the *Church,* and *Churches* of *Christ Jesus* all the world over" (7). The "setled" church and the "moving" one seem at first to be meta-phors for a lazy and an active approach to salvation, as in the poem quoted above. But later, Williams insists that legal regulations respecting physical space be altered to protect the fluid movement of godly conversation. It is "an *inven-tion* of *Satan*," he writes, "to divide the *Land* for *gaine*, into *Nationall, Provin-ciall, Diocesan, Parochiall,* so that there is not a foot of land left in the whole *Nation,* for the holiest . . . to finde a resting place out of such a *Church* compasse" (30). As Williams's readers would have known, nonconformist preachers were often of necessity itinerant, and their listeners sometimes traveled many miles to receive their ministry—some congregations had, like Scrooby's, sought refuge beyond England. Williams's argument counters, by revealing, the strategic pro-duction of space in England by its rulers.[29]

Reading this logic back into *A Key into the Language of America,* Native spatial relations emerge as crucial to Williams's assessment of the comparative potential of English and American salvation. The Natives' "flying" mobility argues for their compatibility with the primitive model of the church favored by English nonconformists. The Algonquians Williams has met have the "strong Conviction naturall" of the existence of a divine being of highest power. "I know there is no small *preparation* in the hearts of Multitudes of them," Williams writes; "I know their many solemne *Confessions* to my self, and one to another of their lost *wandring Conditions.*" Conviction and preparation are two of the initial stages of conversion. As the influential Puritan divine William Perkins wrote, "Beginnings of preparation, are such as bring vnder, tame, and subdue the stubburnenesse of mans nature"; preparation meant "the apprehension of gods anger against sinne."[30] Preparation's precise mechanics were much debated in Puritan theological circles; for Williams, the uncoerced, ambient nature of initial preparation hinged with the subsequent stages of the pursuit of grace, the catching by God of a convert upon hearing the gospel.[31] Paradox-ically, *Indian* wandering, not ministerial wandering, would produce Native conversions—if the English could be hospitable enough to allow them to wit-ness prophesying in church.[32] Having given them the ability to make trails in stone with their bare feet, carry soaked Englishmen safe to shore, and find their way without man-made paths, God seemed to have equipped Native Ameri-cans ideally for the only kind of conversion still legitimate in the absence of sanctified proselytizing.

The eligibility of the Narragansett polity for a proper sense of space, move-ment, and Christian regeneration was rooted for Williams, as it was for John Eliot and other missionaries, in the belief that God was no respecter of per-sons. In Williams's case it was also founded on evidence of Native protocols that encouraged detachment from specific places and attentive, noncoercive communicative behaviors. "Hence it is," Williams claimed, "that so many glorious and flourishing *Cities* of the World maintaine their *Civill* peace, yea the very Americans & wildest *Pagans* keep the peace of their *Towns* or *Cities*" without a godly church.[33] The form of Native governance itself, he suggests, is structurally resistant to the corrupt model of the "Nationall Church."

Before looking more closely at how *A Key into the Language of America* depicts those protocols, it is important to point out that Williams's assessment of the possibilities of Narragansett governance may not have been the result of his political theology alone. Ethnographers and anthropologists have suggested that the sociopolitical behavior of southeastern New England tribes was in flux at this time. Hereditary kinship connections, ecologies, and medical practices, forms of agriculture and hunting, tribute and warfare, and the comparative significance of trade among Native polities were all changing as a result of shifting intergroup alliances and European disease, settlement, and trade. Not organized strictly in band or tribal cultures, Algonquians during the mid-seventeenth century were centralizing power, formalizing tributary relations, and specializing authoritarian roles. This transition was uneven, and there is considerable debate about how best to describe such sociopolitical organizations. Anthropologists have used many terms, all debatable, to describe mid-seventeenth-century Algonquian affiliation, from "band" to "kinship group" to "village" to "small-scale variable societies." Williams began interacting with the Narragansetts at a moment when their practices harmonized unusually well with his valorization of tension and agonistic debate in the design of public authority—during the Pequot War, when he operated as a go-between for the Narragansetts, Mohegans, and Massachusetts Bay.[34] What were the practices and protocols that caught Williams's attention?

Narragansett Communications Systems

The Narragansetts probably shared Williams's habit of linking communication, mobility, and spiritual truth. "Speech located the community in the temporal continuum," Kathleen Bragdon observes of the Algonquians of this period, "and also tied it to the landscape, by being richly marked with significant locations." Brush and rock piles were used to commemorate people and events, while landscape features in the undulating New England topography, often considered to have been created or placed there by spirits or heroes, were used to structure storytelling. These practices, Bragdon explains, are only the most persistent of a range of techniques, the full extent of which is not known, for managing communication and temporality.[35] With his eye on an ideal configuration of communications systems in church and state governance, Williams found himself drawn to particular techniques used by the Narragansetts to transmit and store knowledge. *A Key into the Language of America*'s chapter "Of Discourse and Newes" offers a dense analysis of these.

"Their desire of, and delight in newes, is great, as the *Athenians*," Williams tells us, "and all men, more or lesse; a stranger that can relate newes in their owne language, they will stile him *Manitióo,* a God." In this typically packed sentence, Williams first links Native audiences explicitly to classical republicanism through their valorization of information circulation. But in referencing the Bible as well (Acts 17:21), Williams opens the possibility that American Indians, when spoken to in their own language, were prepared by this republican attitude toward news to hear the spiritual Good News as spoken through a representative—just as John was the voice of Christ.[36] The audience dynamics that accompanied Narragansett news delivery, too, indicate such a sociopolitical preparation when described by Williams:

> Their manner is upon any tidings to sit round double or treble or more, as their numbers be; I have seene neer a thousand in a round, where *English* could not well neere halfe so many have sitten: Every man hath his pipe of *Tobacco,* and a deepe silence they make, and attention give to him that speaketh; and many of them will deliver themselves either in a relation of news, or in a consultation with very emphaticall speech and great action, commonly an houre, and sometimes two hours together. (55)

This was an ideal audience for the still-common practice of publication by the spoken word. That Natives were customarily patient in a crowded audience and maintained close, silent attention would have been striking for readers accustomed to London crowd dynamics. "Emphaticall speech and great action" are here distinguished from the "Antick Gestures" of the Natives' unchristian priests. Williams intimates that the orderly speaker-audience relation of classical oratory may be found in Narragansett culture, implicitly differentiating it from *pawwaw* practices that, he argues, impeded spiritual progress. Such an organized public communicative sphere evidences Narragansett structural preparation. The aural customs depicted here conform both to ideal Congregationalist meeting protocols and to English notions of civil public behavior.

Shifting attention from the structure of news telling to its content, other fundamental, haunting questions from English public debate frame Williams's discussion of Narragansett audience dynamics: what produces belief and what evidence points to truth? Taking advantage of the dramatic weight of those moments in oral reporting in which an audience member claims the speaker to be lying ("Cuppannawāutous. | *I doe not believe you.*"), Williams offers the example of the Narragansett response to his own account of Christian soteri-ology: "Pannóuwa awàun, awaun keesitteóuwin | *Some body hath made this lie*" (56, 57). But after a brief list of terms whose recognition helps a Christian to know whether his Narragansett audience is receptive—a list that character-izes Natives as polite and reasonable, if rigorous, listeners—Williams turns to the earthly, political problem of truth that impedes Native religious conviction:

> Wunnaumwáyean. | *If he say true.*
> *Obs. Canounicus,* the old high *Sachim* of the *Nariganset Bay* . . . once in a solmne Oration to my self, in a solemne assembly, using this word, said, I have never suffered any wrong to be offered to the *English* since they landed; nor never will: he often repeated this word, *Wunnaumwáyean, Englishmen;* if the *Englishman* speake true, if hee meane truly, then shall I goe to my grave in peace, and hope that the *English* and my posteritie shall live in love and peace together. I replied, that he had no cause (as I hoped) to question *Englishmans, Wunnaumwaúonck,* that is, faithfulnesse, he having had long experience of their friendlinesse and trustinesse. He tooke a sticke and broke it into ten pieces, and related ten instances (laying downe a sticke to every instance) which gave him cause thus to feare and say; I satisfied him in some presently, and presented the rest to the Governours of the *English,* who, I hope, will be far from giving just cause to have *Barbarians* to question their *Wunnaumwāuonck,* or faithfulnesse. (57–58)

This is one of the most quoted passages of *A Key into the Language of Amer-ica,* and for good reason. Most readings of it take the scene as evidence of Williams's keen eye for indigenous mnemonic systems or as an indication of the uncommonly reciprocal relationships Williams could generate with Native Americans.[37]

In the larger context of Williams's political relationship with those "Gov-ernours," particularly with respect to the mechanisms that produce truth in testimony or evidence in belief, the passage becomes more complex. When Williams reports the phrase, "If the *Englishman* speake true," he raises a ques-tion in which he had deep interest, since it was in part responsible for his exile: the validity of oaths. A scene depicting simultaneously the theory of truth telling operative among the Narragansetts and the mechanisms by which such declara-tions were recorded resonated profoundly with ongoing English debates over the relationship between private conscience and public duty. The stakes of a national debate were expanded to those of colonial policy in the American woods, where Englishmen operated between (at least) two forms of authority.

"When we read early modern debates over the 'abuse' of ecclesiastical insti-tutions," Ethan Shagan observes, "we find an active struggle over the line be-tween public duty and private conscience—or between the church as a branch of government and the church as a spiritual body—in which divergent religious predilections produced dangerously divergent ways of thinking about the state." Oaths ex officio were a particular flashpoint for debate. These permitted the interrogation of individuals in the absence of a formal charge, which could result in self-incrimination. Punishing people for their ideas, not their actions, was a practice suspiciously similar to that of the Spanish Inquisition. Oaths, Shagan observes, "occupied a liminal position between outward behaviour and inward belief, a point where people were required by law to align their words with their thoughts, potentially giving the courts direct access to their consciences."[38]

Defenders of the oath ex officio navigated the boundary between common and religious law by claiming that an oath was an act and thus a ritual. While the monarchy claimed no authority over thoughts, it did claim authority over ceremonies, rituals, and forms.[39] An oath forced a deponent to convert an ineffable and secret thought into words; while under oath, such declarations were considered actions—what are known in linguistics as speech acts. With good reason, especially in a culture that understood aurality and textuality in performative terms, most English wanted to keep the meanings of words flexible. For many, opposition to the oaths' transformation of words into deeds was part of a broader resistance to the forced clarification of legal and religious boundaries, both in the political structure of the English polity and in its public speech. Williams insisted that the "Holy name of God [is] highly dishonoured by the Legall Oaths of this *Nation*" because the practice presumed that it was a converted believer who was taking an oath, which in "Millions" of cases was not true.[40] Presbyterians and some radicals argued that ritual acts were not to be so lightly altered by the monarchy and thus that the oaths were inappropriate, but moderates were more convincing. Williams's mentor Edward Coke was one of these, basing his influential critique of oaths ex officio on the claim that the policy permitting them violated English common law traditions.[41]

In Williams's account of Canonicus's complaint against English perfidy, the detail of the broken stick hints at a material means of accounting for truth that would have been well-known to English readers, the tally. Used for hundreds of years for transactions involving long-term debt, the tally was a wooden stick carrying notches that indicated the amount owed. The stick was then split down the middle, with each party to the exchange taking half (the payor took the larger portion, known as the "stock"). This method of accounting debt was still in use during Williams's time and would not completely be supplanted by bills of exchange or notes until the early eighteenth century.[42] As an authentication method, the tally had the advantage of being unforgeable. The unique contours of the stick as it broke were essential to the technology's success. While the tally had ancient roots, it would in this instance have functioned uncannily as a textual version of itself: a reminder of the past but an agent that authenticates the present. Native and English practices appear to be taking "stock" of each other. As a merchant Williams might have felt the tally to be a particularly apt response to the problem of accounting for mutual commitment. Its use by Canonicus suggested a shared understanding of the limitations of negotiation and of the power of material objects to record such wrongs. The advantage of the Narragansett stick—at least, in Williams's account—was that, like the tally and unlike the oath, it made no pretense of authenticating truth in the name of a supernatural power.

On display in this scene is Williams's mastery of both Native communications systems and English ones—indeed, his superior conceptualization of the ideal means of representing "trustinesse" and truth. But given that such mastery is a chief object of the passage, a reader must be suspicious of Williams's ethnographic verisimilitude. He chooses to emphasize a homograph, the broken stick—mnemonic of trust, as depicted here, for Natives, yet resonant with the English tally—and insists to English politicians that the work of producing truth is also a work of faith, bringing his text into the larger English debate over the relationship between civility and the self.

In telling this story in *A Key into the Language of America*, Williams engaged in some selective concealment himself. His correspondence reports that Williams himself had broken "a straw in two or three places" in opening that conversation with Canonicus, in tandem with showing the sachem a "copy of the league, (which Mr. Vane sent me,)" between Miantonomi and Massachusetts Bay.[43] Williams's experiences in the Pequot War crucially shaped his openness to the Narragansetts, as well as his suspicions of the truthfulness of other Native groups—and of the English. "Sir concerning Indian affaires," he wrote to John Winthrop Jr. after the war, "Reports are various: Lyes are frequent. Private interests both with Indians and English are many." Indeed, he came to trust the Narragansett sachem Miantonomi as much or more than his English interlocutors during this conflict; his estimation of other Native groups remained skeptical. As he revealed to John Winthrop Sr., Williams and Miantonomi collaborated to conceal information from Miantonomi's own followers: "Sir, Miantunnomu is close [i.e., uncommunicative] in this his project, and therefore I thinck the messenger is sent only for the Beades." In this episode, Miantonomi and Williams walked a fine line between normal diplomatic hierarchies of information access and deception, since the Narragansetts did not all agree about the alliances with the English or the policies forced on them in the aftermath of the war.[44]

One of Williams's many defenses of Miantonomi against the machinations of Massachusetts Bay emphasizes questions of ethnicity, truth telling, and religion. To disbelieve Miantonomi (as Massachusetts Bay seemed to be doing merely for political and economic leverage) meant one was trusting the reports of other Indians. In that case, the question of truth telling rested on the quality and truthfulness of the interpreter and the goodness of the motives of the questioner:

> Sir, let this barbarian be proud and angry and covetous and filthy, hating and hateful, (as we ourselves have been till kindness from heaven pitied us, etc.) yet let me humbly beg belief, that for myself, I am not yet turned Indian, to believe all barbarians tell me, nor so basely presumptuous as to trouble the eyes and hands of such (and so honoured and dear) with shadows and fables. I commonly guess shrewdly at what a native utters, and, to my remembrance, never wrote particular, but either I know the bottom of it, or else I am bold to give a hint of my suspense.[45]

This (somewhat self-serving) claim of openness is belied by his concealment in *A Key into the Language of America* of his own use of stick breaking with Canonicus. Williams also extensively employed the tactic of concealing his informant network from his English interlocutors. "Mr Stoughton hath bene long assured that *Meiksah*, Canounicus eldest Sonn hath his Squaw," he wrote in one letter, "but having enquired it out I find she was never at the Nanhiggonsicks." Inquired of whom? "It is true," he would say in later years of approaches to negotiating, "that Honestie and Innocencie, Reason and Scripture are infinitly Excellent in their Way, but are they Sufficient to charme (except God please to give his Spirit) Adders Serpents, Foxes, Wolves etc. yea or to order tame Beasts without Bit or Bridle as David speaks by wch we all know what David meanes."[46]

But once the wolves were charmed, Williams felt, one had to come through with one's promises. In the international context the failure of English promises might herald war. In his correspondence during the Pequot War, Williams explicitly reminded Winthrop of this risk; in *A Key into the Language of America* the lesson appears in more suggestive ways. Once again, Williams offers unsettling knowledge, this time about Narragansett military communication:

> If it be in time of *warre,* he that is a *Messenger* runs swiftly, and at every towne the *Messenger* comes, a fresh *Messenger* is sent: he that is the last, comming within a mile or two of the Court, or chiefe house, he *hollowes* often and they that heare answer him untill by mutuall *hollowing* and answering hee is brought to the place of *audience,* whereby this meanes is gathered a great confluence of people to entertaine the *newes.* (60)

Depicting not "howling" but "hollowing" (hallooing, or shouting "hello"), Williams depicts the reputedly chaotic soundscape of the forest as, instead, an efficient means of uniting a community: a single technique is used to guide the outsider to the proper space of public speech as it gathers a local audience. Here Williams, like Winslow, takes his readers behind the scenes of the mysteriously rapid Native regional communication. But as in the case of indigenous mobility, he offers no comfort for those anxious about the fact that the Natives have specialized systems for expediting information dispersal "in time of *warre*."

Indeed, in a comment that appears offhand to us today, Williams suggests that the adaptability of Native information architectures is particularly crafty in episodes of international conflict. While they usually use the shouted alarm to "give notice of strangers," Williams reports, "yet I have knowne them buy and use a *Dutch* Trumpet, and knowne a *Native* make a good Drum in imitation of the *English*" (18–19). This is not an adoption of European technologies but a tactical disruption of their functioning—both a refusal of the system and a manipulation of it at the same time. Are those Indians, Dutch, English, or something else listening, drumming, trumpeting in the woods, preparing to attack? Williams suggests that Natives understand systems as systems, that the boundaries between cultures do not prevent the strategic parasiting of both technologies and semiotic habits to Native ends, and that such parasiting might well be a necessity for all humans.

The Moving Page

Such a suggestion is amplified by Williams's performance of a similar tactical irruption on the very pages of his book. Williams and his printer deftly manipulated both English generic conventions and readerly expectations about the physical format of printed texts. Analyzing the shape of *A Key into the Language of America*—its origins in a particularly heterogeneous mixture of generic and morphological antecedents—and the print-culture environment of early 1640s London suggests the complex way Williams addressed his native audience through both spirit and letter.

A Key into the Language of America was printed in the shop of Gregory Dexter.[47] Scholars have noted many variants in the extant copies of the text; Lawrence Wroth concludes that without any evidence of any single copy being the first issue, it is likely that all of these variants were issued simultaneously. Given also the presence of corrections that only Williams would have been likely to make (as in the case of a Narragansett word set incorrectly), it is possible that Williams was in Dexter's shop during the printing, and likely that he was there to inspect at least the beginning of the text. Certainly the two men by 1643 shared a commitment to challenging "prelatical authority." Dexter had been subpoenaed for printing a tract by William Prynne and had in the previous few months been cranking out controversial pro-Parliament pamphlets, broadsides, and books.[48]

In the same year *A Key into the Language of America* was published, John Cotton chose to have Dexter print the second edition of his *The Doctrine of the Church,* claiming that he changed printers because the previous shop was not as artful at laying out "Marginall proofes."[49] As we saw in chapter 1, the margins were often where one found the main show in seventeenth-century theological texts. Like many writers of his class, Williams was conscious of the space of the inscribed page. In manuscript correspondence he was master of a range of hands and layout conventions for indicating social deference.[50] What Williams was looking for in *A Key* was even more challenging than such letters or the theological marginalia of Cotton's *Doctrine of the Church*—not just sophisticated dialogue layout, but also poetry and commentary, all in an octavo format (the smallest Dexter is known to have printed). A printer with a reputation for good layout manipulation was essential.

The visual features of the book resulting from the Dexter-Williams collaboration have significance for any interpretation of *A Key into the Language of America.* The work has caught the eyes of a series of literary historians, but its visual features have seldom influenced interpretations of the text's peculiar interplay of poetry, dialogue, and commentary. Here I focus on *A Key*'s lineated layout and typography. These features play with the temporality of reading, analeptically and proleptically restructuring interaction with the text. By calling attention to process and questioning the conventions of genre, layout and typography bolster Williams's analytical technique and his argument for civic reformation. Williams's book looks like a phrase book, but its visual elements refuse the sense of categorical difference between cultures such translation manuals sometimes promoted in his time.

The vertical lines separating English from Algonquian phrases are one of the most conspicuous and commented-on features of Williams's text. The presence of the line has raised questions about the relationship between Algonquian and English phrases as represented in *A Key into the Language of America.* Most commentators have seen it as a prophylactic structure, typography promoting phylogenic difference despite a pretense of conceptual continuity. David Murray writes that if we "read the lists of words and phrases horizontally, there is a strict correspondence. Narragansett word is matched with English word— or so we assume, but since we cannot make anything of the Native words or fit them into any linguistic framework" they recede into the background as compared to the English dialogue.[51] Yet there is internal consistency, redundancy, and ambiguity within the Algonquian word list: the phrases "You are heavie" and "You are light" are translated twice with only minor differences, while some words are untranslated, offered as equivalents whose particular local accents Williams does not reveal (see Figure 10).

The chapters on seasons and numbers, while certainly lacking the dense cultural context such concepts demand, present linguistic tools for assembling sentences and extrapolating words for figures (see, for example, the list on page 147, depicted in Figure 11). From the standpoint of a linguist, the internal consistency of *A Key into the Language of America*'s Algonquian vocabulary, along with fugitive instances of untranslated terms, suggests a complex recording of Narragansett language that does not restrict it to correspondence with English.

For scholar John Canup, the vertical line between the two vocabulary lists emphasizes the otherworldly quality of Algonquian rather than its accessibility through English. The rigid spatial division between the columns "could thus perform the distancing function of the cultural barrier the English sought to maintain between themselves and the native people."[52] But on closer examination, that line, in the original text, appears to be made up of many small vertical lines—it is perforated. The page bearing a translation of "Come hither friend" and "Come in" is typical: the vertical line is not a barrier, but something more reminiscent of Canonicus's broken stick, each fragment of which represents an exchange between the English and the Narragansett (see Figure 12).

The establishment of new relations via "coming in," or crossing a spatial threshold, poetically resonates with the porousness of the vertical bars. Williams's ubiquitous and often passive-aggressive *et cetera* ("&c") too, strays into Algonquian passages, indicating at times an unknowable continuation of a set. The *et cetera* challenges English readers to reconstitute some lists from previously presented information (as in Figure 1, for example), but baffles in other cases (see Figure 13). How are European readers to know which words correspond to the categories of the creation indicated by "&c" in the Algonquian column, or even which people's categories Williams would have one use, when launching into the conversation about spirituality modeled on this page? Here visual layout enhances the unsettled spatial configuration on which Williams insists in the content of his work.

For some critics, the genres on which Williams drew in constructing *A Key into the Language of America* have offered an explanation for this uncanny visuality. John Teunissen and Evelyn Hinz argue that books of emblems are

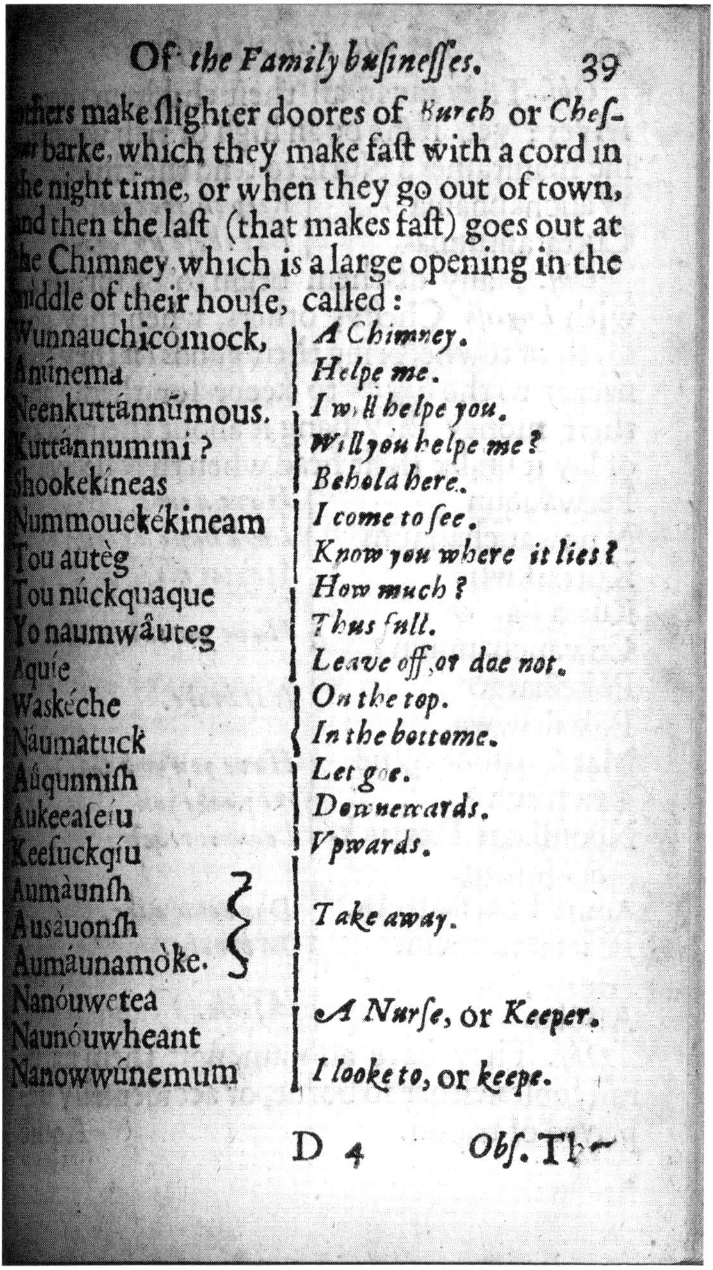

Of the Family buſineſſes. 39

thers make ſlighter doores of Burch or Cheſ- barke, which they make faſt with a cord in the night time, or when they go out of town, and then the laſt (that makes faſt) goes out at the Chimney which is a large opening in the middle of their houſe, called:

Wunnauchicómock,	*A Chimney.*
Anúnema	*Helpe me.*
Neenkuttánnūmous.	*I will helpe you.*
Kuttánnummi?	*Will you helpe me?*
Shookekíneas	*Behold here.*
Nummouekékineam	*I come to ſee.*
Tou autèg	*Know you where it lies?*
Tou núckquaque	*How much?*
Yo naumwâuteg	*Thus full.*
Aquíe	*Leave off, or doe not.*
Waskéche	*On the top.*
Náumatuck	*In the bottome.*
Aûqunniſh	*Let goe.*
Aukeeaſeíu	*Downewards.*
Keeſuckqíu	*Vpwards.*
Aumàunſh, Ausàuonſh, Aumáunamòke.	*Take away.*
Nanóuwetea, Naunóuwheant	*A Nurſe, or Keeper.*
Nanowwúnemum	*I looke to, or keepe.*

D 4 Obſ. Th-

Figure 10. The nuances of some words are untranslated in *A Key into the Language of America.* Photograph courtesy of the Newberry Library, Chicago, Illinois.

important formal precedents for Williams's text. Francis Quarles's book of emblemata, for example, mixes engravings, memorable moral epigrams, and poetry. For David Murray, it is wonder-cabinet works and books whose layout and narrative structure were based conceptually on this cataloging of marvels that are significant.[53] Others have compared *A Key into the Language of America* to contemporary grammars and dictionaries, and one could extend this comparison to disciplinary guides such as *A Key to Galen's Method of Physick* (1654).[54] If *A Key into the Language of America* looks odd to us, these analyses suggest, it is because we see with modern eyes; the book was less visually unsettling in its time.

The particular tactics and genres chosen for synthesis (or to produce dissonance) are significant in the analysis of any given work, but we must be wary

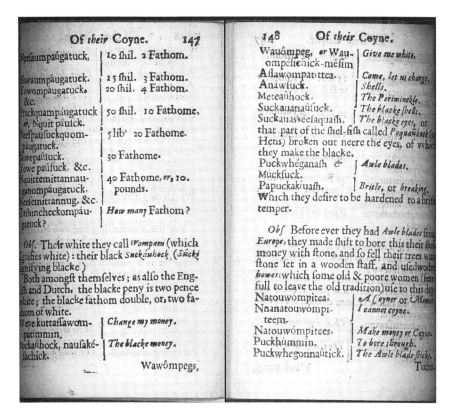

Figure 11. Roger Williams's chapters on seasons and numbers offer linguistic tools for assembling sentences and extrapolating words for numbers. Photograph courtesy of the Newberry Library, Chicago, Illinois.

of allowing generic precedents to determine our readings. As I have suggested in previous chapters, generic destabilization is a key tactic for writers of settlement texts, for whom establishing one's authority meant exhibiting a command of both difference and similarity. In this task, disturbing an English audience's formal expectations was a potential advantage, the better simultaneously to attract readers and to reassure them that in the strange environment of America there were nonetheless writers and administrators who could perceive and implement order.

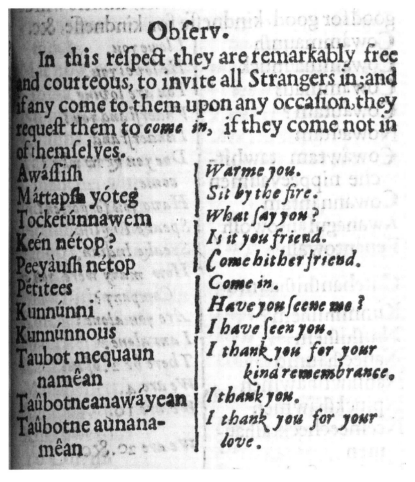

Figure 12. The vertical lines in *A Key into the Language of America* are made up of a series of fragments. Photograph courtesy of the Newberry Library, Chicago, Illinois.

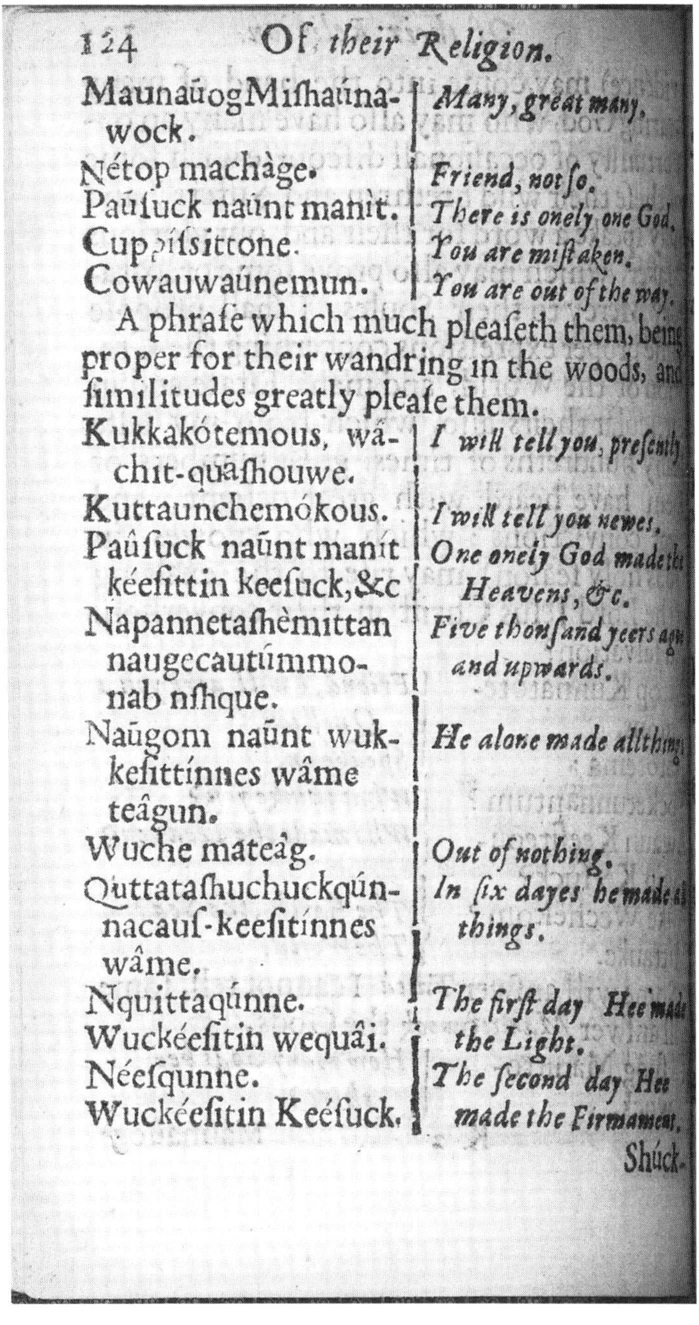

MaunaúogMiſhaúna-wock.	*Many, great many,*
Nétop machàge.	*Friend, not ſo.*
Paúſuck naúnt manìt.	*There is onely one God,*
Cuppiſsittone.	*You are miſtaken.*
Cowauwaúnemun.	*You are out of the way.*

A phraſe which much pleaſeth them, being proper for their wandring in the woods, and ſimilitudes greatly pleaſe them.

Kukkakótemous, wá-chit-quáſhouwe.	*I will tell you, preſently*
Kuttaunchemókous.	*I will tell you newes,*
Paúſuck naúnt manít kéeſittin keeſuck,&c	*One onely God made the Heavens, &c.*
Napannetaſhèmittan naugecautúmmo-nab nſhque.	*Five thouſand yeers ago and upwards.*
Naúgom naúnt wuk-keſittínnes wâme teâgun.	*He alone made allthings*
Wuche mateàg.	*Out of nothing.*
Quttataſhuchuckqún-nacauſ-keeſitínnes wâme.	*In ſix dayes he made all things.*
Nquittaqúnne.	*The firſt day Hee made the Light.*
Wuckéeſitin wequâi.	
Néeſqunne.	*The ſecond day Hee made the Firmament,*
Wuckéeſitin Keéſuck.	

Shúck.

Figure 13. Williams's "&c" sometimes lacks a clear referent. Photograph courtesy of the Newberry Library, Chicago, Illinois.

Williams's evocation of, but departure from, a text that is not often seen as one of *A Key into the Language of America*'s antecedents is instructive. Marten Le Mayre's *The Dutch schoolmaster* (1606) consists of a grammatical outline followed by dialogues in Dutch and English—often ones that playfully engage with the inevitable oddities produced in learning by repetition. Concluding the text is a section on Christianity, with an emphasis on brotherhood that likely addressed Anglo-Dutch political tensions of the time. It is plausible that Williams would have known of this book. He learned Dutch at Cambridge in the early part of the century and taught it to Milton while he was in England obtaining the Providence Plantations charter.

At times Le Mayre's work exhibits the narrative equivalent of Williams's "Implicit dialogue" in addition to the layout features of vertical lines, typographical distinction, and vertical side-by-side translation.[55] The choices of words to use for pronunciation exercises with the letter *K,* for example, suggest the complications of familial sexual politics: "Knowledging kunningly komelinesse kinswoman keepe-silence." Similarly bawdily, for the letter *N,* readers are to practice pronunciation with the sequence, "Naughtinesse, Nakednesse nethermost neuerthelesse notable notwithstanding." (The comma inserted after "Naughtinesse" is perhaps accidental, but it signals the presence of such cryptosentences.) Other lists treat politics or religion, in particular the vocabulary of religious persecution.

In the section "To buy and *sell,*" both the textual flow and the physical layout of the dialogue are similar to those in Williams's work but with a difference that illuminates *A Key into the Language of America* (see Figure 14). In Le Mayre, English is in roman type on the left and Dutch in black letter on the right; in Williams, Algonquian is in roman type on the left and English is in italic on the right. In the early seventeenth century, the layout conventions for texts of this kind were in flux, but the moods and politics attached to different typefaces were comparatively conventional. Black letter was associated with the authority of the Word of God as printed in the Bible; it also bore connotations of authority from the longer history of Continental print culture. Representing Continental Dutch (an increasingly competitive language of trade and banking) in black letter and English in roman suggests something of a contest between Dutch and English, with English holding primacy of place and Dutch primacy of typeface and perhaps pedigree.[56] In *A Key into the Language of America,* the choice of italics may indicate emphasis or aurality in the rendition of English. It thus seems to position the language in a subservient position by way of both type and spatial position on the page. Yet the multiple uses of italic to indicate emphasis and properness (as in the italicization of nations, proper names, or biblical figures) and citations of oral statements (before the widespread use of quote marks) balances the page, suggesting, as in Le Mayre's text, difference but not inequality. That is, although *A Key*'s layout suggests English as a target, and thus secondary language, its fonts read authority the other way around. Such a suspension was difficult to compose; using italics to represent Dutch, for example, would have swung the balance in favor of English, while using black letter to represent Native American language would have strongly suggested the author's subscription to a theory, current at the time, that American Indian languages, because closer to Hebrew, had not fallen so far from the linguistic and moral tree as had English.[57]

Early modern dictionaries and phrase books like Le Mayre's were not merely consulted for reference, as readers would do today. "Early modern dictionaries were not always read from cover to cover," John Considine observes,

Figure 14. Marten Le Mayre's *The Dutchschoolemaster* features a layout similar to that in *A Key into the Language of America* but uses different typefaces. Photograph courtesy of the The Bodleian Library, Oxford, United Kingdom.

"but they were written with reading, which would often be sustained over a paragraph or more, and sometimes over several pages, in mind. . . . Persuasion was one of their primary activities."[58] Vernacular dictionaries or phrase books were often designed to persuade readers of the natural superiority of the language, and by extension the governance, of a particular nation or empire.

Early modern English dictionaries and phrase books were no exception to such national designs: they were often dedicated to the perfection and expansion of English power. They were, in effect, tools of the state as it was imagined by the patrons concerned—and the patrons could range from royalty to academics. In many cases this meant that dictionaries were textual projects fusing church and state. The *Thesaurus linguae Romanae* of Thomas Cooper is a good example: *"Cooper's Dictionary,"* reported Anthony Wood at the end of the seventeenth century, "was so much esteemed by Q. *Elizabeth,* that ever after she endeavoured to promote the Author as high in the Church as she could."[59] Other examples, touching close to Williams's future territory, were John Florio's *Worlde of Words* (1598) and its sequel, *Queen Anna's New World of Words* (1611), whose title exhibits national ambition through an imperial pun.[60]

Williams's use of the phrase book for religious argument was in line with the general tendencies of dictionaries and phrase books to make claims as part of a collation of information not yet narrativized and hence seemingly disinterested. His use of the dialogue also had relatively recent precedent in transnational and multilingual texts. In form and content, *A Key into the Language of America* was similar to unusually cosmopolitan phrase books such as Le Mayre's. Williams affiliated his portable, small-format text morphologically and formally with a textual practice that resisted the conflation of national destiny with linguistic particularity. His combination of this visual form with textual renderings of Narragansett politics and signifying practices, and the argument he made out of them, struck at the heart of the church-and-nation fusion that other dictionary projects had often worked for in the past. It did so at a moment in English politics when the relationship between the two was hotly debated.

Williams did not have much chance of winning this argument. Most English believed that some relationship between the Church and civic government had to be maintained or chaos (or, more likely, a foreign Catholic takeover) would ensue. But that this claim does not come up explicitly in *A Key into the Language of America,* as it does in many of his other publications, might be telling. It was an uncertain moment in English politics. With *A Key,* ostensibly a mere "help to the *Language* of the *Natives"* and a set of wholesome observations, Williams could practice his brand of negative capability. The visual, linguistic, and generic features of *A Key* imply, rather than insist on, a separation of the religious garden from the civic realm. Formally (where the formal includes material and linguistic structures) it models the mode of passive proselytization for which Williams argues. Though Williams exhorts Englishmen to seek grace by comparing their fallen state to what he depicts as the relative innocence of American Indians, the political implications of his theology emerge only as the negative space of his ethnographic and linguistic narrative. At the same time, Dexter's visual choices work against resolvability, against positive foundations or iconological status: the broken line becomes the center of the text.

Williams and his printers tapped into a received vocabulary of layout when shaping *A Key into the Language of America*. But the fluid and reciprocal referentiality of its visual choices, when combined with its literary allusions, metaphors, secular implications, and overt religious accusations, makes *A Key*'s visual quality gestural or figurative rather than categorical. It emphasizes what Anne Myles terms "the syntax of relationship" among text, world, and readers.[61] To turn the pages of Williams's book as a seventeenth-century reader was not to enter the comforting space of Comenius's pedagogy or the illuminating realm of emblemata but instead a forest of gestures whose paths were laid by a peculiar vision of the primitive church.

"Noonapuock Naūgum": Anthropology and Williams's *A Key into the Language of America*

Like some other readers of Williams, I have been suggesting that *A Key into the Language of America* unsettles categorical interpretations of Native America that limit its interpretation to old-world paradigms. "Linking acts and footsteps, opening meanings and directions," writes Michel de Certeau of early modern travel accounts like *A Key*, "these words operate in the name of an emptying-out . . . of their primary role. They become liberated spaces that can be occupied. A rich indetermination gives them . . . the function of articulating a second, poetic geography on top of the geography of the literal, forbidden or permitted meaning."[62] But if *A Key* perforates colonial rhetoric, it does so nonetheless at the cost of real Natives' mobility. To say this is not to say that Williams's text must be read as either an example of colonial rhetoric or not; all cases of colonial rhetoric seek to restrict indigenous mobility, but not all restrictions of indigenous mobility are examples of colonial logic. Between these there are, as in the case of the Pequot War discussed in chapter 4, many ways a representation can go.

From the Narragansett standpoint, the mode of access to the "rich indetermination" of which Certeau speaks is, in the case of *A Key into the Language of America,* limited to the audience for transatlantic print culture. Powerful members of that audience gave Williams title to Rhode Island in part as a result of his book's publication. Despite the fluidity of Williams's page and the radical way the book as a whole offers Native culture as a model for the constitution of English politics, we must remember its Native audience beyond the terms Williams offers. As part of a successful public relations strategy to establish ownership of part of southern New England, *A Key* made an argument about property boundaries.[63] It matters who is watching, or reading, when American Indians move, a fact that unveils some of the assumptions made by Certeau's theory. Who is the audience for Certeau's walkers in the city? Is it only other city dwellers? If to walk "is to lack a place," if it is a liberating "indefinite process of being absent and in search of a proper," such freedom resonates more positively with Williams's ideal eternal pilgrimage than with today's likely American Indian readings of such movement—the Trail of Tears, frustrated attempts at gaining federal recognition, the persistent enforced separation from the topographies on which one's stories are built.[64]

In the previous chapters of this book when reaching this point in my analyses of publication events, I have tried to demonstrate that because of the mixture of necessity and threat involved in plugging into indigenous communications systems, the major texts of early settlement call for rereadings with Native audiences in mind. This chapter departs from that narrative in order to suggest a methodological caution. There is certainly evidence for a Narragansett reading of paths and of Williams's activities that would complicate the assumption that only English people made up Williams's audience. The "forest of gestures" was a political space for coastal indigenous people. Places accrued spiritual significance in ways that contradicted Williams's notion of history; animals, feces, and refuse largely absent from Williams's account sent reliable signals up and down Algonquian paths. Those paths were marked by more than feet, as tree carvings, early maps, stone and branch piles, and rock paintings all attest. Europeans other than Williams sensed how mobility shaped southeastern Algonquian lifeways.[65]

   But elaborations of such readings would be, like those in preceding chapters, based on anthropological and archaeological interpretations that are themselves based in large part on Williams's *A Key into the Language of America.* These might be considered reasonably reliable sources in the sense of their having been written by two of New England's most successful and least violent diplomats, Williams and Winslow, or in Morton's case by an outsider to the dominant theocracy and one who spoke some Algonquian. It is equally true, however, that they have been privileged in part for their capacity to depict southeastern Native groups as coherent and continuous according to modern definitions of "culture."[66] Instead of speculating about the Native audience, as in the first two chapters, in the case of *A Key* we might better consider its implications for modern Native audiences by questioning its evidentiary status.

What exactly makes a Narragansett, a Wampanoag, a Nipmuc? Is it culture, kinship, political affiliation, religion, or all of these? In speaking of the colonial era, who gets to decide what constitutes belonging to these groups? The stakes of such questions are high. The Mashpee Wampanoags offer a famous example (and one that will return with a new significance in the next chapter). When they attempted to win tribal recognition in the court of Judge Walter Skinner in 1976 and 1982, the Mashpee found that the mysterious standard of recognition required at least two elements: consistency and coherence. The Mashpees were recognizable as a tribe—implying coordinated activity both cultural and political in nature—only intermittently throughout the colonial and modern periods. As a result, the court rejected their claim that an 1870 decision by Massachusetts to declare the reservation a town (which led to its common land being sold) was an illegal abrogation of federal power.[67] Along with it went further control over the allocation of natural space and the political process in Mashpee. Southeastern New England recognition cases still await consideration by the Bureau of Indian Affairs; anthropologists and historians play key roles in these decisions.[68]

Influential answers to these questions have been offered by the work of Kathleen Bragdon in a series of articles and her book *Native People of Southern New England*.[69] Like other scholars, Bragdon is heavily dependent on Williams's *A Key into the Language of America*. Amassing and synthesizing vast amounts of information from historical, linguistic, and archaeological sources, Bragdon points out that neither the traditional universalist mode nor the globalist trend in anthropology answers the challenges of depicting what she refers to as the "Ninnimissinuok" (using Williams's rendering of the Algonquian word for "people"). The major differences among southeastern New England indigenous social groups emerge, she argues, out of ecological differences among coastal, riverine, and upland societies. She calls this "ecosocial" variability. Such a framing, Bragdon argues, allows her study to proceed from the inside of Native communities outward, rather than offering "a portrait of their relations with others" (xiv). European contact, in this account, did not much change American Indian culture until later in the century. Bragdon's work is invaluable; it has made possible the proliferation of studies of indigenous culture in the region, demonstrated new complexity in Native cosmology through close linguistic analysis, and brought attention to the richly complex issues facing anthropologists of contact-era Native societies.

The attraction of this analysis for scholars across the disciplines—its distillation of southeastern Algonquian identity—might also be its weakness. *Native People of Southern New England*'s portrait of the Ninnimissinuok could be said to exemplify the kind of coherence anthropology James Clifford warned against long ago in his essay "On Ethnographic Authority." Like literary critics still trying to prove authorial intention, Clifford charges, when ethnographers represent social groups as "whole subjects, sources of a meaningful intention," their corralling of the chaotic elements of culture obscures "ambiguities and diversities of meaning."[70] Insistence on an inside out approach to these societies deemphasizes the consequences of intertribal (and tribe-to-empire) communication. Bragdon shows persuasively how language, pottery, trade norms, and kinship dependencies circulated among Eastern societies. Yet once interactions with Europeans enter the discussion, she insists that the Nipmuc and the Narragansett, for example, require utterly different interpretive frames. This demand signals a theoretical tension that characterizes many studies of New England's indigenous past. Bragdon's summary appears to acknowledge critiques like Clifford's:

> The seemingly static character of indigenous societies increasingly appears to be an artifact of the perspectives of the observer, rather than being inherent in so-called "cold" or traditional cultures, for each has its own unique history, a history that colors contemporary events and actions. The dearth of first-hand accounts of Native reactions to European presence makes cultural adjustments difficult to detect, but Ninnimissinuok ritual in particular demonstrates ways in which structures and symbols were transformed in the crucible that was southern New England in the early seventeenth century.[71]

These are unique societies with unique histories, yet southeastern New England is nonetheless imaginable as a "crucible." While "structures and symbols" were transformed, culture and identity somehow were not. Archaeologist Patricia Rubertone offers a more skeptical reading of Roger Williams but nonetheless arrives at the same paradox of change and stasis in her descriptions of Narragansett life. "Here they would have conducted their everyday lives," Rubertone writes of Narragansett homelands, "in much the same manner as did their mothers and fathers and the generations who had preceded them, despite the incorporation of foreign commodities and the acquisition of new technological skills." Even if the question of how commodities and skills might alter culture or social relations is set aside, this picture downplays shifts in culture and politics known to have been in process in southeastern New England *before* colonization.[72]

This tension is a product both of political commitment to indigenous sovereignty and of the evidentiary challenge presented by the colonial texts on which anthropological descriptions of seventeenth-century Algonquian life are necessarily based. Rubertone argues convincingly for the interweaving of archaeological approaches with historical anthropology, uncovering in the process the history of uses of Roger Williams's work in arguments against Narragansett sovereignty. Yet even with the flood of archaeological data recovered by Rubertone, Paul Robinson, and William Turnbaugh (among many others), the narrative of coherence and continuity remains—and not unreasonably. Western property concepts and text-based notions of evidence privilege coherence and continuity under the rubric of a culture concept that is imagined to prove, with referential integrity, the validity of a people as a sovereign entity.[73] The concept is particularly shifty in relation to Native groups since they were declared, by Justice John Marshall, to be "domestic dependent nations," whose primary diplomatic relations are not with the localities or states in which Native reservations lie but with the federal government.[74] Claims of intermixing threaten the integrity of physical boundaries by undermining the cultural coherence that structures recognition, while to claim that American Indians have always been, like all humans, capable of deception or individual action might hazard the future of the few agreements that benefited Native Americans.

Other ethnohistorians have challenged this narrative even as they appreciate the dilemma faced by analysts sympathetic with the consequences of a more complex depiction of Native life. Peter Thomas has argued that because for most northeastern Native societies the primary political and economic unit was the village (and mobility was both a key economic strategy and a deeply seated cultural value), affiliation with and definition of social groups was a product of "cooperation among communities in response to outside pressures." The shadow of internal coherence cast by modern interpretations of archaeological findings obscures the complex ways in which individuals negotiated the tangled web of colonial power plays. "Persistent tribal unity is a figment of everyone's imagination," Thomas concludes; the "'tribe' as such was episodic."[75]

David Silverman has observed that the question of Native American religious conversion is an issue around which, for scholars as for Williams, theoretical questions cluster with respect to the relationship between individual and ethnic change. To address this, Silverman identifies a rhetorical tactic that he terms "religious translation," which was neither a permitted crypto-syncretism to help Puritans answer difficult Native queries nor a pseudo-Christianity on the part of Natives trying simply to preserve their own beliefs. It was a complex "acknowledgment that Christian and native beliefs were analogous at several critical points." Like Thomas's, Silverman's approach offers a new mode of historical thinking about tribal identity that allows for multiple definitions of sovereignty and detaches them from specific media or ritual behaviors. "Amid familiar accounts of cultural clashes and cultural misunderstandings in early American encounters," Silverman concludes, "were processes of cultural convergence, however ambiguous and incomplete."[76]

Williams's peculiar attention to mobility and to the structures of communication, rooted in his vision of Christian society, shaped his depiction of Narragansett country. In *A Key into the Language of America,* Williams offers a Narragansett culture more fluid and more self-aware with respect to its communication tactics than has hitherto been depicted. Such a picture should not be altogether dismissed in the consideration of Narragansett pasts—after all, historically, the ability of those who identify as Narragansett to survive at the most literal level has had as much to do with thinking beyond categories such as race, nation, and religion as with transferring traditional beliefs into new forms or protecting old forms. For Williams, Indians were, like all people, capable of both deception and sturdy friendship.[77] The most reliable lessons in Williams's text may lie in his willingness to value flexibility as a concept in communications systems—a concept that necessitates a material response in the design of social order. My point is not to invalidate Williams, Morton, or Winslow as sources, but to alter our relationship to those sources. Our own desires might appear more explicitly in our arguments about Native societies. At the same time, we should be open to the ways in which skewed accounts can be used productively, with caution and reading against their grain, to represent past societies and the processes by which they communicated, worshipped, traded, or fought.

Williams's text explores the relationship between communication and sovereignty, and while it emphasizes the kingdom of God, it nonetheless ruminates spectacularly on the failures of language to secure truth, nationhood, or justice. It serves as an entrée into the history of alternative approaches to conceptualizing relations between colonial powers and Native American communities. As such, it is an occasion not so much to recover the truth about the past as to see current issues and past conflicts in a mutually shaping relation. Recent work in Native American studies emphasizes that it will require more nuanced conceptions of indigenous affiliation, belief, and motivation to alter Western sovereignty concepts in a way that does justice to the complexity of the American Indian past.[78] The demand for continuity, and indeed the perception of it from outside a tribe, is a product of a legal structure and a logic of history that certain state powers have relied (as they have insisted) on as constituting recognition. Arguing for coherence is a way of defending Native self-governance for many scholars, who are well and justly aware of the significance of what academics say about the indigenous past for current courtroom decisions. But order is in the eye of the beholder, making it a weak tactic in the face of current technologies of U.S. imperialism. Understanding a polity is not required in order to respect its right to self-government at the scale of international justice.[79] As many tribal polities themselves emphasize, flexible understandings of sovereignty are needed, and then, in what is always the more difficult step, the cultural and social means of preserving the conditions of possibility for flexibility.

Making paths in the forest of gestures was a fraught enterprise for Roger Williams—whether that forest was an idol-infested England or a barbarian-ridden American wilderness. It is a commonplace in the critical literature to claim that *A Key into the Language of America* was "designed for the information and use of the English."[80] Paths made by Native American feet, and their departures from those paths, made a way for Williams to exhort an anglophone print audience. But in an important if indirect way, Native Americans were its audience as well. Williams turned to Narragansett thought in part because he wanted to see how *they* spread words—and how the Word might come into their sphere and circulate along the paths of the forests of gestures. When Williams wrote that the book was "for *All*," he meant it literally: Narragansett natural preparation was a model for English people and, in turn, the civil conversation that would result from the change in English government Williams demanded would be a model, bringing Indians to more godly ways. Such a program invited suspicion from both indigenous and English people. When Williams wrote in the name of what he termed the "publike *exercise* of the *word*," he meant something more threatening than usual to those who had banished him because he had tapped into both Native American and metropolitan circuits of controversy.[81]

Williams was not a characteristic thinker or writer of his time. His peculiarities offer us neither unobstructed access to the Native American mind nor a pristine example of cultural tolerance and reciprocity. Instead, they offer us a lesson in our own desire to produce understanding and how it is sometimes premised on a narrow imagination of the relationship between medium and meaning. For Perry Miller, what was remarkable and salvageable about Williams was his resolute insistence on breaking with the past for the sake of salvation. For Edmund Morgan, it is that he "dared to think." For some scholars, it is his sympathy with Narragansetts and his ability to see all humans as equal candidates for salvation—by extension, equally as human as Europeans. For others, it is his insistence on what they see as a precedent for church-state separation.[82]

What he thought may be of less importance for us today than what Williams's speaking was doing. Williams advocated an agonistic public sphere of religious debate, whose existence it was a chief goal of government to protect. In print, in moving through Indian country, in negotiations, and in private letters, Williams liquefied the viscous lines of communication in New England. He did so in the name of making Christ's voice heard and making the garden of the church's perfect separation from the corrupt world a possibility. If he saw Native society in more detail than other observers, and if he was favored by some Natives with a closer look at it, it was not because he differed from other Europeans who saw New World cultures through their own or in seeing his wishes fulfilled in America. It was because his vision was a complex mixture of discourses and logics whose shared ground was an insistence that the inextricability of medium, message, and messenger demanded the utmost attention to the flow of information. Such a vision problematizes the evidentiary basis of the very interpretations I have offered in previous chapters with respect to indigenous readings or uses of publication events in early New England.

As we have seen, for Williams the experience of negotiating the Pequot War shaped his developing appreciation of the cross-cultural difficulties of truth telling. For other English people, the experience of anxiety during the war took a host of forms other than linguistic ones. Pequot warriors were hard to tell from other Natives, made strange sounds, were difficult to see in combat, and wore the clothes of dead Englishmen. The next chapter responds to the problems of evidence in representing the Native past and future by suggesting that we consider the long-running multimedia struggle that shaped, and continues to shape, southern New England.

Four

Multimedia Combat and
the Pequot War

Quantify the myths
symbolic utterance of the Grandfather (Lenape)
count/years on the Red Score
which does not
count for history
(qualifiers)
(quality)
What mode allows me to understand
ten or sixty million dead (records fail us)
purple blood in rivers
burned villages seven hundred or a thousand in flames who knows in the
particular time the sequence undefined, time answered, held in by the stockade
wall, the Puritan army, the Narragansett allies: no one to escape fire or
sword.
How does documentation change genocide into grace?
(Paula Gunn Allen, *Off the Reservation*)

It is the Saturday after Thanksgiving, 2005, and I am on the Pequot reservation, Mashantucket. In the sunlit passage leading to the section of the Pequot Museum devoted to the Fort Mystic massacre of 1637, I pause; it is one of the rare places in the museum that is not dense with information. For a brief space there are only a few signs to read, and no videos or life-size reconstructions of Pequot daily life packed with sound effects, anthropological detail, even odors (as was the case in the massive display of the sixteenth-century Pequot village just adjacent). While glancing at my notes, I overhear an awkward discussion between a museum docent and a visitor. As she talks, the middle-aged female visitor is half engaged, half continuing her walk toward the next exhibit, which documents the famous massacre. She has thrown off a line to the docent about it being all well and good to claim that humans had been on the continent for as long as the Pequots say, but that, of course, "we all know that's not true."

"What makes you say that?" asks the interpreter.

"Archaeological evidence proves it; Indian stories don't change the evidence," the woman replies. She speaks with a regional accent, perhaps Connecticut, New Jersey, New York.

"But surely," responds the interpreter, with perhaps practiced indirection, "each culture has its own stories about creation?" Waving her hand and side-stepping toward the entrance to the Pequot War exhibit, the visitor offers a dismissal wrapped in a concession: "Oh, yes, each culture has its own stories. Sure, yes."

This was apparently as far as such a conversation could go that day, on the Pequot reservation, surrounded by the state of Connecticut and by ongoing legal combat over land and sovereignty between Native and non-Native people. This wasn't just any reservation, after all; with the world's largest casino generating over a billion dollars a year and a rapidly expanding resort, the Pequots have been at the forefront of the transformation of Native America by the gambling industry, controversial exemplars of what might be seen as a colossal inversion of historical power relations. Since the 1980s, when federal recognition was granted to the Pequots and the tribe began to acquire land and build a gambling business, regional residents have looked with a mixture of wonder and anger at the development of the tribe.[1] The 300,000-square-foot Mashantucket Pequot Museum and Research Center attracts a substantial number of locals—but it appears not to have ameliorated the tension between the tribe's vision of its future and non-Native residents' suspicions or fears. As I watch her enter the exhibit's shadows, I wonder how the visitor will read the next Indian story in the museum—telling of the infamous, history-shaping destruction of hundreds of Pequots by English and Mohegan allies in 1637.

If societies tell themselves different creation stories, they also tell themselves different stories about destruction. In her elegant history *The Name of War,* Jill Lepore shows how the meanings and effects of war are generated both during a conflict and by narratives about it. Describing the uses of English literacy by warriors of the allied Native communities of southeastern New England in King Philip's War (1675–76), Lepore emphasizes the importance of communications systems both during the fighting and afterward, as each party laid claim to a legitimate use of violence. Wars are, paradoxically, occasions for opposed groups to pay unusually close attention to each others' communications cultures. But they are won in part by rigidly controlling one's own society's systems of communication ("Loose Lips," Americans were alliteratively instructed during World War II, "Might Sink Ships"). For Lepore, Native Americans were doomed to lose control over the meanings of King Philip's War because New England's indigenous people lacked printing presses and because alphabetic literacy was a risky skill for a Native to possess. Puritan ministers and historians and former wartime captives took control of the story of King Philip and, through extensive publications, assured the glorification of colonial violence—guided by God's providence—against deceitful, uncontrollable Indians. "Whether illiterate or literate," Lepore laments, "New England's Indians had little chance to win this kind of war, or even to wage it."[2]

Yet New England's Native people *did* tell, distribute, and pass down their own stories about the colonial wars. Lepore only retells a couple of brief Native accounts, neither of which constitutes important evidence for her narrative. More important, she is reluctant to discuss the implications of her *own* storytelling—print-culture based, reliant on Western ideas of evidence and linear causality—in the trajectory of Native-U.S. negotiations over sovereignty today. Reflecting on Lepore's claim raised a question for me, as I listened to that exchange in the Pequot Museum hallway in November 2005: if in the multicultural age, a debate about Native sovereignty is displaced onto a conversation about creation and narration, what happens to the conversation about war and communication?[3] U.S. troops were still in Afghanistan and Iraq, with few images or voices from those contests represented in U.S. media; federal recognition cases for a number of New England tribes were still pending or under appeal. The future and the past of war and cultural and political boundaries, and the way communication shapes all of these, resonate in historical narratives, whether published in books or constructed in museums.

The deprecation of Native stories is not uncommon in sweeping histories of early America. This is not just because, as Devon Mihesuah and Angela Wilson put it, "the colonial institution does not yet require [historians] to utilize Indigenous voices or to focus their energies on the needs of modern Indigenous peoples."[4] Most history and anthropology of the pre-eighteenth-century period is done by non-Native scholars, and relatively few direct material expressions by Native people of the region remain from the contact period. In the case of New England's indigenous population, successive fragmentations of communities and families by war, displacement, and disease were exacerbated more recently by reservation policies that often made it impossible to stay on the reservation (and thus to retain tribal privileges) while also earning a living wage. Such conditions disrupted the storytelling traditions of southeastern New England's Native people and encouraged the development of representational practices that, in a more pronounced way than in other groups, defeat the analyst's dream of access to pure, unadulterated information about a society. Many Native New Englanders do not bear the stereotypical phenotype of Indians or other markers such as language, and their stories are mosaics, heavily recombined histories designed not to recover an abstract real thing that happened in the past but to promote and recount survival in the face of colonial land grabs, cultural identity theft, and racism.[5]

Such histories add an epistemological problem to the technical problems with representing Indian voices. Indigenous scholars have contested the notion that history involving Native Americans can be told apolitically, or from an evidentiary regime heavily dependent on printed textual sources, or within a narrative of strict linear causality.[6] The history of the Pequots—and in particular the Fort Mystic massacre alluded to in Paula Gunn Allen's poem—emblematizes the tangle of methodology and politics that inevitably faces a historian of early America. The Pequot Museum tells the tale of the massacre from the point of view of a certain idealized Mashantucket Pequot tribal perspective. It is not the only indigenous account of the massacre, as Allen's poem attests, but it is a spectacularly public one, constructed by representatives of a tribe recently made wealthy through the establishment of a reservation casino. What might it mean to use the museum as a source equivalent in importance to the seventeenth-century published narratives of Captain John Underhill, one of the leaders of the attack, or the Reverend Philip Vincent, who was not present for it?[7]

As I have been arguing in the cases of specific publication events, the relationship between "documentation" and "grace" (seen broadly as a hope of future salvation), shockingly linked in Allen's poem, is an ongoing problem, not a fixed entity. As Allen and other Native American scholars and spiritual leaders have emphasized, stories about the past—and the forms of evidence they validate—help make the future. Scholarly detachment, in such a political ecology, is not so much unethical as impossible. Paul Chaat Smith, in reflecting on the difficulties of representing the Native past and present in the National Museum of the American Indian (NMAI), observes that since both knowledge about and visions of a group's history vary substantially within tribes, things sometimes taken to be important in history telling—the existence of discrete cultures, authoritative informants, reliable evidence—are thrown into flux. "I wanted," Smith writes, "to introduce the idea of history itself as something we had to fight for, it was never just there for us to know, and the notion that we all carried on these wonderful intact deep narratives of our past seemed . . . like so much colonial bullshit." Such contests for tribal identity are ongoing—indeed, a tribe will be considered in this chapter as a strategic, historically fluctuating representational choice—and in the case of the Pequot tribe, they have been embodied in events like the Pequot War and in institutions like the Pequot Museum. "Each story," Smith observes, "is spun out of the ideology of the moment—and the event—of its telling."[8]

As we have seen in previous chapters, the *means* by which the story is told offer insights as well. The Pequot Museum's use of advanced technology, of simulacra, and of confrontational rhetoric offers suggestions for how to read settlement texts. The representation of colonial-era violence is both a source for depictions of information circulation and itself a site of contest over communications flows. Beginning with a description of the Museum's Pequot War exhibit, this chapter uses the museum's emphasis on simulacra and multimedia to rethink the first accounts by William Bradford of Pilgrim conflicts with the local Native Americans. John Underhill's account of the Pequot War—the first major English-Native conflict in the region—shows the complex development of tensions about deciphering Native wartime communication that were nascent in earlier accounts. Anxieties over the flow of information and the decipherability of Indian motives shaped the Pequot War and the telling of history in ways that may be familiar to us in what we think of as the new age of information warfare.

Native simulacra frightened English settlers. In particular, imitative utterances threw colonizers' notions of legibility and truth not so much into confusion as into disturbing self-recognition. As we saw in chapter 3, the early seventeenth century witnessed widespread debates about truth telling, taking oaths, interrogation, equivocation, and how to know positively if someone were "saved." These debates required English people to theorize about the connection between words or gestures and things or inner truths every bit as much as Renaissance intellectuals, shaken by the discoveries of the New World, were doing. That the Natives wore the clothes of English people they had killed, imitated animal sounds, and asked leading questions instead of stating their desires directly reminded the English of the disturbing absence of a standard of clarity and truth telling. Such phenomena in turn threatened the generation of proper, just, and hierarchical authority that narratives trying to justify English violence were meant to instill.

The tactics Natives used in wartime communications—which blended acts of violence with those of transmission—caused an accompanying ambiguation of the "Indian" and the "English" in Plymouth's first encounters. As Joyce

Chaplin has shown in her pathbreaking work on technology and English colonization, American Indian warfare on the east coast usually involved both an acknowledgment of social boundaries and an awareness that cultural permeability could be a source of strength. These beliefs were evidenced in the adopting of war captives into the community to replace lost members or the staging of long, athletic battles with low casualty rates to show courage and maintain territorial boundaries.[9] Thus it is not, as Richard Slotkin puts it, that the Pequot War shows a mindset that "presumed no common ground between the groups."[10] Rather, English violence was an attempt to argue that there was no common ground unless on English communicational terms. Imitation and dissimulation were associated with notions of outdated or savage modes of combat (sometimes explicitly compared to Irish practices), but at the same time they prodded at the core of contemporary English problems of communication and hermeneutics. It was a tactic that the Pequots had likely been using for some time before contact and that, it might be claimed, they have used again in the twenty-first century.

The two Native communities examined in this chapter—the Nausets and the Pequots—valorized such deception as a form of war, and their ideas were likely rooted in both eastern woodlands politics and spiritual beliefs about the permeability of the human and other-than-human worlds. The clash of military cultures was in part a result, as Lepore argues, of the English tendency to define how cruelly an aggressor could act in terms of how savage one's enemy could be made out to be.[11] Because for indigenous peoples of this region the ability to intimidate and deceive were signs of courage and cleverness, and because Americans tended not to kill large numbers of each other in war, they were difficult for the Europeans to read. Yet, as in all combat, control of the flow of information was the fulcrum of victory. When the English recorded their narratives of these combats, they revealed struggles with and shortcomings in their establishment of such control. Knowing what Natives were communicating to you was hard enough. Knowledge of what you meant to them and how information circulated within American societies was frustratingly difficult to obtain in the early settlement period—but at the same time it was necessary in order to tell a comforting military story to audiences back in London.

In turn, a look at the difficulties facing English writers trying to tell stories about violence in the politicized atmosphere between London and New England suggests new ways of looking at the Pequot Museum as a representation of tribal identity. Instead of critiquing the Pequot Museum according to a more authoritative history, I view it here as a tribal expression—built mostly by non-Native anthropologists, architects, and archaeologists, to be sure, but at the direction of the tribal council. (The council, like all representative bodies, represents a subset of enrolled members' interests and varies in the degree to which it weighs external audiences in its evaluation of exhibits.) The museum enunciates a tribal history to audiences that include Pequots, other American Indians, and non-Native tourists and scholars. As we will see in the conclusion of this chapter, that expression is contested in ways that an individually constructed history is not. But before looking at the relationship between the history of the Pequot tribe and its museum, we must take the museum as one of several documents that tell us about the Pequot War and its meanings. The mode and media of storytelling are as important as the museum's story. Its use of simulation and simulacra helps us reread other kinds of evidence of the war for an attention to communications technologies that, seen in the long view of history, form a pattern that, if not uniquely Pequot, certainly characterizes the history of the Pequots as a social formation.

They Soon Lost Both Them and Themselves

By the time visitors reach the Pequot War exhibit at the Pequot Museum, they have passed by and around hundreds of life-size sculpted figures of Pequots placed in reconstructions of past eras in Pequot history. One 20,000-square-foot exhibit depicts a mid-sixteenth-century village complete with a guided audio tour, scent simulation, and sound effects. Through detailed synthetic trees, people, and even fish and dogs, the Museum's staff have attempted to capture the best guess about what precontact life looked like in the southern part of what was to become Connecticut. The multimedia range widens as visitors enter the Pequot War exhibit: there is a diorama of the fort; actors on video screens telling stories about the prelude to the war from the Pequot, Dutch, and English points of view; a large reproduction of John Underhill's famous picture of the attack on Mystic (included in his 1637 narrative of the war, *Newes from America*); artifacts; photographs; and the pièce de résistance, a half-hour-long, $7 million feature film—*The Witness*—running in two circular theaters.

The interpretation of the event is unsurprisingly sympathetic to the Pequots—the English perpetrated a characteristically violent takeover of indigenous land and attempted to eradicate the Pequots as a polity and a culture in the wake of the war. The plot is one generally agreed on in current anthropological and historical scholarship. As the use of wampum in the fur trade became pervasive, it seemed as if the Pequots and their tributary tribes—the Mohegans, the Western Niantics, and others—were minting money by virtue of controlling the most important shell-gathering and bead-production zones.

The murders of John Stone (a retaliation for the Dutch murder of Pequot sachem Tatobam) and John Oldham (by a tribe subject to both the Narragansetts and the Pequots) strained relations between the English and the Pequots. English settlers began to move into Connecticut from Massachusetts Bay, Plymouth Plantation, and directly from England, crowding the Dutch and Natives present. English interests in controlling Native politics and the wampum trade were catalyzed by rumors of imminent treachery spread by former Pequots interested in taking over the tribe. Connecticut and Massachusetts Bay demanded excessive (and misdirected) restitution for the murders. They also insisted on political subjugation from the Pequots, whose control was weakening due both to a recent plague and the difficulty of overseeing trade in the large area they had established. A series of military actions followed: Massachusetts Bay attacked first at Block Island and then in the Pequot home territory; the Pequots retaliated at Wethersfield; a coalition of Mohegan, Narragansett, and English forces led by Captains John Mason and John Underhill destroyed the Pequot community at Mystic; and finally Pequots were systematically hunted down and massacred or enslaved by the English and their allies. The Treaty of Hartford prohibited anyone from self-identifying as Pequot and demanded tribute payments from all tribes that adopted former Pequots.

But locating the authority in the museum's various tellings of this narrative is difficult. The assembled media compete with each other, both for attention and for hermeneutic supremacy. The dramatic quality of *The Witness,* which as one commentator observes is more docudrama than documentary, leaves the impression not of reality but of fiction, prioritizing the emotional effect of inducing sympathy.[12] Before the film begins, visitors are seated in a circular space whose vertical sound baffling and black ceiling with randomly illuminated recessed lighting resonate with the famous circular paling of the fort. The audience is put, metonymically, in the position of the victims of the massacre depicted in the film, just before the attack. But from the film's first image—text explaining the difficulties of reconstructing the war on film—the question of its relation to reality is opened. The story is told predominantly from the point of view of an invented Pequot witness to the war. This young man is assigned to be the "story-keeper"; such a role is reasonably consistent with, if partly an extrapolation from, evidence of Algonquian practices of assigning individual tribal members the task of remembering parts of treaty negotiations or narrative traditions.[13] But the film contains scenes in which the story-keeper is not present, and some of what we see is at odds both with historical sources and with the presentation of the war in the media featured in galleries outside the theater: for example, John Underhill, whose famous illustration of the Mystic battle features in two exhibits in the museum, takes no noticeable role in the film. The video screens outside the theater, featuring actors dressed as Dutch, English, and Pequot historical figures giving monologues on the increasing tensions in the region during the 1630s, create the same distancing effect. Visitors are encouraged to see the war as a complex product of political tensions among many nations by the aggregation of a range of performative technologies, each with its own rules for creating an illusion of the real.[14]

The aggregate effect of the museum is as much to call attention to visitors' standards of the real—to make that process of reading the object of the Museum—as to transmit a particular interpretation.[15] The character of the witness, dressed in a hybrid costume of English and Native clothes, calls attention to the as-told-to quality of the narrative while insisting on the legitimacy of oral traditions. The film itself, of course, is as much an aural as a visual experience. Visitor responses suggest a range of reactions to the exhibits. Looking at stills of characters from *The Witness* outside the theater, one group of middle-aged women (well-dressed and perfumed, perhaps casino-goers) asked a docent, "We're wondering where these pictures come from, since in the 1630s they didn't have cameras, right?" The question may seem naïve out of context, but the signage only indicates the characters' names and significance; from an evidentiary standpoint, these images appear equivalent in the visual field to the artifacts or maps that have just preceded them in the gallery. At some level, this question was about why such an unhistorical object as a film still would be included in a museum.[16] For some, perhaps more for the young, the multiplicity of media and the valorization of sensory media other than texts or artifacts as forms of evidence is exhilarating. Equally, the mannequins filling the museum—based on Iroquoian people who modeled for them in the 1990s—strike some as fascinating. But for others, like the woman who doubts Indian stories, such a shift in evidentiary privileges is disconcerting, eliciting performances of resistance, while the mannequins, I can attest from my own reaction, strike some as uncanny, even eerie.[17]

Such effects have been much discussed by scholars interested in what has been termed postmodernism, and their appearance in the Pequot Museum, which was opened in 1998, may well be a deliberate use of simulacra designed to unsettle visitors or appeal to a postmodern tourist sensibility. Before exploring that question, let us turn back to representations of violence from the early settlement era in New England. In these narratives can be found concerns reminiscent of those that characterize the Pequot Museum: concerns about the power of representations to shape authority, about demonstrating a knowledge of the real ways in which Natives communicated, and about decoding Native "deceptions." Tracing these questions offers a new way of thinking about Puritan fury during the Mystic massacre.

The complete destruction of the palisaded village at Mystic and the killing of hundreds of children, women, and elders—with accompanying celebrations of these deaths as evidences of God's favor—have hitherto been explained in two ways. Either these events are seen as logical extensions of European war practices or, more often, a product of an othering of the Native in which Puritans measured their civility in proportion to their violent domination of supposed Indian savagery.[18] Turning back before the Pequot War, to the first violent encounters on the shores of Cape Cod between the Pilgrims and local Native families, we can begin to trace a different story of the war through the crucial role played by control over embodied practices of communication.

William Bradford's account of the first few days of the Pilgrim arrival in the New World, in two publications, exemplifies the anxiety induced by English confrontations with Native communications systems in violent situations. Bradford's history *Of Plymouth Plantation* is one of the best-known works of the early settlement, self-consciously fashioned as an account designed to be "profitable" both to Plymouth and to future leaders of the colony.[19] The text is careful to demonstrate Bradford's suitability as a leader through his mastery of the flows of communication in and out of New England, both those involving the investors and sympathizers back in Europe and those involving God, via providential messaging or communal expressions of thanks or contrition. But it is not the only account of incidents in which the governor was involved. The earliest published example of a violent New World encounter in the settlement of New England comes from the 1622 text whose publication seems to have bothered Edward Winslow, Mourt's *Relation*. It is the story of Bradford's falling into a deer trap with which I began this book.[20]

> [A]s we wandred we came to a tree, where a yong Spritt was bowed downe over a bow, and some Acornes strewed vnder neath; *Stephen Hopkins* sayd, it had beene to catch some Deere, so, as we were looking at it, *William Bradford* being in the *Reare*, when he came looked also vpon it, and as he went about, it gaue a sodaine jerk vp, and he was immediately caught by the leg. (7–8)

As I argued earlier, the fact that this amusing incident does not appear in *Of Plymouth Plantation* suggests an editorial concern over communication as a system that shapes Bradford's narrative. In particular, this scene reveals two shortcomings in the Separatists' signaling systems from the English standpoint. First, the inability of the party's scouts to prevent Bradford from falling into a trap they were in the process of examining demonstrates the failure of the party's communications chain. The unknown recorder of this incident (possibly Edward Winslow) insinuates that the blunder was Bradford's, that in his eagerness he came around the examining group from the wrong direction without asking first.

The second shortcoming in the system is revealed in the way it was published. At first Bradford's hoisting was only a New World publication event, signaling to Native hunters that there were foreigners in the area and serving, no doubt, as a bonding moment for the exploring party and a good fireside story for the larger group. But in Mourt's *Relation,* published in England without Bradford's consent and, as we have seen, against what Winslow considered the best interests of the colonization project, the event suggested the sorry state of tactical knowledge of indigenous systems, particularly among the colony's leaders. In the uncertain early years of the settlement it was thought crucial for the colony to present a unified front in the London public print marketplace. Though not the public relations disaster that the nonconformist leaders in America would fear Thomas Morton's *New English Canaan* to be a decade later, moments like this one in the *Relation* opened the door uncomfortably on the unsteady process of learning Native practices.

Of Plymouth Plantation, composed many years later, bears evidence that Bradford had learned his lesson. Bradford dramatizes, in his tenth chapter, the broad question of how social authority was justified by moments of decoding or threatened by its failure. The first major expedition on land began, he tells us, on November 15, 1620. Within a mile's walk, the Europeans saw "five or six persons with a dog coming towards them, who were savages" (64). These Indians (of the northern branch of the Nauset society) fled the newcomers, first heading into the woods. Seeing that Bradford's party was inclined to follow them, "they again forsook the woods and ran away on the sands as hard as they could, so as they could not come near them but followed them by the track of their feet sundry miles and saw that they had come the same way" (65). This last comment about seeing that the Nausets had come the same way is a reassuring detail, but Bradford leaves out a telling one. The detail was included in Mourt's *Relation*: the Europeans followed "about ten miles by the trace of their footings . . . and at a turning perceived how they ran vp an hill, to see whether they followed them" (20).

This detail is suggestive, because the Indians, having decided that they were being followed, returned to the part of the shore where their tracks could easily be traced. They then continued up the coast, turning inland only when they had reached an area where, upon pursuing the footprints, the explorers would find themselves trapped. Having taken the bait but lost the trail, Bradford reports that his party "still followed them by guess, hoping to find their dwellings; but they soon lost both them and themselves, falling into such thickets as were ready to tear their clothes and armor in pieces; but were most distressed for want of drink" (65). Once again, Bradford has demonstrated himself incapable of avoiding Native traps. By omitting the detail that the Nausets deliberately surveilled the English progress up the coast before setting the final trap, Bradford shores up the shaky account offered in the *Relation*.

Native traps involving this kind of use of the landscape together with herding or encouragement from the hunters were, as historians and archaeologists have discovered, not uncommon in the northeast. The hedge drive trap—a wedge-shaped channel made up of stakes or natural hedges that guide deer into a containment area for slaughter—is analogous to the tactic used by the Nausets to guide the English into a thicket. The dog, too, is an important detail: dogs were used as alarms, but they were more broadly authenticating mechanisms. (Pequot oral history still reads dog sounds this way; William Simmons reports one tribe member as saying, "A dog howling is a sign of death. That's what my mother always said.")[21] Dogs could find their way in the woods and they knew who was in and who was out of the family or community in elemental ways. On a path, or perhaps more importantly off of it, dogs are drawn to evidence that humans do not always notice: offal, in particular, but any body fluids will catch their notice and in woodlands life could be important information.[22]

Dog or wolf howls figured prominently in the next interaction with the Nausets. The Plymouth men were more cautious the next time they went adventuring, this time farther south on Cape Cod. But once again, they could not read the signs. After some exploring, the party heard "a hideous and great cry," and fired off a few muskets in response, which seemed to end the conversation. Bradford writes that the men concluded that the cry was made by wolves or other animals, "for one of the seamen told them he had often heard such a noise in Newfoundland" that had a natural, not human origin. But as Bradford tells us later:

> presently, all on the sudden, they heard a great and strange cry, which they knew to be the same voices they heard in the night, though they varied their notes; and one of their company being abroad came running in and cried, "Men, Indians! Indians!" And withal, their arrows came flying amongst them. (69)[23]

This is a densely meaningful passage, from the confusion of "Men" and "Indians" (reminiscent of the earlier confusion of "them and themselves") to the emotional exclamation and the ghostly origins of the Nauset arrows. But equally important is Bradford's claim not merely that he recognized the voices but that he could distinguish the "notes" and that he could tell that they were deliberately "varied." This claim may or may not be true; certainly it plays to Bradford's advantage that he finally—and at a key moment—shows the ability to decipher a Native American signifying practice.

Though the English were taken by surprise, with their party split in two, and though the combat was pitched and point-blank, no one was injured in this attack. No doubt adrenaline-filled, as their assailants retreated on a signal from their leader, the English went (what they imagined to be) native, chasing the Nausets, firing into the air and shouting "once or twice," "that they might conceive that they were not afraid of them or any way discouraged" (70). This "protesting too much" underscores the longing to communicate that underlies the battle (with longing on the Nauset side as well). At the same time, it implies that, emotionally excited as they were by the Indians, Bradford and his men were concerned about public relations. Having left vague the issue of whether or not the Pilgrims were actually afraid, yet having stated that they tried to signal courage, the account may have unsettled English readers even as it attempted to reassure them. Effective communication in this instance meant departing both from civility and from the English language itself.

Nevertheless, Bradford shows two forms of mastery in this episode. He convinced us earlier in the story that the "great cry" was beasts, creating the suspense that draws us into the panic of the moment when the attack comes "all on the sudden." In a move calculated to wind his readers up with anticipation, the plain stylist deceives them, preparing them for the renowned confusion of pronouns that characterizes the battle scene between the Nausets and the English. Bradford emerges as the decoder to be trusted. His leadership was premised in part on his godliness, but since he was governor and not minister, it was also premised in large part on his being a model and a guide for the creation of systems of communication that preserved the social order while giving access to the spirit. This helps explain the significance of a remainder to this story of deception and decoding: that seaman, whose interpretation of the horrible cries Bradford used to set us up for the surprise, emerges as a source of misinformation. He is an outsider, a laborer—one with experience, but experience that in retrospect is life threatening. The confusion of interpretive categories (wolf/Men/Indian) that results in hysteria is framed by Bradford as originating in a failure to command information properly.

The Nausets with whom the Pilgrims fought had recently had conflicts with the English. A few years earlier, Thomas Hunt had come to the area, and "[a]long with his fish," as Neal Salisbury describes it, "captured about twenty Indians from Patuxet (on the site of the future Plymouth colony), including Squanto, and seven from Nauset for sale into slavery" (101).[24] Only a year or so before the Pilgrims encountered the Nausets, Thomas Dermer and his crew were captured and threatened by them. The English gained release when Tisquantum, who had befriended Dermer, negotiated their freedom. But Dermer's report lacks resentment toward his captors; when compared with the casualty-free result of the Nausets' subsequent engagement with the Pilgrims, it seems likely that intimidation and what might be called "generous conflict" were a tactic commonly employed by the Nausets, though they could certainly kill when provoked. One telling of an Onondaga creation story suggests that this sophisticated approach to contact has a broader cultural history and spiritual underpinning in the region. It describes the pregnancy of the mother of the twins—one a creator and one a destroyer—who would go on to shape much of the world in which humans would come to live. The creature (perhaps a turtle) who is the twins' father places two arrows on the mother's body, one with a point and the other without. The story emphasizes not that the arrow without a point is better, but that the creation emerged from the process of interaction between the son who invented beneficial creatures, sought happiness, and observed tradition, and the son who destroyed and interrupted these.[25]

The Nausets likely had a long history with European fishermen of various nationalities. Sending the message that they were a fierce but not completely untrustworthy tribe was a strategy that may have been designed to produce a cautious approach to Nauset territory. Other combat options were certainly available—ones that would become familiar to the soldiers at Saybrook Fort at the mouth of the Connecticut River during the Pequot War. The English were comically easy to track; they were noisy in the forest, the matches on their weapons put out a strong smell when lit, and they never bothered to mask their odor with bear grease or some other animal scent.[26] "Waiting in hidden positions along well-traveled trails," Patrick Malone writes, Algonquians "struck without warning when their victims passed by" when they meant to kill or capture opponents. The howling that the English heard was designed not just to intimidate listeners in the moment but, as in a horror movie, rhythmically to construct silence as comforting—and it was in silence that Native attacks intended to kill began. If the Indians deliberately refrained from killing the exploring party, then Bradford either continued to misread the signs or deliberately reinterpreted them for his readers. The shirts hanging up to dry, he reports, were shot "through and through"; this repetition as likely signified a power of death the Indians *chose* not to employ that morning as it did a divinely ordained providence that favored the Pilgrims.[27]

It is possible that the circle of imitation and simulation, from Natives imitating the wolf to English imitating the Natives, is even more complex. As we will shortly see in the case of the Pequot War, the Natives of southeastern New England also mimicked their opponents, sometimes for emotional effect and sometimes for purposes of stealth. Once again a passage left out of Bradford's history, but included in the printed *Relation,* opens an interpretive door. It comes in the midst of the description of the fight, as the Pilgrims, one group trapped at the camp and the other with their boat at the shore, attempt to coordinate with and cheer each other:

> [O]ur care was no lesse for the Shallop, but we hoped all the rest would defend it; we called vnto them to know how it was with them, and they answered, Well, Well every one, and be of good courage: . . . The cry of our enemies was dreadfull, especially, when our men ran out to recover their Armes, their note was after this manner, *Woath woach ha ha hach woach*: our men were no sooner come to their Armes, but the enemy was ready to assault them. (19)

Perhaps because of its tantalizing ambiguities, what might be called a kind of cryptolegibility, the scene has elicited many readings by scholars. The paradoxical specificity of the attempt to capture the phonetics of an Algonquian utterance, presumably in the midst of pitched combat, as well as the unresolvability of the meaning of the phrase, emblematize the challenges of studying early colonial encounters. It is possible that Edward Winslow recorded this Native sound; as we have seen, his interest in acquiring Algonquian was more keen than most of his fellow settlers'. Too, this is military information: communication is a drama central to any combat, and the English understood themselves to be equipping both their arms-bearing men and, through publication, other possible colonists for interactions with New England Native societies.

With this in mind, some analysts argue that the *Woath* phrase is an attempt to transcribe a specific Algonquian saying—one that has remained elusive. For others, such as Jon Coleman, it is an animal sound, an imitation of one of the howling sounds wolves make, designed to terrify the enemy and give courage and energy to the howler. It might even be something in between the two. In his *Key into the Language of America,* Roger Williams records the Narragansett phrase for "*Ther is an alarme; or there is a great shouting*" as "Wauwháutowaw ánawat" or "Wawhautowávog," phrases that bear some phonetic similarity to those recorded in the *Relation.*[28] But if the English shouts across the field of combat preceded this particular utterance—that is, if this came in reply to the English making themselves visible, as the narrator says, when going after their guns and after having called out "Well, Well . . . be of good courage"—then another possibility emerges. The Nausets may have been imitating English speech, perhaps in an attempt to confuse the enemy while gaining themselves some knowledge of their opponents' communications tactics. That the cry was "dreadful" may well have been because it was strangely familiar; though slightly out of tune, it was just the sort of thing the English would do within moments, as the Nausets disappeared and the Pilgrims shouted after them.

Violent encounters demonstrated the necessary yet frightening permeability of different signifying systems: animal, English, Indian, and divine.[29] When the first full-scale war between the newcomers and a Native society came, the question of how to decipher the Natives would become as important an element of English war as the question of how to publish combat would be for its historians. The density of Native communication across a range of media—clothing, sound, spoken language, singing, and others—called forth a corresponding multimedia response on the part of at least one of the war's most influential chroniclers.

Sufficient Intelligence, Sufficient Light

As Captain John Underhill sailed to Block Island in 1636 under a commission to punish the Pequot people for offenses against the English, he no doubt had occasion to reflect on preceding Indian combats, like Plymouth's with the Nausets. The success of surprise attacks by both sides—such as Myles Standish's assassination of Wituwamat and other Native leaders at Wessagusset, or Opechancanough's massive assault on Virginia settlers in 1622—called the utility of formal European military procedure into doubt.[30] Native warriors were deceptive, good at camouflage, and, if the reports coming from savvy Lieutenant Lion Gardener at Fort Saybrook were right, constantly surveilling English movements. The Pequots were hiding in the woods, waiting for Gardener's ill-disciplined men to wander off hunting, away from the strong house; they were lurking in the hay meadows in ambush; they were invisibly patrolling the rivers, from whence they allowed English bodies to float back down to Saybrook, such as one "with an arrow shot into his eye through his head."[31] Underhill's twenty or so soldiers were comparatively inexperienced when it came to such chilling communiqués from an enemy. Most were in the company for the same reasons he was: a belief in English superiority (as ordained by God and evidenced by His wonders) and a desire for the land or booty that would likely come with successful service. Underhill himself had been granted one hundred acres of land for fighting the Natives near Brookline a few years earlier.[32]

This mission against the Pequots was not likely to be as easy. Pequots were rumored to be fierce opponents, and on the European side, motives for the attack were mixed. The Pequots held land, tribute, and trade access desired by at least five colonial entities: the Dutch, the Plymouth planters, the ever-grasping Massachusetts Bay Company, the nascent towns of the Connecticut River valley, and the new corporation that had hired Underhill to fight.[33] If the Pequots were watching from the woods, Underhill knew, so were New England, Old England, God, and the Dutch. And without question the "eyes of all the Indians of the country," as minister John Higginson warned, "are upon the English."[34] Few knew this better than Roger Williams, as we saw in the last chapter, who channeled (and influenced) the desires of the Narragansetts and the Mohegans. The outcome of the conflict was sure to reshape colonial relations.

No less was it likely to shape Underhill's career. Underhill tended toward unorthodox religious beliefs (he was one of John Cotton's congregants and a follower of Anne Hutchinson) and had a streak of rowdiness that would get him in trouble periodically for much of his life. Successful service in the war would increase his international reputation at least, if not his social capital back in Massachusetts Bay.[35] Fighting the Pequots and their allies held for Underhill the opportunity to demonstrate his faith and his mastery of Native ways. In the end it would open the door to a career fighting Natives for the Dutch. His narrative of the war would play a key role in such a demonstration, and because his many motives for publishing made it beneficial for him to record details about Pequot communications practices, I turn to it in this section.[36]

Underhill's military model of information control attuned him to a certain class of communications and induced anxiety when he could not decipher them. That anxiety sometimes made him recoil into comfortable English interpretations or expectations, but just as often pushed him to consider his enemy's perspective. The control of information in warfare requires an immersion in the enemy's systems that Bradford never quite engaged—or at least, never depicted himself as willing to engage. Even in the so-called information age of today, new military strategies have made headlines in the United States because they blur cultural and political boundaries. The discovery that the U.S. military tracked domestic war protests and protestors caused one such controversy. The Department of Defense claims to have dropped this program. Yet the explicit directive of the department's *Information Operations Roadmap* indicates that it broadly considers it essential to provide domestic spin to war stories from the front, insulate domestic media from propaganda projected at the enemy, and control the flow of information about war into the United States.[37] Such an approach to systems muddies the distinction between citizen and enemy in frightening ways. Yet as Gilles Deleuze and Felix Guattari have observed, it is the paradoxical nature of an effective military to be at its best when it is both aware of and capable of violating socially significant boundaries.

Seen in this light, John Underhill was what Deleuze and Guattari have termed a "war machine." When a technology of war is created or appropriated—or in this case, when a mercenary is trained—the latitude it is given to understand and hence defeat its enemy renders it to a degree uncontrollable by its maker. The war machine, at its best, is a generic technology that can decipher and destroy any enemy; it is powerful when it is working for you, but like an army returning to Rome, always brings with it the fearful question of whether in fact it is working for you.[38] A war machine model of information flow is porous and accepts espionage and deception as conditions of existence.[39] For Bradford, the boundaries of the community had to be policed rigorously. Bradford's model of information flow, as we saw in the differences between the *Relation* and *Of Plymouth Plantation,* conforms to the boundaries of a community—the community's elected leaders should be, or should control, the conduits to other information worlds. In the case of Underhill, who kept moving among many polities in the colonial Atlantic, a narrative resulted that celebrated English victory but was likely to unsettle readers, giving them a sense of their dependence on the skills of a rover like Underhill.[40]

The trigger for Underhill's first foray to the south was the English reaction to the murder of trader John Oldham on Block Island. Interpretations of the political motivations for the attack vary. The Manissean people of Block Island, key manufacturers of wampum, were once tributaries of the Pequots, and the two groups probably shared relatives.[41] At the time of the murder of Oldham and his crew, however, the Narragansetts and their leader Miantonomi controlled the island's tribute. Miantonomi, seeking alliance with the English against the Pequots, launched a raid on the island in an attempt to demonstrate his control over his tributaries. But he also suggested to the Massachusetts Bay leaders that the killers had sought refuge with the Pequots. The Bay took advantage of this rumor and resurrected an old complaint against the Pequots, their alleged murder of John Stone. Massachusetts' leaders ordered John Endicott—Thomas Morton's recent enemy—to attack Block Island and then demand that the Pequots deliver up the killers (and tribute) in order to prevent war with the English. They counted on Roger Williams to persuade the Narragansetts, who might be insulted at the attack on the Manisseans, that this strategy would be to their advantage.

Algonquian dissimulation was on masterful—and effective—display at Block Island. The show began before the raiding party arrived. Perhaps tipped off by the Narragansett raid just before, or by news that the Puritan boats were underway, the Manisseans knew when and where the attackers were going to arrive. "Comming to an anckor before the Island," Underhill reports, "we espied an Indian walking by the shore in a desolate manner as though he had received intelligence of our coming. Which Indian gave just ground to some to conclude that the body of the people had diserted the Island."[42] This affective information, an early manifestation of the melancholy Indian stereotype, seems odd in context. But extending such emotional complexity to the Block Islander allows Underhill to stage a heuristic drama. Though "some" on "just ground," we are told, speculated that the Manisseans had decamped, Underhill demonstrates his superior perspective. Like Bradford, Underhill offers readers a moment in which the colonizer has to show the home audience that he has a superior decoding technology, violating narrative trust, temporarily, to secure a certain authority over transmission. An English interpretive practice ("just ground . . . to conclude") is posited, given a rationale and a piece of evidence (Indian "desolat[ion]"), and then dismissed—but is spectacularly included despite being a detail inessential to the combat description. "But some knowing them for the generality to be a warlike nation," Underhill tells us, "were not perswaded that they would upon so slender termes forsake the Island, but rather suspected they might lye behind a banke," which, as it turns out, they did, attacking from hiding as soon as the English came ashore. Underhill thus reveals that the lone Native's emotion has its cause in information technology unknown to most Europeans, hidden channels of communication suspected only by experienced men like himself (and, though Underhill does not make the reference specifically, perhaps only by men who remember the story of a similar trick pulled by Sinon and the Acheans in their wooden horse).

While Underhill and his men escaped the kind of shoreline trap that had caught Bradford's party, they did not manage to take advantage of it. The hidden Manissean bowmen ended up being almost all the Natives the war party saw on Block Island, "the *Indians* being retired into swamps," Underhill complained, "so as wee could not find them" (7). Scorched earth then became the policy of the frustrated English—a targeted destruction of all Native resources and dwellings only interrupted when Underhill feared "lest wee should make an alarum by setting fire on them" and again risk losing what he has suggested they already lacked, the element of surprise (8). (The colonists killed the islanders' dogs, perhaps in rage, perhaps symbolically—or perhaps for the same reasons Native warriors often did, to prevent alarms and interrupt an important communication channel.) "The Block Islanders," Alfred Cave writes, "were virtually invisible" (112). More precisely, seen from the Manissean point of view, they were camouflaged. What is camouflaged is made to appear as environment; what the English took for trees, reeds, brush, or animals, along with their sounds and smells, included scores of Natives sending out what the English would receive as noise—wilderness—across the sensory spectrum. Despite Underhill's estimate of fourteen killed, only one death is confirmed by other sources, and one Block Islander may have been captured.

The next journey of Underhill's party, up the Pequot River (now the Thames) through Pequot and Niantic country, has attracted much attention. With good reason, it inspired Richard Slotkin to compare Underhill's narrative to Joseph Conrad's *Heart of Darkness*. As the English approached the mouth of the river, the Niantics appeared on the shore, running alongside and hailing the Englishmen. The Natives "spying of us," Underhill writes, "came running in multitudes along the water side, crying, what cheere Englishmen, what cheere, what doe you come for? They not thinking we intended warre went on cheerefully untill they come to Pequeat riuer. We thinking it the best way did forbeare to answer them" (9). The five ships' worth of well-armed Englishmen refused to reply, Underhill specifies, in order to get the drop on the Indians. Such has been the dominant interpretation of this interchange. A series of critics has claimed that this is a scene of disillusionment and the failure of intercultural communication, as the Niantics and Pequots come to realize for the first time that the English are angry.[43] But there is suggestive evidence that the silent treatment did not work and that the Niantics might have known what the English were up to before they ran to the shore. If lethal Native attacks, as we saw before, sometimes began in silence, and if an Englishman interested in trade was generally a chatty one, it would have been immediately clear what the visitors intended, even in the absence of news from Block Island about the recent raid. But the smoke from burning Manissean villages, fields, and dogs likely had attracted enough attention to begin the spreading of that news. English silence may have been a tactical failure induced by fear.

When the English reached the river, the Niantics' tune changed—"what cheere, are you hoggerie, will you cram us? That is, are you angry, will you kill us, and doe you come to fight," as Underhill records it. They may have been taunting the invaders, not expressing naïve astonishment. The Niantics had appeared "in multitudes," showing their strength of numbers; they had dogged the ships even after not getting an answer from a boatload of what appeared to be warriors (as far as is known, no women were on board). This tactic of transmitting interference continued after darkness fell. "That night the *Nahanticot* Indians, and the *Pequeats,* made fire on both sides of the River, fearing we would land in the night," Underhill claims. "They made most dolefull, and wofull cryes in the night, (so that wee could scarce rest) hollowing one to another, and giving the word from place to place, to gather their forces together" (9). Niantic and Pequot communications systems, noisy rather than furtive like the Manisseans', seem transparent; Underhill somehow knows what the "cryes" mean (he conceals the assistance here, which is likely ubiquitous, provided by a Native translator). Comprehension does not aid sleep, however; Underhill is careful to keep readers thinking about the uncertainty of war, the threat of "multitudes," and the gathering Native forces despite his confident decoding.[44] The effect is enhanced typographically: marginal notes begin to appear on this page, calling out like the Niantics from the shore, surrounding and qualifying the text, not disappearing until just after the Fort Mystic battle.

This manipulation of *Newes from America*'s medium becomes even more crucial in the next scene of Native deception. When morning comes, an ambassador for the Pequots answers the English charges by telling a story about how the Pequots were wronged by the English in the early settlement and one of their citizens killed. In the margins, a note insists "* This was no wayes true of the *English,* but a devised excuse" (11). At this point in the text, Underhill is deep into a first-person ventriloquization of the ambassador's speech, telling the story of the Dutch assassination of the Pequot sachem Tatobam. The use of the marginal note, whether it was Underhill's choice or an editor's or printer's, suggests the problem of giving too much voice to Native Americans. The English reader, absorbed by the Pequot's story, might begin to see the story as the ambassador is trying to tell it: the Pequots, he claims, did not distinguish "betweene the Dutch and English, but tooke them to be one Nation" and thus should be excused owing to cultural confusion in the contact zone (12). Underhill was, in other words, in a rhetorical jam, and the spatialized textuality of the marginal comment offered a safe way out. To capture the "wit" of the ambassador, and hence to show his own tactical decoding skill, Underhill chose to reproduce the seductive Pequot-centered view, its emergence from the semiotic politics of Pequot trade and combat. Yet such a simulation of the Pequot viewpoint risked capturing an English audience in an Indian trap. As with Morton's marginal notes about Native history markers carved in trees, the marginal note here betrays the permeability of Native American and native English audiences.

Underhill's response was simply to assert that the ambassador's speech offered not a simulacrum of what happened in the killings, but dissimulation.

"Our answer was," he reports succinctly, "they were able to distinguish betweene *Dutch* and *English,* having had sufficient experience of both nations" (12). The measures of sufficiency here are left ambiguous—for good reason, given the English colonists' difficulty distinguishing among the Natives. (Roger Williams later requested on behalf of the Narragansetts that the captains mark their Native allies with bright colors so that the soldiers could distinguish them from the Pequots.) Indeed, the ambassador's story was partly, as Underhill records himself suspecting, an elaborate ruse to buy time for Pequot civilians to decamp, a ploy just as effective as the "desolate" Block Island point man's attitude had been. To a modern reader, the deception begins to look patently comic when Underhill writes, after two hours' delay and three separate messages, "There came a third *Indian* perswading us to have a little further patience," after which the Pequots "did laugh at us for our patience" (14). The maneuver—that is, the storytelling—saved many Pequot lives that day.[45]

Perhaps the most disturbing Native simulation—more than the storytelling, the camouflage, or the howling—was the wearing of clothes taken from slain English people. After the Wethersfield attack, the Pequots had rigged English clothes as sails symbolically in their canoes, a macabre mockery of English seagoing technology. They then upped the ante, using the clothes as trophies and as an emotional weapon:

> [S]ome of their armes they got from them, others put on the English clothes, and came to the Fort jeering of them, and calling, come and fetch your English mens clothes againe; come out and fight if you dare: you dare not fight, you are all one like women, we have one amongst us that if he could kill but one of you more, he would be equall with God, and as the *English* mans God is, so would hee be; this blasphemous speech troubled the hearts of the souldiers, but they knew not how to remedy it in respect of their weaknesse. (16)

This is finely honed information warfare. The Pequots, playing English, as it were, reanimate the English soldiers' dead countrymen, all the while morphing them into Indians who mock them both as live opponents and in the guise of ghostly figures of the dead calling for revenge. Such practices are endemic in the world history of warfare, and they were richly haunting for Puritans. The way this jibe plays on gender ideology, English perceptions of Natives as heathen, and the confessed unpredictability of the Puritan god suggests how closely the Pequots had been observing the settlers.[46]

The Puritans' distaste for idols, Ann Kibbey argues, extended beyond man-made objects into the world of human body movements. Through a trope known as *figura,* which indicated a gestural quality unique to a body or phenomenon, the same evils brought on by the use of imagery, crosses, sculptures of saints, and other material renditions of faith could be engendered by human movement. Just as *figura* named that sense that made it possible to recognize an acquaintance from far away by her gait, so it could be used to tell when the devil had possessed a person, inducing "antick" movements and unholy sounds. For Kibbey, the Puritan tendency to find blasphemy even in bodily movements and attitudes contributed to the dehumanization of the Pequots that resulted in the massacre at Mystic.

In this case, the use of *figura* is complicated by the Pequots' appropriation of English clothes. If the Pequots had noticed the English tendency to understand civility as a function of outward behavior and dress, then did not their mockery indicate a deliberate refusal of such standards rather than a natural barbaric tendency? Logically, such a gesture conformed to other important Puritan tenets—a constant appreciation of the fleeting quality of life and the deprecation of such outward matters as sartorial choice.[47] If there was something devilish about Pequot movements, such gestures made in English garb reflected back questions the Puritans were asking themselves about the justice of their prosecution of the war. Such questions (which had been raised by Lion Gardener early in the conflict) rise to the surface in Underhill's account of the climactic battle at Fort Mystic.[48]

Underhill ran the same risk in telling about the massacre that he faced when recording the words of the Pequot ambassador earlier in the narrative. Comforting the English reader meant bringing that audience into the narrative in a way that would convince it of two (dubious) assertions: that the Indians were not a threat and that the violent governance of the colonies would not be turned on the godly. But modeling his mastery of information management tactics required him sometimes to conceal his sources or the means by which he knew what Natives were thinking. On the last night's march, Underhill writes in a typical passage, "[W]ee set forth about one of the clocke in the morning, having sufficient intelligence that they knew nothing of our comming" (36). Knowledge of Indian movement accrues as a proprietary technology here, silently becoming the possession of a military man privileged to cross over. As in the example of the ambassador's speech, with the term "sufficient" Underhill establishes the line of authority as one involving the proper management of the connection between flows of information and the decision to exert violent force. The most famous use of this term comes in Underhill's concluding justification for the massacre of hundreds of noncombatants trapped in the furnace of the fort: "We had sufficient light from the word of God for our proceedings" (40).

The problems of textualizing Native deception, of putting on paper what Peter Charles Hoffer has termed the full "sensory warfare" of American Indian combat, seemed to Underhill—or those who handled his manuscript—to call for an equally multimedia response.[49] *Newes from America* is best known for an image, "The figure of the Indians' fort or Palizado," that was included in the beginning of each book (and possibly, though there is no direct evidence of it, sold separately as well).[50] This image has become a favorite one for historians—it is used on the cover of many a book about early New England, including this one (Figure 15). It is commonly read as an example of the colonizing vision: a scene from above, as if seen by God, simultaneously commanding the entire battle and righteously rendering organized and geometrical the messy spaces of the Pequot wilderness. The space inside the fort, sometimes described as reminiscent of a vagina, yields to English cultivation by violence of this "virgin" land. The Mohegan allies neatly encircling the fort outside the English soldiers bear evidence of proper management, compared to the chaotic gestures and disorganization of its interior. The weaving of English soldiers between

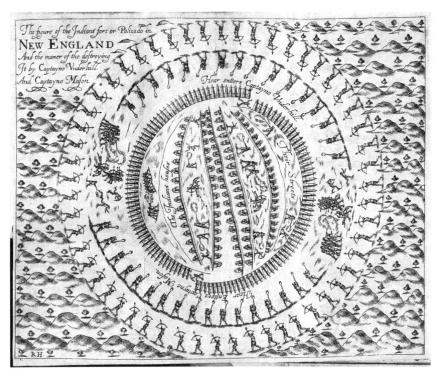

Figure 15. The engraving of the attack on the Pequots at Mystic from John Underhill's *Newes from America* has become iconic. Photograph courtesy of the Newberry Library, Chicago, Illinois.

layers of Native people may symbolize English dependence on American Indians for both survival and identity. But this irony notwithstanding, in this image the Pequots are frozen in time as history's losers, and English violence against women, children, and the elderly disappears from the scene as only male combatants are depicted.

Without arguing with this interpretation, I would like to suggest that this image was more animated than readings have given it credit, and that this was part of the continued combat against the animation of Underhill's enemies. Underhill was, after all, a bit of a dissimulator himself, and the map had an important role to play in saving his reputation as a military man no less than the text had in proving him godly.[51] (Even these goals may have been at odds. To strict nonconformists the image, which is not a map but explicitly the "figure" of the Native fort, that is, an image of a gesture, might well have been seen as an icon itself.) The command view offered here is more earthly than godly, pressing its case for Underhill's knowledge through the performative uses of material media open to English readers.

When a reader opened the "figure" (about 10.75 inches by 13.5 inches) in public, it would have attracted attention and probably comment. As a visual representation of the combat, the image could invite conversation about the war across the bounds of literacy. It also made the book more attractive to buyers; macabre though it might seem today, it is possible that, given the English affection for hanging maps on the walls of homes or taverns, this figure appeared in public in this way as well. But its folding—in the copies at the Huntington and Newberry Libraries, into six rectangles—and its containment within the book would also have enhanced the figure's telescoping effect. If this image condenses space and time, it is itself also condensable, collapsible for containment within the text. The spatial fantasy of the Indian village, surrounded by a fantasy of how space is allocated in war (into neat rows of archers and gunmen facing a single circular target), is made possible by another spatial fantasy, the figure, contained within the tight space of a small (octavo) book. The figure depicts the creation of colonial physical space out of an already populated place through two tactics: its difficult negotiation of planar dimensions and its emergence out of the book, the act of its unfolding involving the reader. The scene is shown as from a full bird's-eye vantage, but landscape, architecture, and bodies are seen in profile, as if from the ground. The rendering of the combatants' faces further fragments the perspectival scheme. Looking away from their aim (as if in shame or disapproval, which Jennings argues deterred the Narragansetts from participating), the Native archers face us directly, while the English are facing their targets, depicted in profile (Figure 16).

It is in the fourth dimension—time—that the map is animated. It was common in books of the time, especially on title page engravings, to depict disparate scenes from the book's narrative in the same single-page space. And, as we have seen, readers in London's print culture would have been particularly alert to typographically generated meanings from layout to font choice. Following the orientation of text in Underhill's figure reveals a temporality much more like man's linear one than God's simultaneous one, despite the initial impression made by the map on modern eyes. A legend in the top left corner initiates the linguistic content of the figure, with text oriented left to right and parallel and perpendicular to the edges of the support, as in a book. Two elements of the figure pull this linear, left-to-right reading off center: the dominant axial orientation of the image and the next logical words for the reader to pick up. These suggest that the image is meant to be read in a circle, clockwise from the legend. An axis of symmetry is formed by an invisible line connecting the two entrances to the fort and, perpendicular to that and buttressing it, the near-symmetrical depictions of two small battles outside the fort. This axis is slightly off the perpendicular, pulling the reader clockwise to seek out the phrase "Hear entters Captayne Underhill," which begins in roughly the same parallel orientation as does the caption and then turns away from it clockwise. (This turn away from standard orientation happens almost precisely at the letter *s* in "entters," which is coincidentally rendered backward—a mistake much easier for an engraver than a typesetter to make.) Keep rotating, and the temporal sequence develops, as the battles outside the pale become simultaneous with some of the events inside: the phrase "Their Streets" appears in proper orientation, parallel with battles inside and below the fort in the first turn, then the words "The Indian houses" appear with fighting inside and below the fort in the final orientation before returning to the map's original position.[52]

Figure 16. Native archers face us directly in the Underhill engraving, while the English, depicted in profile, face their targets. Photograph courtesy of the Newberry Library, Chicago, Illinois.

The letter *p* in "Captayne" on both sides of the image overlaps with the palisade wall in perfect symmetry, pointing to the precise entry points without representing either captain in person, enacting the fantasy of textualization of authority through (simulated) typography itself. Because of the sequence initiated by the clockwise reading, however, this symmetry does not establish equality. Mason's position is upside down—not at the beginning of the battle but in media res. This was a response to Reverend Philip Vincent's published claim that Underhill had hesitated upon entering the palisade and was an attempt to preempt a similar accusation in Mason's account of the war. In the body of his text, Underhill explicitly dismisses Vincent as having been misinformed—but his map (despite contradicting Underhill's own description of where he entered the fort) made a more vibrant and complete refutation of Vincent's report.[53]

Underhill's heroic entrance, depicted as primary, has by the time Mason enters the picture turned the landscape surrounding the fort upside down, suggesting the confusion of a battle already pitched. The pattern of the landscape and its depiction at a higher angle of vision than the profile rendering of the warriors induces a visual frenzy and confusion that weaves a clear, heroic chronology into a hectic sensory experience reminiscent of that of combat.[54] While the parenthetical containment of the fort's rendering and the top-down mastery of the angle of vision of the map in its original orientation suggest stasis and bracketing, the reading practice it encourages reanimates the combat. Performatively, too, a reader trying to interpret this map will call attention to him or herself in the act of examining it in a spectacular way. If there was nowhere to hide for the Pequots slaughtered at Fort Mystic, there is nowhere to hide for readers of Underhill's figure, either, as it complements the work of unsettling military and cultural boundaries enacted in the text's performance of decoding Native America.

Assimulation

Underhill's map is a connector between the past and the present. His figure has been reinterpreted, even put into a new medium, by the audience he might most have feared—the Pequots themselves. Though the Treaty of Hartford that ended the war declared that no one might use the name "Pequot" again, families identifying as Pequots quickly bounced back and, in various altered forms, have persisted to the present. When the tribe, bolstered by billions of dollars in casino profits, built its museum, it elected to use a design that incorporated Underhill's famous map. The gathering space—which cuts a striking figure in the skyline of Mashantucket and creates a massive, luminous common area at the museum's entrance—is based on the interlocking half circles that made up the palisade at Mystic according to Underhill's design (Figure 17).[55]

That such an element of Pequot cultural history owes its recovery and its historical resonance to Underhill's account points to the large political and epistemological issues raised by the museum, both in its own design and in the arguments of its critics. The use of mannequins throughout the exhibits, and the simulated smells and sounds too, raises the question of whether this is a postmodern museum, an ironic play space depicting a fluid tribal identity to a cynical tourist audience. For some critics, human uses of simulations are key to understanding cultural change; the expression of a relationship to the past in a modern-day museum would, in this argument, inevitably be a simulation rather than a collection of real things. Recent scholarship focusing on the museum agrees that it (together with the representation of Indianness in the nearby Foxwoods Casino) conveys a postmodern tribal identity, decentering

Figure 17. The architecture of the Gathering Space at the Mashantucket Pequot Museum and Research Center is based on the Underhill engraving of the Pequot fort at Mystic. Mannequins like those pictured here feature prominently in the museum. Photograph reproduced courtesy of the Mashantucket Pequot Museum and Research Center.

old notions of tribalism and offering a Pequot community with a knowing wink. These scholars insist that the Pequots are a legitimate tribe nonetheless. But labeling the Pequots "postmodern" displaces Native categories of self-representation; if to survive in the allotment era an Indian was told she had to become modern, now in late capitalist times, the survival mode would seem to be postmodern.[56]

If we return, with warnings from recent studies of indigeneity in mind, to one of the original postmodernist theorizations of the role of simulation in culture, we can find a way to read the museum's exhibits that relates them to the Pequot past beyond the level of visual content. Jean Baudrillard's influential text *Simulacra and Simulation* suggests both why indigenous American simulations were so disturbing to English viewers then and why they might be now. "Parody renders submission and transgression equivalent," Baudrillard observes, "and that is the most serious crime, because it *cancels out the difference upon which the law is based*" (21). For English settlers, as I have suggested, the ambiguation of difference induced fear. Baudrillard suggests that it was not merely that Indians thus became *figurae* of the devil's minions, but that they more fundamentally challenged the representational order itself. Law—and thus the legitimacy of interactions with Natives over land, trade, or religion—depended on differentiating among individuals and among nations. Pequot mockery suggested that they knew this was the English way but that they did not choose to participate in differential categorization except on their own terms.

But what about today? In a world now filled with machine-made objects, advertising, and visually driven one-way communication forms such as television and film, the real thing no longer really exists, Baudrillard claims. "It is no longer a question of imitation, nor duplication, nor even parody," he writes, but "a question of substituting the signs of the real for the real, that is to say of an operation of deterring every real process via its operational double, a programmatic, metastable, perfectly descriptive machine that offers all the signs of the real and short-circuits all its vicissitudes" (*Simulacra and Simulation*, 2). Yet the Pequot Museum is a performance rather than a simple expression of an adaptation to a dominant culture, no less than was the Pequot ancestors' wearing of English clothes in a seventeenth-century wartime negotiation. The "vicissitudes" of which Baudrillard writes, far from being short-circuited, are an important plank in their representation of reality. The Pequots' use of simulacra is strategic and has a long history. As Baudrillard insists, such playing with reality is directed at opening up possibilities for the future. With enough simulation, he writes, "Never again will the real have the chance to produce itself—such is the vital function of the model in a system of death, or rather of an anticipated resurrection, that no longer even gives the event of death a chance" (2). But the "real" of which he speaks is itself a Western, colonial concept; here it is more helpful to think that the Pequots are attempting to preserve and show the history of relationships rather than to preserve and show real states of being, environments, or genetic maps. The current mode of protecting the future of the families and the tribe is a strategy that points back to a coexistent, even commensal, process of differentiation. This process might be described as a calculated parasitism (in the sense that the museum both borrows terms from U.S. culture and makes a "para-site," a village beside a village) rather than as a desertion of reality.[57]

Today the question of Pequot fidelity is bound up with the hotly debated issue of wannabe Indianness. The notion that some Indians are simulacra is a concern not just for white folks afraid of losing their houses in the wake of federal recognition but also for other Native Americans. The museum's simulacra are animated by the question of recent Pequot sovereignty and how it was attained. At least three books have been published by trade houses in the last six years that describe the establishment of gaming enterprises at Pequot. Some of these suggest that the Pequots are a legal fraud yet there is something admirable about this simulacrum, while others are less friendly.[58]

The recent increase in Pequot power has been equally controversial among Native Americans. On one hand, the success of the tribe's approach to recognition, which involved court challenges and legislation rather than the Bureau of Indian Affairs (BIA) recognition process, offers tribes new tactics. The establishment of resort casino gambling, too—vastly increasing tribal income by adding slot machines and high-risk games to hitherto small-scale operations—established precedents that have helped increase tribal income across the United States. Contributions by tribes like the Pequots and the Mohegans to American Indian welfare interests such as prescription drug programs or resource and development consulting benefit tribes directly. Monetary donations, such as those to lobbyists working in support of legislation beneficial to tribes, have established a new era of Native self-determination and influence in politics.

Yet as the Jack Abramoff lobbying scandal shows, such influence can come at a cost to tribal reputations. What is more, massive increases in income, as the Pequots' recent history of tension (between their substantial black and white populations, and across those lines among members more and less interested in traditional practices) and consequent upheaval on the tribal council suggests, neither guarantee tribal harmony nor, some argue, represent a continuity with Native traditions of reciprocity, giving, and incorporation of commodities into a broader spiritual fabric. The people amassing wealth from what has been termed the "new buffalo" of gambling, some claim, are attracted to tribalism not by a desire to restore Native communities nor, often, by real blood affiliation, but by greed. Moreover, the Pequots, in the words of one writer, "created a new modern-day paradigm that changed the face of the country—not Native American but Casino-American." The very definition of what an Indian is seems to be at question.[59]

The case of the Mashpee Wampanoag, who failed to achieve recognition in the 1970s but were awarded tentative recognition in March 2006, offers telling ironies. James Clifford's influential essay "Identity in Mashpee" convinced many scholars that the Mashpee should be considered a tribe and that the concept of a tribe needed to be considered in context. As anthropologist Orin Starn puts it, "Modern-day Indian identity no longer entails a fixed address or cultural purity, and perhaps never did. If languages and traditions have survived, they have also changed with the times."[60] U.S. legal definitions demanding social continuity, Western-style evidentiary proof of genealogy and culture, and consistently recognizable governance trumped a tribe's own mechanisms or understandings of identity. Such a situation worked to the poverty of tribes with non-Western self-governance schemes and also of the United States' own philosophies of identity. When the BIA reversed its decision on the Mashpees decades later, was it driven by the cumulative effect of these scholarly redefinitions of identity and sovereignty? Was it activism? Or was it lobbying by casino development interests and the influence of the success of reservation gambling in neighboring Connecticut (where reservation gambling is now one of the largest sources of the government's income) that made recognition more likely? Probably all of these were factors.

The Pequots herald, too, the next set of issues facing many tribes. Tribes running resort-casino businesses are now often caught in a familiar entertainment industry development cycle that demands continual expansion in order to maintain competitive advantage. The latest fear has become that instead of a few real Indians having sovereignty restored in the limited space of a reservation, wannabes are using federal recognition to acquire noncontiguous property, put it into federal trust, and develop it in competition with nonsovereign local and regional entities. Many times, as in the case of the Pequots and the Mohegans, resort and casino development is funded by foreign capital or by gambling interests. The Mohegan recognition pursuit was funded in part by a South African resort and casino developer; the most recent Mashpee attempt was bankrolled largely by Detroit developer Herbert J. Strather.[61] A number of tribes are making the same moves the Pequots are, diversifying geographically and establishing branch industries offshore as a way of compensating for the development cycle's pressure on geographically limited reservation land bases.[62] Such a situation raises questions for some observers about the degree to which tribal sovereignty and existence are motivated by Native needs or what the "self" in "self-determination" might mean in these cases. This self-colonization, some might claim, is little better for the overall well-being (at the levels either of *ethos* or *ethnos*) of indigenous peoples than European colonization. An extreme criticism would say that the strategic use of tribalism may be a cynical postmodern evolution of such colonization.

Just as in the colonial period, the Pequots have managed to anger both invaders and indigenes. But if the major accusation against the Pequots is that they are fake Indians, it could be argued that this itself can be considered a source of continuity or, more appropriate to southeastern New England indigenous traditions, a cyclicality of collective expression in several ways. First, the Pequots have been a lightning rod for critiques and defenses of complex definitions of tribal belonging for centuries.[63] The most famous enemies of the Pequots, Uncas and Wequash, were once part of the group; Uncas even rejoined several times. When the tribe reestablished its autonomy in the 1650s, it was through yet another splintering—this time, of enslaved Pequots away from their Mohegan and Narragansett masters. Because kinship relations, for the Pequots in particular, with an emphasis on households, dominated political affiliation, the Pequots were notoriously difficult to pin down as a group, and members flowed in and out by marriage, enslavement, adoption, and capture. In the rebuilding of the tribe, leadership conflicts based on familial and intertribal tensions, far from demonstrating the absence of a real tribe, as at least one observer has suggested, call to mind the events of the early seventeenth century.[64]

Other resonances emerge when the frame is enlarged to include international economic interactions. Lynn Ceci has argued that seventeenth-century Pequots occupied a key geographic zone for the production of wampum. This position linked Native trade networks into a broader set of markets through Dutch, English, and French trade in wampum and furs. The Pequots found themselves in the forefront of economic and political reconfigurations leading to a new, imperial world economy.[65] The Treaty of Hartford that ended the war—and that many observers suggest indicates the primary motives for English attacks on the Pequots—explicitly took control of the interface between Native wampum production and European trade networks. "With conquest of Pequot land and control of other bead makers," Ceci writes,

> the value of the English pence doubled to six beads per penny. The future stability of that rate was gained by controlling the quantities of wampum in circulation after the 1638 Hartford Agreement stipulated the tributes to be

paid by all Indians who harbored or were assigned Pequot refugees: "one fathom of white Wampum for the Pequot man, and half a fathom for each Pequot youth, and one handlength for each male child." Other bead makers, frightened by attacks on the Pequots, dared not disobey.[66]

Ethnic diversity suddenly had a direct, literal price. With this stipulation, the English tried to convert tribal identity into money and eliminate their enemy in the same gesture.

In the 1990s, the Pequots found themselves in a position analogous to the one they occupied in the 1630s. While Justice John Marshall's ruling in *Cherokee Nation v. Georgia* long ago prohibited tribes from making treaties with other countries by declaring them "domestic dependent nations," it by no means precluded tribal relations with transnational capital.[67] When the Pequots went looking for someone to invest in Foxwoods, they found no willing partners in the United States but several interested takers in Asia. Funds from the Malaysian corporation Genting Berhad came to a domestic dependent nation in a small state within the United States because the Pequots offered a unique combination of location, cultural cachet, and political independence. With no federal taxes to pay, a location that was strikingly beautiful and within one hundred miles of 10 percent of the U.S. population, and a ready-made theme, the investment made clear sense to an international resort and gaming company but not to U.S.-based underwriters who would insist on alienable property as collateral. If the relations among cash, goods, and nations were rearranging in the sixteenth and seventeenth centuries, in the twentieth century it was the relations among cultural identity, national economic sovereignty, and globalization that were in flux.

Commentators have cried foul at the legal maneuvers that got the Pequots federal recognition without a BIA investigation. The Pequots, led by charismatic chairman Richard Hayward, hired the best lawyers, lobbyists, and researchers they could find and accepted the fact that if tribes like the Mashpee could not prove continuity, the Pequots would be a tough sell. But given how quickly the Pequots of the 1630s picked up on and exploited the economic system of the Atlantic and the sartorial and theological predilections of the English, Hayward's approach to gaining recognition might be seen as consistent with Pequot community-building tactics in the past. If we view Pequot history in a more circular or episodic way, a pattern does emerge: the Pequots, for whatever reason, exploit the governmental, economic, and cultural logics of their neighbors in order to create and protect their self-determination. Such an approach to community formation cannot even really be understood in terms of sovereignty (as Taiaiake Alfred would point out), unless in an ecological sense of that term that would recognize the complex interdependence under-lying Pequot approaches to boundary creation.[68]

Reflecting on the present-day demand by the federal recognition process that tribes demonstrate cultural and political continuity over hundreds of years, James Clifford has written, "When the future is open, so is the mean-ing of the past. Did Indian religion or tribal institutions disappear in the late nineteenth century? Or did they go underground?"[69] Perhaps there is even another possibility—some might be cyclical, designed to accommodate and outwait colonization until, once again, forms of political interaction based on reciprocity become widespread. W. Richard West, director of the National Museum of the American Indian, has said that with the establishment of the tribal museum the Pequots "have come full circle."[70] For many Native North Americans, the cycles of history cannot be described by linear causality alone because they were divinely instantiated in a rhythmic, undulary, or circular way. Human history is thus both linear, in that individuals interact with spirits in shaping their destinies, and cyclical, in that with periodic regularity pros-perity, power, or difficulty will fall on a given community.[71] Even the jury in the first Mashpee Wampanoag recognition case, while not awarding recognition, found that the Mashpee recurred—not just that they emerged, passed away, or never were.

This is only one way of looking at the Pequots. The lessons of the debate about their legitimacy lie elsewhere, I suggest, than in demonstrating the truth or falsehood of Pequot tribal existence. Today's Pequot power bears many simi-larities to and many differences from the past; religion was less at contest in Pequot sovereignty in the 1980s, for example, while phenotypical notions of race are more important now than in the 1630s. It is probably as risky to claim the primacy of a cyclical history as to insist on linear causality or naïve ratio-nalism; legal cultures can be designed to treat both of these temporalities with equal justice. Instead, I conclude with the modest suggestion that the lessons to be drawn from the Pequot case have in part to do with the media by which affiliation happens and the way these shape the imagination of a group's agency. The groups concerned here are roughly the Pequots as a historical phenome-non and those for whom the Anglo-American concept of property and legal ownership have been a persuasive and fundamental phenomenon. The Pequot nation in this case reemerges not from the ashes of a primordial group but instead from the cultural policies of Anglo-American society and their atten-dant laws and juridical practices.

In discussions of Native-English relations, the individual property concept is often named as the foundation of sociocultural difference. Natives had communal, use-based, and reciprocal notions of the relationship between particular people and particular places, while colonists brought a concept that linked individual ownership to bounded space. Colonial historians have shown that English notions of land ownership were in fact in flux at the time of settlement, so such a sharp difference cannot be foundational to America's shared history. Current notions of individual property, too, are more a fiction or an ideology than a fact. Anyone who has paid for title insurance knows this; some of the old notion of *vacuum domicilium* survives in the legal concept of adverse possession, while eminent domain laws qualify individual holding rights in—ideally— community interests.[72] In fact, at least one local government in Connecticut has recently used such laws to remove property from its citizens. Just a few months before I visited the Pequot Museum, a hotly contested (and widely controversial) Supreme Court ruling permitted a private company under the control of the city of New London to displace a working-class neighborhood in order to build, not roads or parks, but facilities for private business offices and retail stores.[73]

The Pequot nation's resurgence has been expressed in the form of a massive expansion of its land base, from about two hundred to over two thousand acres. But it has also taken the form of public relations campaigns, advertising, charity, outreach programs, funding for scholarly research, and the Mashantucket Pequot Museum and Research Center. These images of an Indian nation, in the face of controversy over the tribe's authenticity, are a reminder of the instability of property ownership, its constantly contingent and representational status: one can never stop communicating about property, even about one's own property, lest it be deemed available for use by someone else. Property, imagined as fixed, must circulate in order to remain attached. Attachment by circulation, gathering by distribution: these basic tenets of Algonquian social organization send anxious, sometimes violent ripples of reaction through the legal and representational systems of the United States.[74]

William Apess, a descendant both of Pequots and of their Wampanoag enemies, used the conjunction of media, race, and history to make a point in 1836. Courageously berating Boston audiences for their racism and religious hypocrisy, Apess offered himself—literate, eloquent, religious, and Native—as visible proof that past and present shape each other in an ongoing way. The current state of Native Americans was, he argued, a product not of natural Indian degeneracy but of a history of unequally applied principles. In a famous passage, he asks his audience to imagine the story of each race's treatment of others written on their skins. "I should look at all the skins," Apess said, "and I know that when I cast my eye upon that white skin, and if I saw those crimes written upon it, I should enter my protest against it immediately and cleave to that which is more honorable."[75] Wresting the language of rights and honor from legislatures and Indian hunters, Apess wrote this claim on the imagined bodies of his opponents and made a spectacle of his Indianness in order to take control of the narratives of the time. The spaces in between, whether the sunlit marginal passageways of museums or the margins of books, continue to evidence the tense relationship between stories of war and readers' reactions to them.

It is not the Pequot War that, as several popular accounts would have it, has been won by the Pequots in Mashantucket. Nor is Foxwoods Casino, as another book's title proclaims, the revenge of the Pequots.[76] The struggle continues over the concepts of sovereignty and history. The Pequots call the systems that surround them into question. Those systems are legal and evidentiary, but they are also cultural. Taking a cue from the curved parentheticals of Paula Gunn Allen's reminder that "(records fail us)" and of "the particular time the sequence undefined" that the idea of "documentation" violently makes graceful, Pequot reemergences can be read beyond the lines imposed first by Puritan narratives and later by historians.

Coda

It is a stark, cold day in early April at Saybrook Point, near Old Saybrook. A stiff wind blows and occasional raindrops dart through the air. It is clear to me, standing here in person, why the site was chosen for the fort that Lion Gardener commanded in the 1630s: you can see for miles in several directions from this small space of solid ground on a marshy arm of land in southern Connecticut. Such a position gives the wind more force, though, and the contrast with the artificial environment of the Pequot Museum at Mashantucket, not many miles away, couldn't be more palpable. The remains of Fort Saybrook are not visible; they were leveled when a railroad turnabout was put in late in the nineteenth century. There is a raised area that may correspond to the original site, with an abbreviated, largely symbolic palisade outline. But visitors cannot tell for certain, despite the many historical signs posted in the area, if this is the fort's actual spot and its real earthworks. The preservation of the eighteen-acre area, to judge from the signs, was justified principally by its being protected as marshlands.

The site is a palimpsest, not simply of architectural remains (part of the railroad turnabout, which was abandoned in 1915, is still visible) but of messages and of histories. In the early colonial era, animal communication and Native American messaging were interpenetrating spheres that worried English settlers. Today, because of low visitor traffic and little surveillance, the site is popular among people with dogs to walk. The evidence of dog visits is everywhere, a kind of chat room from a canine perspective and a signal that keeps humans off the grass (even if those humans are using their dogs as an occasion to socialize). The human-generated messages in the site are mixed. Aging, hand-made signs inside the reconstructed fort detail aspects of the fort's history and the area's ecology. According to these, the English had "no trouble making friends" with other Connecticut River valley peoples but could not, for reasons left to the reader's imagination, "pacify" the Pequots. Patient English settlers resorted to war only after first harassment and then murders by Natives (see Figure 18). But the relatively new, official-looking signs in the parking lot offer a comparatively balanced introduction to the history of the area, carefully rephrasing the content of the earlier signs. The Pequots were, in this version, "frustrated" with English invasions, which led to resistance and ultimately the war. During the war "gruesome massacres" were committed, not attributed to either party by the signs, tacitly acknowledging guilt on both sides.

The use of typography, which was key in recording the Pequot War, also appears here, interestingly. In this case the older signs bear a calligraphic appliqué that conveys a sense not only of the "hand" of the commemorators but of the "antique" quality of the site. The handwriting style may or may not

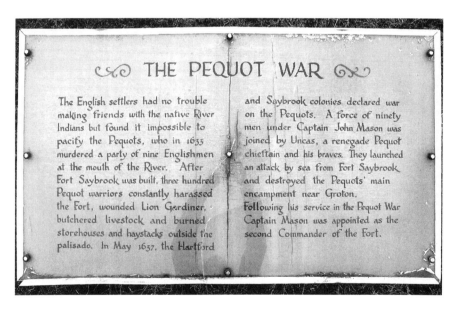

Figure 18. Hand-lettered historical markers like this one for "The Pequot War" stand beside more recently created machine-made ones at the Fort Saybrook site, Saybrook Point, Connecticut.

be based on the one used on Underhill's map, but the sense of authoritativeness that such a lettering style was, and is, meant to summon for readers is unmistakable. The sign commemorating Lion Gardener, in particular, serves as a testament to the importance of the means of carrying the written sign in shaping meaning. The environment of Fort Saybrook—damp and windy, quite cold in the winter—plays havoc with the plastic and metal signs, cracking them in the summer and flooding them when it rains. An uncanny repetition of the reversed *s* on Underhill's famous figure of the Mystic attack haunts the place in the deformation of the letters on the signs: the Gardiner family put up a statue and sign to memorialize their famous relative, but the sign's deterioration renders unclear the detail of his date of death, with an eerie trailing off of twisted letters, trapped and submerged in the water that has gathered behind the glass, like one of Gardener's soldiers during the war (see Figure 19).

The technologies of monumentalization and alphabetic writing do not triumph here. The tension between the characterizations of the Pequots on the different signs that represent the war betrays a recent historiographical and political struggle over Indianness. The presence of a real ruin of a railroad contrasts with the ambiguously real, muffled outline of the more famous fort. Lieutenant Lion Gardener's memory is preserved in text but in a fragmented, decaying form that conveys not permanent significance but a realization of the impossibility of fixity or separateness, of the interpenetration of environment

Figure 19. The letters of the "Lion Gardiner" historical marker drift away into oblivion.

with text. It may not be apparent to visitors that the Warwick Patent and Fort Saybrook would hardly be worth commemorating, by their own cultural standards, were it not for the Pequot War. Fort Saybrook was, after all, largely symbolic, a placeholder in a colonial contest that other colonies eventually won.

Some might object to the persistence of the hackneyed, racist depiction of the Pequots found in the fort. But it might also be argued that as long as the tension between the signs outside the palisade and those within it remains, the strata of history and historiography are visible, the efforts of generations of Native activists and advocates to change the story evident, even if unattributed. As we increasingly come to think of visitors to museums and historical sites less as passive consumers and more as shapers of meaning, as disputants and interlocutors, we must temper our interpretations to account for such possibilities. It may be that if Fort Saybrook functions as an information hub for dogs and preserves valuable marshland animal and plant diversity, and if the tensions of its current state make visitors wonder about how they know their own history, the place will be doing more good than it did in the seventeenth century.

We tend to imagine that the modern anxiety of technoculture is a product of a unique situation in history. The spread of technologies that speed up communication and interaction on a wide scale began in the nineteenth century and their development seems to have accelerated recently. What we think of as the modern consciousness or attitude, it is widely believed, was a result of the tensions brought about by the spread of such technologies: humans' cultural and individual boundaries were challenged with increasing frequency, the world seemed smaller, and time seemed to be compressed. The modern condition is one in which the tools that constitute advantage also scramble their users' sense of self.[1] But in the early colonial settlement, just such a confrontation with instrumentality and technologically induced social turmoil was the everyday experience. Here, Indians, Dutch, and strangers were ever-present challengers to the New English; here "instruments" referred to the agents of God in human or other-than-human form, not just to tools; here communication was sometimes fast, sometimes irritatingly slow; here encounter was always unpredictable. Reading Edward Winslow's insistence in *Good Newes from New-England* that the settlers must strive to be "instruments of good to the Heathens about vs," it may seem to us that Puritan instrumentality knows no bounds (6). Everything—humans both English and Native, natural disasters, trade, foods, animals—could be an instrument if rightly considered; nothing was not a machine. The perception of communications realms as systemic wholes—even in a more complicated way as porous systems, with membranes rather than rigid walls—was expressed in multifarious ways in the early settlement of New England. Transatlantic reporting about the New World contributed to the creation of scientific authority and the challenging of communicational hierarchies in the Old World, leading to radical social change during the following century.[2]

Many ideas about language and human relations, about technology and communication, that fueled fear, catalyzed racial hatred, and underwrote unjust policy in the seventeenth century remain firmly embedded today. Seventeenth-century Europe's dreams of communicational clarity haunt some of the most advanced research in the United States today. In this book I have suggested ways of reading beyond the oral–literate divide that continues to shape both questions about and the uses of colonial North American history. The persistence of a notion of Native Americans as living within an oral culture and those who have displaced them as possessing a culture of literacy is but one part of a larger misperception about technology, about, as Marshall McLuhan put it so compellingly, the medium as the message.

Examples are not hard to find. The U.S. Defense Advanced Research Projects Agency (DARPA) supports some of the most risky and influential research in North America. In an earlier incarnation it sponsored research that led, for example, to the creation of the Internet. It is also, of course, home to projects explicitly designed to maintain U.S. military supremacy. Recent projects sponsored by DARPA, touted as being oriented toward a radically different future of communications technology, are nonetheless disturbingly reminiscent of ancient dreams and notions—of a universal language that would triumph over the punishment of Babel, or of *figura* as a key to the moral character of a person. The Babylon project was funded in 2002–3 to create "rapid, two-way, natural language speech translation interfaces and platforms for the warfighter for use in field environments for force protection, refugee processing, and medical triage" and promised "full-domain, unconstrained dialog translation in multiple environments" (see Figure 20). Human Identification at a Distance (HumanID), funded through 2004, was designed to develop "automated biometric identification technologies to detect, recognize and identify humans at great distances" by using "characterized gait performance from video."[3]

The goal of such programs, of course, is not to produce understanding or clear communication. These technologies might conceivably reduce war zone mortalities for both U.S. and non-U.S. people, in part by aiding medical communication. But they are likely supported principally to reduce liability—to produce a lexicon of phrases or gaits against which an enemy's utterances or movements, "antick" or otherwise, can be compared for justification in the case of a lethal interaction. Language, however, particularly in occupied or combat zones, changes and becomes textured by accent or emphasis far too quickly for a machine-based system to capture—even if the machine's updaters can be trusted. As Michel de Certeau might add, what is true of talking is true of walking, too. Like walkers in the city, human speakers change language in response to machines' abilities to reproduce language. Another DARPA project features a diagram that suggests the litigious nature of the seeming miracle of translation offered by these projects. Global Autonomous Language Exploitation (GALE) sets as its goal "eliminating the need for linguists and analysts and automatically providing relevant, distilled actionable information to military command." In its visual model, a soldier is abstracted from the translation

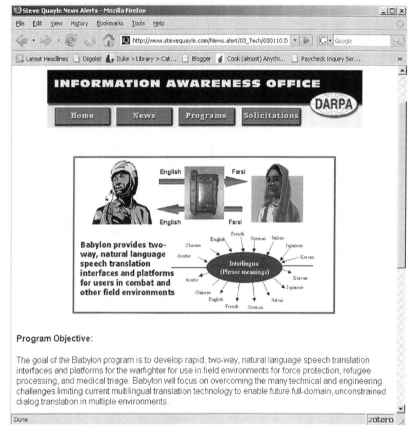

Figure 20. A figure from the description of the DARPA Babylon project depicts translation equipment facilitating peaceful relations between military personnel and combat area civilians.

process by a linguistic distillation engine (computer-based) at the other end of which is an analyst in suspiciously lawyer-like dress. The analyst, as Figure 21 shows, is no longer, like Tisquantum or Thomas Morton, a translator with the messy task of mediating during conflict: he receives input only in English, buffered from combat and from linguistic complexity by transcription, translation, and distillation engines.[4]

These DARPA projects suggest that, like people in early colonial New England, we find ourselves in another moment of uncertainty about the laws of nature and those of nations. The human is being redefined in the genetic age, but military policy still features torture and illegal surveillance; territorial zones of problematic legal status like Guantanamo Bay contain prisoners, the truth of whose innocence or guilt is no more ascertainable by technology than it would have been three hundred years ago. Holy war, too, lurks behind the terminology of terrorism. These facts stand in a mutual developmental relationship to economic globalization and the proliferation of high-speed, mobile technologies of communication. If today's injustices belie the failure of technology to solve our problems, they are nonetheless cited to justify the development of notionally better or more pure signaling systems.

Simply to say that communication should be thought of only in terms of flow, accent, and cultural contingency—that in a postmodern world, nothing grounds communication—is to risk deserting ethical responsibilities. David

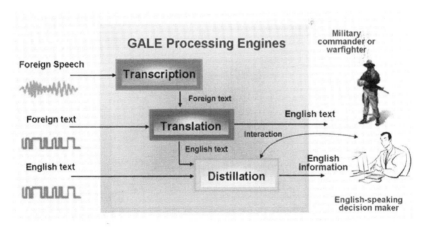

Figure 21. In this figure from the DARPA project description for the GALE (Global Autonomous Language Exploitation) project, a translator in business attire away from the battlefield assists front-line military personnel. The caption accompanying this image reads, "Figure 1 — Processing Engines (For simplicity, inputs to each engines *[sic]* from data bases, etc are not shown)."

Harvey writes, to "accept the general argument that process, flux, and flow should be given a certain ontological priority in understanding the world" requires us also to "pay so much more careful attention to . . . the 'permanences' that surround us and which we also construct to help solidify and give meanings to our lives."[5] Roger Williams hinted, in his complaints about the fusion of church and state, that it was precisely the fluidity of English law and language that made it possible to dispossess Native people of their land in North America. "Christenings make not Christians," Williams warned, as he argued that the English must observe Native political practices and engage in negotiations with them as sovereign entities.[6] Planned interactions between cultures that might result in territorial or economic change must be entered into with ontologies of law and history suspended, but they should also be subject to consensually devised rules, mutual respect, and extraordinary patience. It is that constitution of consent—a social relation designed as a fulcrum to mutual advantage—that is the technology of justice.

In 1636, Lieutenant Lion Gardener, repeatedly appalled at his abandonment at Fort Saybrook by the other colonies and his own employers, decided to send a message that might startle even today's DARPA engineers. He tells us,

> [W]hen I had cured myself of my wound, I went out with eight men to get some fowl for our relief, and found the guns that were thrown away [in retreat], and the body of one man shot through, the arrow going in the right side, the head sticking fast, half through a rib on the left side, which I took out and cleansed it, and presumed to send it to the Bay, because they had said that the arrows of the Indians were of no force. ("Leift Lion Gardener his relation of the Pequot Warres," 122)

Here the disfigured, dead body of an Englishman itself becomes the medium of communication. But it is not disassembled in the common way, perhaps beheaded and displayed in order to frighten an enemy—it is instead used to send a message within the English camp. More precisely, it is a hybrid document, fusing Native technology with English nature. The message draws on the logic of the rattlesnake skin and bundle of arrows sent by Canonicus to the Pilgrims and told about by Edward Winslow. In claiming that Native technologies had plenty of force, and in suggesting that only a message of bone and arrowhead, not text, could convey this truth, Gardener reversed the hierarchies of power characteristic of later English descriptions of weak Native natures and strong English instruments. The message was something more than the media used to send it; fatal misconceptions about technology might lead to fractures within a culture rather than to its triumph over another.

Figure 22. In her work *Strawberry and Chocolate*, Gail Tremblay (Onondaga) uses traditional techniques and form with nontraditional materials to make baskets that address the depiction of Native people in modern media. Courtesy of National Museum of the American Indian, Smithsonian Institution. Photograph by Ernest Amoroso, National Museum of the American Indian.

Such a co-optation of the media and means of communication (though not always as macabre as Gardener's) persists today as a strong strain in Native American art. It is with a basket, then, not a book, that I conclude. In the National Museum of the American Indian, in November 2005, a basket made by Onondaga/M'ikmaq artist and poet Gail Tremblay was on exhibit (Figure 22).

Baskets are devices for storing and transporting—for separating, in their mechanical essence, but for gathering, in their social essence. They have long been considered central evidence of the coherence of particular Native American cultures in their fusion of local materials, tribal decorations, and traditional construction. Tremblay plays with such connections in *Strawberry and Chocolate*: instead of ash splints she uses 16 mm film, whose translucence, when developed, breaks down the visual barrier of the basket wall and whose role as a communications technology suggests many ironies. Only recently have Native Americans been able to move behind the motion picture camera, producing films, such as Victor Masayesva's *Imagining Indians* (1992), that critique Hollywood's exploitative and often objectifying relationship to Indian country.[7] Here Tremblay offers a different kind of technological signifying, using film against its cultural grain to build an indigenous object for preservation. In doing so she emphasizes form no less than she plays with substance: this is a fancy basket, built using the same skills and techniques that northeastern Natives have used for centuries. The title of the piece appears to refer in part to the particular qualities of the film medium: chocolate for the color of the undeveloped emulsion or leader, woven into one part of the basket, and strawberry for the hue of the developed film in another part of the basket. The associations suggested by the title are both local and cosmopolitan—strawberries are one of the famous staples of northeastern life (strawberry leaves were part of the cure for Massasoit's illness), while chocolate is a Mesoamerican invention. Film is a different kind of communications technology in the hands of Gail Tremblay, embodying more than one medium at a time. The basket transports us from the dangerous fable of a medium's clarity, its supposed revelation of the patterns of the world, to a different pattern, different audiences, and perhaps a different future.

Acknowledgments

I am deeply grateful to have been a part of the conversations from which this book emerged. If I am true to them, these chapters will give fuel to those conversations. I will forget to thank some people—partly out of the frailty of my memory and partly because I did not always realize they were helping me at the time—for which I apologize.

I certainly didn't know it was happening when it first began. This book grew from unanswered questions in my dissertation on bachelors in nineteenth-century America, written at the College of William and Mary. Jim Axtell reassured me that Thomas Morton was worth much more attention, while Liz Barnes, Richard Lowry, Susan Donaldson, Arthur Knight, Chandos Brown, and Grey Gundaker all taught me how to read signs in new ways. When I wrote that first essay on Morton, I had in mind Alan Wallach's lessons about academic writing and Robert Gross's about the history of the book. They guided the emergence of this book through chapter drafts, helped map its path to publication, introduced me to the people behind the scholarship I was reading, and, at just the right times, encouraged me. I was lucky, too, in my fellow graduate students there, who will recognize their influence on the pages that follow; my thanks and love especially go to Robin Veder, Tim Barnard, Catherine Lunt, Renée Sentilles, Emily Mieras, Kelly Mason, Marland Buckner, Chris LaSota, and Eric Allman.

Having an opportunity to teach at Duke University has been fortunate for me. The intellectual environment in the Department of English exhibited the energy, beauty, and healthy intimidation of a powerful storm from the first minute of my first interview there. I am grateful to all the faculty and staff in the department, but this book owes much of its shape to Tom Ferraro, Priscilla Wald, and Robert Mitchell in particular. They read it, ran it ragged, and made it much, much better. More important, they provided a model of mentorship: I learned from them just how much more I have to learn. Sean Metzger, Rebecca Walsh, Houston Baker, and Jennifer Thorn discussed parts of the book with me and offered friendly critiques that were very different but equally influential. Outside my department I found support of many kinds, from the encouragement, strategic advice, and good humor of Elizabeth Fenn, Beth Eastlick, and David Jamieson-Drake to the unusual, energizing combination of athletic and academic partnership of Orin Starn.

The greatest source of brainpower and new ideas at any school is its students. The undergraduates in my early American survey classes have been good questioners, testing the parts of this book that, I have claimed to them, inflect American literary history. But the genesis of many of my ideas here was in my early American literature and culture graduate seminar of fall 2002. I owe much to conversations with Kinohi Nishikawa, Russ Leo, Erin Gentry, Hillary Eklund, John David Miles, Monique Allewaert, Melinda DiStefano, Lauren Coats, Bart Keeton, and Lena Tashjian (the argument in chapter 3 is indebted to Lena's challenging observations). For discussions of networks, thanks to Pat Jagoda; of American Indian politics, to Jessi Bardill; and of English ideas about nature, to Vin Nardizzi. I hope I grafted these topics in a way that does those exchanges justice.

As the manuscript developed, the conversation about it widened fruitfully beyond Duke University. Audiences at Harvard University, the Newberry Library, meetings of the Society of Early Americanists, Northwestern University, and the University of Chicago asked hard questions that I have since tried to answer; I'm particularly grateful to Eric Slauter and Yvette Piggush from Chicago and Katy Chiles at Northwestern for their critiques. Laura Mielke has been a constant source of inspiration and trenchant insight; I'm thankful to her for her friendship and for introducing me to Hilary Wyss, who is an energizing interlocutor. Early drafts were read and critiqued by Christopher Grasso, Fredrika Teute, Kelly Wisecup, and anonymous readers for *Book History* and for the University of Minnesota Press; their responses have made this book better.

Over meals and between conference sessions, I have had the benefit of good insights about my work from colleagues at other institutions. I spent an illuminating day in New Orleans with Carolyn Podruchny and Heidi Bohaker that made the book stronger, and my colleagues in the Whitman studies community, particularly Betsy Erkkila, Kenneth Price, Ed Folsom, and Jay Grossman, have been sharp analysts of my claims about media. Paul Chaat Smith, Ivy Schweitzer, Wai Chee Dimock, Michael Elliott, Gail Tremblay, Chia Yin Hsu, Jonathan Beecher Field, Orit Halpern, Dennis Moore, and Betty Donohue all at various times helped me understand what this book could be. I am grateful to my colleagues in colonial and early modern studies who spent time and care with the manuscript: Ralph Bauer, Ethan Shagan, Jane Calvert, Andrew Newman, Sarah Rivett, and Jeffrey Glover each navigated the book to straighter, smoother paths.

A straight path isn't necessarily a swift one, however. For speed, I thank my research assistants over the years: at Duke, Melissa J. Miller, Socorro Finn, Derek Womack, and Emily Helser; and at William and Mary, Joanna Fairbairn. I also had time provided by funding from several institutions. This project received a Reese Fellowship in American Bibliography and the History of the Book from the Huntington Library; a long-term National Endowment for the Humanities fellowship at the Newberry Library; and a long-term fellowship from the American Council of Learned Societies. The views, findings, conclusions, or recommendations I express do not reflect those of these institutions. I am grateful to the Arts and Sciences Research Council at Duke University for funding to support my research assistants, and deeply thankful for the consideration of Duke's administration (especially for Chuck Byrd's good advice) in allowing me to accept these awards. For managing my departmental business with skill (even with broken air conditioning during a North Carolina summer), I thank Catherine Beaver, Sharon Brown, Thomas Nickles, and Toya Wallace.

The research assistance at the libraries I have been privileged to visit has been extraordinary. At the Huntington, I was guided by Mona Shulman and Kate Henningsen; at Duke's Perkins Library and its Rare Books, Special Collections, and Manuscripts group, Elizabeth Dunn and Sara Seten Berghausen were inestimably helpful and encouraging; and at the Newberry Library, Frank Valadez and Carla Zecher made my fellowship a delight.

If these institutions polished what began at William and Mary and at Duke, it is because I have been lucky enough to be surrounded by mentors and friends who sustained me all along. Todd Lapidus, Stephanie Lerner, Gerda Lerner, and Camilla Fojas shaped this book in ways that they will recognize, though reading it for the first time. My uncles David Earnest, Richard Steiger, and Bob Bourdette set high standards both for prose and fun. I miss Bob dearly; his passing while I was finishing the manuscript gave me much on which to reflect. I am lucky to have patient and kind in-laws in Fred and Norma Filios, who opened their home to me when the book needed the experience of walking the land of New England. My friends in molecular biology, Mignon Keaton, Maria Rodriguez, Adrienne Wells, and Rose-Anne Meissner, have been both loving and patient with my humanistic bent, happily explaining signaling pathways and digestion to me. My old friends Robert Nelson, Amy Howard, and Christopher Labarthe read parts of the manuscript and have surrounded me with intellectual and emotional happiness.

Finally, there are the folks without whom this book could not be. In this the last shall be first: I thank Celeste Newbrough for the hard work that made a great index. Ezra Greenspan saw this project's potential in its rawest stage—but more important, perhaps, he explained that potential to me at key moments. Doug Armato at the University of Minnesota Press also picked up on the manuscript's potential, and he and Nancy Sauro, Danielle Kasprzak, and many patient others at the Press transformed it from a project into a book. My mother and father, Katharine and Michael Cohen, tolerated my wanderings early and late, hosted me on the peregrinations during which I wrote much of the manuscript, and critiqued it with rigor and love. Dan Cohen made me speak my ideas plainly and provided the best distractions a brother could hope for with his music and his laughter. To my grandmother Marian Weston's patience, generosity, and joy, I owe an unpayable, delightful debt.

The constant conversation of love in which Bridget Finn and I have engaged since meeting many years ago has added breadth to my life in ways only a pure gift can do. Without that breadth, this book would have been inconceivable. Without her knowledge of science and people, of the worms of the earth and the wrens of the sky, I might have written a chapter, but little more. Without her patience and her care, where would I be? With hopes that this draft demands less patience than the first, I dedicate this book to her.

Notes

Introduction

1. See D. Hall, *Cultures of Print*; Cressy, *Coming Over*; Monaghan, *Learning to Read and Write in Colonial America*; Kupperman, *Indians and English*; Amory and Hall, ed., *A History of the Book in America*, vol. 1; and R. Brown, *Knowledge Is Power*.

2. See Gustafson, *Eloquence Is Power*; Kibbey, *The Interpretation of Material Shapes in Puritanism*; D. Hall, *Worlds of Wonder, Days of Judgment*; St. George, *Conversing by Signs*; B. Smith, *The Acoustic World of Early Modern England*; Kamensky, *Governing the Tongue*; D. Cohen, *Pillars of Salt, Monuments of Grace*; Warkentin, "In Search of 'The Word of the Other'"; Lienhard, "Las prácticas textuales indígenas"; Wyss, *Writing Indians*. My thinking about the media history of colonial New England has been catalyzed by Walter Mignolo's *The Darker Side of the Renaissance*, and in particular his redefinition of the book as a "sign carrier" operating within a culturally specific "graphic semiotic interaction" (81). Mignolo's work builds in part on Brotherston, *Book of the Fourth World*.

3. Two major recent studies in early American history and culture enable and form the point of departure for *The Networked Wilderness*. They also suggest why this period and this region offer such potential for communications studies. Phillip Round's *By Nature and by Custom Cursed* reveals how the very forms of communications systems as such shaped politics and social organization in New England in the seventeenth century. Round's use of Pierre Bourdieu's theoretical approach helps us understand how colonials and Londoners anticipated the effect the various nodes that constituted the transatlantic communications chain would have on their conversations and debates, adopting a new kind of civil discourse. But Round does not engage the question of how Native groups responded to civil discourse, or whether or not they already had comparable systems. (Round's more recent work takes up the question of Native printing and publishing.) Jill Lepore's prize-winning *The Name of War* examines this question in its study of communication during King Philip's War. Lepore retells the war as a contest of cultures of communication. Literacy emerges here in its fully paradoxical form as a pathway to power (and perhaps salvation) for American Indians but also as a threat to cultural and literal existence, dramatically so in the case

of the murder of translator John Sassamon. Of the English chroniclers of the conflict, Lepore finds that "like all literate Europeans in the New World, [William] Hubbard and [Cotton] Mather had a veritable monopoly on making meaning, or at least on translating and *recording* the meaning of what they saw and did" (xviii). Yet there is a big difference between the two sides of Lepore's "or" in this formulation—precisely the difference postcolonial studies points to as a key site for the study of resistance. The translation and recording of the war happened in Native communities throughout the region; Lepore recounts only two brief oral reports of the war still current among local tribes. More important, European reporting of the war has been no less subject to reevaluation by Native American historians than by academic historians, a question I discuss in the context of the Pequot War in chapter 4.

4. Mourt, *A relation, or iournall,* 23.

5. Weston, *History of the Town of Middleboro, Massachusetts,* 351. See also the discussion of this scene in Coleman, *Vicious,* 52.

6. On trapping, see V. Anderson, *Creatures of Empire.*

7. Ong, *Orality and Literacy.*

8. Ong was a student of both technology theorist Marshall McLuhan and American Puritanism scholar Perry Miller, so the persistence of his model of the relationship between representational technology and the mind may not be surprising, in the early American field in particular. Scott Richard Lyons, Robert Allen Warrior, Christopher B. Teuton, and Lepore have found the oral-literate binary still at work in the fields of rhetoric, intellectual history, and cultural history. See Lyons, "Rhetorical Sovereignty," 460; Warrior, *The People and the World;* Teuton, "Theorizing American Indian Literature"; and Lepore, *The Name of War,* especially 26–27. See also the influential theory of the "great divide" between literacy and orality in Goody and Watt, "The Consequences of Literacy." *The Networked Wilderness* does not argue that there is no difference between aural and inscribed forms of communication—indeed, Ong's rigorous analyses of the different formal properties of mnemonic and inscriptive practices and the performative dynamics of oral communication are an essential guideline for interpreting publication events that use these different modes. It is the hierarchization of consciousnesses and the use of a media activity to characterize an entire culture that are both the most inimical and, historiographically, most insidious aspects of Ong's thesis. Books and speeches are different, but in encounter, the performative qualities of things and the material qualities of talking are thrown into relief by the attempt to communicate across semiotic systems.

9. Warkentin, "In Search of 'The Word of the Other,'" 3.

10. Matthew Brown has recently offered such a recasting of book history, insisting that textual materialism be expanded to include emotional, performative, material, and intellectual interactions with texts. See his "'BOSTON SOB/NOT'"; and the more extended treatment in his *Pilgrim and the Bee.* Jacques Derrida discusses the "support" of an inscribed document in *Paper Machine.* In the case of indigenous North American material communications, distinctions among support, inscription, and form may be more difficult to maintain.

11. Lienhard, "Las prácticas textuales indígenas," 78. See also Lienhard, *La voz y su huella.*

12. See Gates, *The Signifying Monkey,* for "signifying" as both a traditional topos describing the tactics of messengers between the gods and men and as a counterhegemonic tactic. Gates's double-voiced approach to formal criticism has a parallel in Gerald Vizenor's concept of "survivance" and other Native American techniques of adaptation and resistance; see Vizenor, *Manifest Manners.*

13. For other work about the relationship between oral and written textuality and the kind of methodology required to capture their complex interplay in North America, see Fliegelman, *Declaring Independence;* Brooks, *The Common Pot;* Rigal, *The American Manufactory;* and Looby, *Voicing America.* The interplay of voice and text that these scholars find so interesting in the eighteenth century has a long foreground in the seventeenth. Richard Cullen Rath argues against the

utility of the literacy thesis, observing that both human and natural sounds were powerful shapers of meaning and interpretation "even in the most literate culture in the world at the time, that of the New England Puritans" (Rath, *How Early America Sounded*, 3). Theater scholar Bruce Smith argues that "systems of communication in early modern England maintained a contact with the human body that seems remarkably different from communication systems today. Rather than imagining a rigid distinction between oral culture and literate culture, between aural media and visual media, we should imagine a continuum between speech and vision" (B. Smith, *The Acoustic World of Early Modern England*, 19). My use of the term "network" is informed by studies in information theory and new media, but it has precedents in the study of New England; for a use of the network to conceptualize transatlantic English affiliation, see Bremer, "Increase Mather's Friends."

14. Finnegan, *Communicating*, 29. See Finnegan's summary and discussion of communications theories of the twentieth century beginning with Claude Shannon's, 3–32. Also influential among American historians and cultural critics have been Habermas's *Theory of Communicative Action* and *Structural Transformation of the Public Sphere*.

15. For this reason, too, unlike Brotherston, Krupat, and others, I do not attempt to characterize Native American sign systems in terms of writing or compare them to European literacies. Writing is a technology that, when separated analytically from the social context in which it happens, often occasions dangerous hierarchizations of social groups. On Foucault's multifaceted treatment of technologies as production tactics, systems of signs, power mechanisms, and ways of relating the self to the world, see Foucault, "Technologies of the Self."

16. See, for example, Kittler, *Discourse Networks 1800/1900;* Luhmann, *Social Systems;* and the essays in *Structure and Dynamics of Networks,* ed. Newman, Barabási, and Watts.

17. Greenblatt, *Learning to Curse*, 32; Jehlen, "History before the Fact," 692. See D. Murray, *Forked Tongues*, for an argument for a similar focus on mediation in the study of colonial encounters.

18. Weaver, *That the People Might Live*, 35; Weaver, *Other Words;* Warrior, *The People and the World;* Pulitano, *Toward a Native American Critical Theory;* Womack, *Red on Red;* Cook-Lynn, *Why I Can't Read Wallace Stegner and Other Essays.* Among similar works in postcolonial studies, see Chakrabarty, "Postcoloniality and the Artifice of History."

19. "Anxiety" has a long history as a category of analysis in American studies; see Wald, *Constituting Americans,* for an argument for the term; and Pfister and Schnog, eds., *Inventing the Psychological,* for essays cautioning analysts about the use of psychoanalytic terms in cultural studies before Freud. I find the word useful in capturing a distinction between fear and worry about the future; while at times in New England's early history such fear rose to a cultural level (most famously during King Philip's War and the Salem Witch Trials), in many cases I will be speaking of the worries of individuals as functions of their rank or their elected role in a polity.

20. For a revision of the history of the idea of communication that puts failure, noise, and breakdown at its center, see J. Peters, *Speaking into the Air.*

21. D. Hall, *Cultures of Print,* 93. This is in fact a rare moment in which Hall means "language" to imply only the written word.

22. Sandra Gustafson's work on the historical period covered here is a recent example of this trend. As she puts it, "The forms of state power that white men designed in the early republic were shaped in crucial ways by their proximity and resistance to the speech of white women, native Americans, and African Americans . . . . The textual prophylaxis that Puritan leaders employed to control the internal threat of multiplicity that women's oppositional speech represented was matched by their use of text to distinguish English eloquence from native speech traditions and thus to contain a threat of multiplicity from outside their speech community" (Gustafson, *Eloquence Is Power,* xix, 33). For a less localized but similar approach, see Greenblatt, *Marvelous Possessions.* For a comparison of English and colonial public performances and "antics," see Abrahams, "Antick Dispositions and the Perilous Politics of Culture."

23. Darnton, "The Heresies of Bibliography," 43–45. See, for example, Darnton, "An Early Information Society."

24. McKenzie, *Bibliography and the Sociology of Texts,* 12–13. Cathy Davidson advocates for a "history of texts" in Davidson, *Revolution and the Word,* 59–72.

25. In McKenzie, *Bibliography and the Sociology of Texts.*

26. Chartier, *Forms and Meanings,* 1, 95, 1.

27. On the permeability of popular and clerical interpretive fields, see D. Hall, *Worlds of Wonder, Days of Judgment;* and Gordis, *Opening Scripture.* On gender restrictions, see Monaghan, *Learning to Read and Write in Colonial America.* Against the category of "literacy" itself, see A. Newman, "On the Literacy Frontier."

28. McKenzie's *Bibliography and the Sociology of Texts* is based on lectures delivered in 1985 (first published in 1986) and on an essay on New Zealand first published in 1984. See also Baker, *Double Fold.*

29. McKenzie takes this phrase from I. A. Richards; see his discussion of Richards and the problem of intentionality in literary study in *Bibliography and the Sociology of Texts,* 37.

30. McKenzie's own work on the Cambridge University Press is one of the best histories of collaborative print production—but again, it was designed to complicate notions of authorial control that he then went on to find enacted in the example of Congreve. The touch or presence of the author in the printing house becomes, for McKenzie, the renewed, now physical foundation of intentionality. See also Darnton, *Literary Underground.*

31. Derrida warns about the difficulties of studying a performance situation in "Signature Event Context." He observes that one must preserve the idea of intention but relegate it to being only one factor in an interpretation. At the same time, it is impossible to confine a speaking situation to such a limited set of conventions that the context of an utterance can be positively identified. Context should be treated with the same suspicion that we bring to intention, but both are analytically significant.

32. "The Sociology of a Text: Oral Culture, Literacy, and Print in Early New Zealand," in McKenzie, *Bibliography and the Sociology of Texts.*

33. Ibid., 79.

34. The *Requerimiento* (1510) declared Spanish sovereignty over Amerindian lands and peoples. It was to be read to indigenous populations on contact but was not always translated—and sometimes was not even heard by those populations.

35. Todorov argues this controversial foundation of European dominance in *Conquest of America;* see among other responses Greenblatt, *Marvelous Possessions,* 10–12; and Cheyfitz, *The Poetics of Imperialism.*

36. For an example of oral–print movement and the social contexts of "original" fairy tales, see Darnton, "Peasants Tell Tales."

37. For more nuanced discussions of the materiality of the archive than I can pursue here, see Derrida, *Paper Machine;* and Steedman, *Dust.* For accounts of the role of definitions of material evidence in Native sovereignty contests, see Sparke, "A Map That Roared and an Original Atlas"; Weaver, *Other Words;* and Boon, *Other Tribes, Other Scribes.*

38. Besnier, "Literacy and the Notion of Person on Nukulaelae Atoll," 582. See also Street, *Literacy in Theory and Practice;* Finnegan, *Literacy and Orality;* and Heath, "The Functions and Use of Literacy."

39. See D. Hall, *Worlds of Wonder, Days of Judgment,* 103.

40. Tuvill, *The Dove and the Serpent,* 60–61 ("Of Negotiation in generall"). The dove and serpent were explicit models for New England emissaries to the Algonquians. Massachusetts Bay officials, for example, once warned John Endicott not to trust the "salvages" to be loyal: "And as wee are commanded to be innocent as doves, soe withall wee [must be] wise as serpents." Shurtleff, *Records of the Governor and Company,* 1:385, 394, 400.

41. There are, as we will see, important exceptions to this generalization, though none of these engage the history of the book. Finnegan's work comes closest to doing so by virtue of her emphasis on technology as a social relation. See also Brotherston's critique of the undertreatment of textual materiality by analysts of indigenous American texts from Lévi-Strauss to Derrida, in *Book of the Fourth World,* especially 9–81.

42. Besnier, "Literacy and the Notion of Person on Nukulaelae Atoll," 571. Amory has proposed the term "ethnobibliography" for an approach to the history of material texts that emphasizes the ways racial and cultural difference affect reception and distribution. See Amory, *Bibliography and the Book Trades,* 12.

43. Merrell, *The Indians' New World,* vii; and see Axtell, *The European and the Indian.*

44. Axtell, "Babel of Tongues," 18, 49.

45. P. Smith, "The Terrible Nearness of Distant Places," 385.

46. See Gustafson, *Eloquence Is Power;* and Matthew Brown, *Pilgrim and the Bee,* 179–207.

47. Butler, *Bodies That Matter,* 95.

48. Lefebvre, *The Production of Space,* 33.

49. Round, *By Nature and by Custom Cursed,* 155. For an elaboration of "textual performance" as the "theater of writing and reading," see Matthew Brown, "BOSTON/SOB NOT," 312.

50. Lefebvre, *Production of Space,* 143. Lefebvre argues that cultural space is produced along the lines of social relations of labor that characterize a given society. Lefebvre observes that to "underestimate, ignore and diminish space amounts to the overestimation of texts, written matter, and writing systems, along with the readable and the visible, to the point of assigning to these a monopoly on intelligibility" (62).

51. See Richter, *Ordeal of the Longhouse;* Sayre, *Les sauvages américains;* Urton, "From Knots to Narratives"; Jaenen, "Native Oral and Inscribed Discourse"; Salomon, *The Cord Keepers.*

52. Lefebvre, *Production of Space,* 143.

53. See in particular the section "Spatial Architectonics" and 192–93 in ibid. My use of theories of space to build on the history of the book is double-edged. Lefebvre's theorization of space, for example, does not stand unqualified by its deployment in Native America. Those parts of his theory that involve modernity and communication are constructed in part on an idea of the premodern that is Eurocentric and that imagines "primitive" peoples as lacking or not needing elaborated spaces. If our understanding of early American publication events can benefit from theories of modernity, it is equally the case that early American texts qualify those theories.

54. Elliott, "Coyote Comes to the *Norton,*" 726-27. See also Lyons's demand for a parallel terrain of rhetorical power that he terms "rhetorical sovereignty," which would produce "the affirmation of peoplehood" for Native peoples from within public discourse (Lyons, "Rhetorical Sovereignty," 456).

55. On Native nationalism, see, for example, Wilson, "Reclaiming Our Humanity," especially 72. For an intellectually syncretic approach, see the work of Vizenor and the analyses of it by Krupat, especially *The Turn to the Native,* chapters 3 and 4. For a critique of the language of sovereignty in indigenous rights discourse, see Michael Brown, "Sovereignty's Betrayals."

56. See P. Deloria, "American Indians, American Studies, and the ASA," 672.

57. For an articulation of this approach with respect to museum exhibits, see P. Smith, "The Terrible Nearness of Distant Places."

58. Such questions animate provocative recent work on the world of books and objects in Renaissance England. Studies by Wendy Wall, Margaret Spufford, Annabel Patterson, Peter Stallybrass, and David Cressy have helped situate colonial texts in a larger world of print production and circulation. Recent research probes more broadly into materiality in English culture, seeing it in an informational continuum with the works that are already familiar to us from the literary canon. Julian Yates's study of error and failure in English objects, for example, asks us to consider ways of thinking of objects as agents, problematizing the idea of subject development from a position that utterly decenters present notions of consciousness and somatic embodiment. We need to account

for the phenomenology of the book, its paper, typography, binding, and for the contexts in which books were bought, read, cited, and destroyed, to see how things also formed a link between New England and old England (and beyond). See Quilligan, ed., "Renaissance Materialities"; and Yates, *Error, Misuse, Failure.*

59. Indigenous information technologies—that is, materials, objects, and the social uses of them in communication—were not uniform in Native America, though some were more widespread than others. In the chapters that follow, such practices will be analyzed first within the culture-specific context suggested by available sources. To offer only two examples, ceremonial posts functioned differently in eastern than in northwestern societies, while the use of fire to communicate was common on the plains but not in the eastern woodlands, where hills and tall cover reduced visibility. See, for example, Krech, *The Ecological Indian,* 109.

60. See Krupat, "Post-Structuralism and Oral Literature."

61. Chantal Mouffe argues that political communication, often troped as negotiation, "should be envisaged instead as creating a relation not of *negotiation* but of *contamination,* in the sense that once the articulation of the two principles has been effectuated—even if in a precarious way—each of them changes the identity of the other" (Mouffe, *The Democratic Paradox,* 10).

1. Native Audiences

1. See also Daniels, *Puritans at Play.* On the literary legacy of Morton and the Maypole, see McWilliams, *New England's Crises and Cultural Memory,* especially 44–73.

2. "Thomas Morton of Merrymount," from chapter 19 of Bradford, *Of Plymouth Plantation,* 204–10. On Morton's comparatively light impact on Plymouth's economics, see Salisbury, *Manitou and Providence.*

3. The literature in this area is voluminous, but among the influential books that take information circulation as a central concern are P. Miller, *The New England Mind;* R. Brown, *Knowledge Is Power;* D. Hall, *Worlds of Wonder, Days of Judgment;* and Lockridge, *A New England Town.* For examinations of the place of literacy and textuality in Native American cultures, see Swann and Krupat, eds., *Recovering the Word;* Monaghan, *Learning to Read and Write;* Brooks, *The Common Pot;* Wyss, *Writing Indians;* Warrior, *The People and the Word.*

4. Another dissenter (and lawyer), Thomas Lechford, returned to Europe to publish his critique of the Separatists in 1642. See Lechford, *Plain-Dealing.* Child wrote *New England's Jonas Cast Up in London* to support advocates of religious freedom in New England who distributed petitions written by hand—for potential signers, the inability to get such a petition printed in New England would have resonated with the argument for religious toleration. See also the discussion of Samuel Gorton's radical challenge to the government of Massachusetts Bay in Gura, *A Glimpse of Sion's Glory.*

5. Grantland Rice writes that up until 1662 there was a "flowering of a unique exchange of transatlantic civic criticism," in large part because of "the New England theocracy's effectiveness in suppressing printed commentary within the colonies, an activity which . . . reemphasized the political nature of public writing, and the concurrent lapse of censorship enforcement in England" (Rice, *Transformation of Authorship in America,* 24–25). Morton opted for the more liberal presses of Amsterdam. On censorship in London, see Patterson, *Censorship and Interpretation;* and Agnew, *Worlds Apart.*

6. Morton's text is reprinted in Dempsey's edition of *New English Canaan,* and in facsimile in Force, *Tracts and Other Papers,* vol. 2. Quotations from *New English Canaan* in this chapter are taken from the Amsterdam edition of 1637 held by the Henry E. Huntington Library, hereafter cited in the text.

7. I draw heavily here on the summary in Zuckerman, "Pilgrims in the Wilderness." Dempsey's biography in *New English Canaan* gives a good sense of the scholarship on Morton. See also Major, "William Bradford versus Thomas Morton" and "Thomas Morton and His *New English Canaan.*"

8. For the story of Morton's unfortunate marital career prior to emigrating, see Dempsey's edition of *New English Canaan*, part 2, 73–81; and Ranlet, "The Lord of Misrule."

9. Ma-re Mount had five names within about a year: Passonagessit, Mount Wollaston, Ma-re Mount, Merry-Mount (Bradford's influential modification), and Mount Dagon (Endicott's designation after cutting down the Maypole). The constant renaming suggests the ideological power of space in a land with small, interdependent settlements. I use Morton's original, punning name, which he claimed meant "mount-by-the-sea" but which also implied the aural interpretation Bradford orthographically cements as "merry." See also Krim, "Acculturation of the New England Landscape."

10. Cartelli, "Transplanting Disorder," 260.

11. Zuckerman, "Pilgrims in the Wilderness," 256; Connors, *Thomas Morton*.

12. Zuckerman, "Pilgrims in the Wilderness," 257.

13. Kupperman, "Thomas Morton, Historian," 661; see also Demos, "The Maypole of Merry Mount."

14. See Zuckerman, "Pilgrims in the Wilderness," 257. Puritan leaders continued for some time to enact this brand of poetic justice directed at the medium; Israel Stoughton in 1635 and Roger Williams at around the same time, for example, had to destroy their own manuscripts as punishment for sedition against the Bay Colony. See Breen, *Transgressing the Bounds*, 21–22.

15. For evidence about the relative literacy of Morton's servants, see Dempsey's edition of *New English Canaan*, 83–219.

16. For a history of the relationship of Puritanism to learning, see J. Morgan, *Godly Learning*. Readings of the poems include Dempsey, "Reading the Revels"; and Murphy, "'A Rich Widow.'"

17. D. Hall, *Cultures of Print*, 52.

18. Shields, *Civil Tongues and Polite Letters in British America*, 162.

19. For a discussion of sixteenth-century theories of Native American language, see Greenblatt, *Learning to Curse*, 16–39. Morton's account and use of Native literacy departs from the binary model outlined by Greenblatt, evidence of an evolution in the politics of colonial linguistics. On settler English literacy education as rooted in religious concepts and discourse, see Monaghan, *Learning to Read and Write in Colonial America*, especially 19–45.

20. Gustafson, *Eloquence Is Power*, 5.

21. See Greenblatt's "Racial Memory and Literary History" for a rumination on what this might have meant in the early modern era. While Morton draws on a philological tradition arguing that culture is embedded in language, his treatment makes clear the contextual powers that shape language and understanding. As Kupperman has noted, this kind of ideological contradiction was often forced by the attempt to textualize evidence from encounters *(Indians and English)*.

22. "cap a pe": *cap-a-pied*. On the historical role of posture and gesture in public speaking, see Gustafson, *Eloquence Is Power;* Fliegelman, *Declaring Independence*. Morton's use of the term "postures" here also suggests a parody of the Puritan iconoclasm discussed in the Introduction.

23. Captain Myles Standish and his men, sent to arrest Morton at his plantation, are also likened to Don Quixote attacking the windmill (142).

24. This is a rhetorical gesture reminiscent of Montaigne's famous essay "Of Cannibals." Bubble is depicted from the beginning as an incompetent communicator, made fun of by Morton for his inability to speak Algonquian words. In general, his performances produce the opposite of the desired effect; Bubble's "oratory luld his auditory fast a sleepe, as Mercuries pipes did Argus eies" (122).

25. Bradford quoted in Major, "William Bradford versus Thomas Morton," 6.

26. The *Oxford English Dictionary* lists a host of early modern meanings for the term "loose," including a connotation having to do with freedom from indenture that may well be resonant in Bradford's comment, given Morton's appropriation of his partner's bonded men. The more

enduring meaning related to digestion may also be active in Bradford's characterization, and I will consider it further in chapter 2.

27. Bradford, *Of Plymouth Plantation*, 205–6.

28. Ibid., 206.

29. Sternberg, "The Publication of Thomas Morton's *New English Canaan* Reconsidered," 372; see also Dempsey's edition of Morton, *New English Canaan*, xxix.

30. See Kupperman, *Indians and English*; and Dempsey's edition of Morton, *New English Canaan*.

31. Morton, *New English Canaan*, ed. Dempsey, 229–30.

32. Kupperman, *Indians and English*, 2. At times, this line of reasoning runs the risk of arguing for the Natives as companions to colonization, rather than as "the colonized"; Morton backs down quickly from several of these arguments, which Kupperman examines in detail.

33. Greenblatt, *Learning to Curse*, 32; V. Deloria, *Custer Died for Your Sins*, 5.

34. Matthew Brown, "BOSTON/SOB NOT," 307; Greenblatt, *Learning to Curse*, 32.

35. Richter, *Facing East from Indian Country*, 9.

36. Hariot wrote that the Roanok Indians seemed to believe that the English could control disease, transmitting epidemics to them "as if by 'inuisible bullets.'" Greenblatt reads Hariot as cynically ventriloquizing Native belief, in Chaplin's summary of Greenblatt's argument, "to enact a morality play for the benefit of an English audience": the passage seems to be about European evil taking advantage of Native innocence, European technology triumphing over Native superstition, or both. But Chaplin shows that Hariot was also a publishing atomist who wanted to propagate the controversial theory that matter was constituted in "discrete, durable particles." For him and for readers who knew the controversy, the term "bullets" had a local, specific meaning in the context of natural science. In the *Briefe and True Report*, Native Americans were deployed as an intervention in a debate about natural philosophy and the composition of matter, and perhaps about technology and imperial morality as well. But Chaplin insists that the episode's legibility should remain, like the "original" conversation with the Roanok, elusive—to do justice to the complexity of Native American technologies and responses to colonization, the question of whether Hariot's reporting of the story is strategic or merely tone-deaf should stay productively open. Chaplin, *Subject Matter*, 29.

37. Mignolo, *Darker Side of the Renaissance*, 20.

38. Nelson, "From Manitoba to Patagonia," 372.

39. Edelman, *Homographesis*, 12.

40. Edelman's use of this term is based in psychoanalytic criticism and a historical account of the politics of homosexuality. Edelman theorizes a queer practice out of the possibilities of the homograph, what he calls homographesis, "a mode of strategic or analytic resistance to the logic of regulatory identity" (ibid., 13). My use of the term attempts to elaborate on the communicative dynamics engaged by Richard White's notion of the middle ground, in which linguistic and cultural misunderstanding is a historical driver no less potent than negotiation or violence (White, *Middle Ground*).

41. Bragdon, *Native People of the Eastern Woodlands*, 185. See also Pauketat, *The Ascent of Chiefs*, especially 185; on the use of poles in Delaware Big House ceremonies, see Tooker, ed., *Native North American Spirituality*, 104; Sullivan, "Mississippian Households and Community Organization in Eastern Tennessee"; and in the same volume, Mehrer and Collins, "Household Archaeology at Cahokia and Its Hinterlands." Ma-re Mount was at Mount Wollaston, now Quincy, Massachusetts.

42. Sturtevant, *Handbook of the North American Indians*, 160. On totems, see Bragdon, *Native People of Southern New England*, 185.

43. Bragdon, *Native People of Southern New England*, 35, 72, 85, 92.

44. Ibid., 143.

45. Ibid., 49. Bragdon argues that hierarchical social structures were changing within Native societies in this area on the eve of the epidemics. Conditional sedentism as the basis of legitimate occupation of land was, she says, "associated with hierarchy, inequality, and centralized authority, in part because of the way in which labor was divided and the products of that labor appropriated, and in part because of the way land, central to production, was allocated. . . . The documentary and archaeological data support an argument for a kind of 'ownership' linked to notions of personal identity, descent, and intimate use" (43).

46. Ibid., 173.

47. Warkentin, "In Search of 'The Word of the Other,'" 12; Wogan, "Perceptions of European Literacy in Early Contact Situations."

48. Warkentin, "In Search of 'The Word of the Other,'" 17. Patricia Fumerton's recent work on homosociality and broadside posting in Renaissance England's alehouses suggests the possibility that Morton might also have been using the aesthetics of public posting to generate camaraderie among his servant-class men of both Native and English origin. Reconciling these two groups would not have been easy, but the social panic it induced suggests that Morton was better than most at the task (Fumerton, "Not Home").

49. United Kingdom Public Record Office, S.P. 16/382/7, *The Complete State Papers Domestic*, ser. 2, pt. 6, reel 129 (Brighton, England: Harvester Press, 1981).

50. Prempart, *A Historicall Relation;* and *The Bible, that is, The holy Scriptures*. See A. Johnson, "J. F. Stam, Amsterdam, and English Bibles."

51. Sternberg, "The Publication of Thomas Morton's *New English Canaan* Reconsidered," especially 372. Puritans were not the only exploiters of the international flow of illegal print; among others, recusant Catholics published on the Continent and established transnational networks of print that troubled the Puritans. See also Woodfield, *Surreptitious Printing in England;* and Allison and Rogers, *Contemporary Printed Literature of the English Counter-Reformation.*

52. Laud, *Works of the Most Reverend Father in God,* 7:544. Laud's incursions into the lives of Separatists in Holland were closely observed by the American colonists. "To the New Englanders . . . the suppression of the English classis in Holland was an important event," Raymond Stearns notes, that "portrayed the perfidy of the prelatical system and particularly of Laud, who would not be quit of English subjects wheresoever they might flee; for if the archbishop extended his authority over the English in Holland, would he not erect a bishopric in the Bay Colony?" (Stearns, "The New England Way in Holland," 790–91). See also J. Murray, "The Cultural Impact of the Flemish Low Countries."

53. The same kind of typographical analysis used today to identify the origins of dissenter texts was used by Laud to hound printers and authors in the Low Countries: "To trace the printers, the English authorities relied considerably upon analysis of literary style and print type by knowledgeable scholars and 'experienced printers'" (Sprunger, *Trumpets from the Tower,* 39).

54. Arminianism shared many beliefs with Calvinism, but its advocates thought that all people could be saved and that a person could earn salvation by working toward it in specific ways.

55. Schmidt, *Innocence Abroad.*

56. Lipking, "The Marginal Gloss," 613.

57. Though Evelyn Tribble, in *Margins and Marginality,* claims that her title is something of a tease, her analysis stays within a resistance-to-authority paradigm that ultimately affirms an ill-fitting mapping of imagined textual spatial hierarchies to struggles for social power. Even when marginalia take their simplest, indexical form, they do not stand so much at the margins of something as above it, participating in the science of cataloging, comparing, indexing, or the *omnium gatherum*. I suggest not that we have to leave center and periphery behind for the seductively unmappable marginalia of poststructuralism, but that we have to leave it analytically and return to it in a new way. The material space of the page makes possible a relation of main to ancillary text, which then gets used by different writers to construct their authority as grounded in the margin or

in the center (or wherever). In turn such possibilities are affected by readers' experiences: once writers begin using a page space for contests over authority, printers and readers must be ready to reproduce, respectively, the physical and the rhetorical conditions for those contests. It is true that at times, as Slights points out, the margin is parasitical and "generates what modern communications experts call 'static,' an interfering signal so strong and so incompatible with the primary communication that all the audience receives is noise" (Slights, "The Edifying Margins of Renaissance English Books," 696). Once this positioning of responses and critiques is recognized as such, it takes on structural qualities of its own—pulling against the central text and giving the reader another narrative path to follow, another decision to make. Part of being a seventeenth-century reader was deciding where, in a given text, the main action was—in the margins, in the text, or somewhere in between? Books like the Bible and Erasmus's *Praise of Folly* had a reputation for their marginalia; any new book could potentially garner one as well.

58. For a detailed discussion of Morton and the authority of "experiment" (experience) in early settlement literature, see Egan, *Authorizing Experience,* 14–31.

59. Book ornamentation like Morton's adds a peculiarly Dutch touch, featuring tulips and other distinctive kinds of flowers, to the customary predominance of acanthus morphologies that dominate the grotesque. See Trent, "The Concept of Mannerism," 3:376.

60. Fuller, *The History of the Worthies of England,* 2:274.

61. Bushnell, *Green Desire,* 70.

62. As Morton's accounts of cultivating Native literacy and sexual relations with Native women suggest, it also raised the question of "national" hybridization. See K. Hall, *Things of Darkness.*

63. For a discussion of Morton's choices in the conclusion and possible interpretations of his use of Horace and Virgil here, see Dempsey's edition of Morton, *New English Canaan,* 199n687.

64. Winthrop, *Journal,* 1:130. Thomas Morton to William Jeffreys, May 1634; letter reprinted in Dempsey's edition of Morton, *New English Canaan,* pt. 2, 269–72.

65. Shea, "'Our Professed Old Adversary,'" 53. Winthrop, *Journal,* 2:154. Shea sees Morton making a philological power play that goes beyond my argument: "His own text prevailing, the literary history continuous with Ovid and Virgil and flourishing contemporaneously in the satires and masques of Ben Jonson would write a different sort of New England from that self-fulfilling prophecy being indited by the Puritans" ("Our Professed Old Adversary," 53).

66. In *New English Canaan,* Morton complains explicitly about the Puritan manipulation of the ritual of official proclamation, saying that instead of resulting in a communally produced document, "the construction of the worde would be made by them of the Seperation, to serve their owne turnes" (159).

67. Woodfield, *Surreptitious Printing;* for comparison, see Robert Darnton's influential work on French book smuggling and print culture, which discusses both calculated subversive publishing and the structures of power in publishing (Darnton, *The Literary Underground of the Old Regime*); see also Johns, *The Nature of the Book.* On Morton and the masques, see Dempsey's edition of Morton, *New English Canaan;* and Abrahams, "Antick Dispositions and the Perilous Poetics of Culture"; see also Alice Nash, "'Antic Deportments and Indian Postures.'"

68. Gustafson, *Eloquence Is Power,* 15.

2. Good Noise from New England

1. Massasoit was facing a difficult political situation when the Pilgrims began to set up houses at Patuxet. The same plague that had wiped out Tisquantum's tribe at Patuxet while he was in slavery had upset the region's matrix of power. The Narragansetts, having lost fewer people to disease, were numerically superior and eager to control trade and tribute relations in the area, particularly upon the advent of a constant English presence. Massasoit's establishment of formal political relations with New Plymouth bolstered Wampanoag power against the Narragansetts

while providing an economic and political bubble within which the fledgling colony could stabilize. The Wampanoag were also known as the Pokanoket during the seventeenth century.

2. Massasoit lived from about 1580 to 1661; there are a number of nostalgic biographies of his life. For scholarly accounts, see among others Salisbury, *Manitou and Providence;* Bragdon, *Native People* and *The Columbia Guide;* Kupperman, *Settling with the Indians;* and on Native biography more generally, Grumet, ed., *Northeastern Indian Lives.* David Bushnell observes, as indicative of a lifelong commitment to Native cultural autonomy, that just before he died "Massasoit unsuccessfully attempted to write a clause against further missionary efforts into the terms of a sale of land" (Bushnell, "The Treatment of the Indians," 69).

3. On Winslow's career, governorship, and fame (from Holland to Barbados) as a negotiator, see the rich recent biography by Bangs, *Pilgrim Edward Winslow.* Previous biographies have been brief and, as Bangs demonstrates, troubled by inaccuracies.

4. Two influential paradigms for technological determinism are represented by the works of Jared Diamond, in particular his book *Guns, Germs, and Steel,* and Marshall McLuhan, whose interpretation of the medium as constituting the message may be traced through the essays collected in McLuhan and Zingrone, eds., *Essential McLuhan.*

5. Bradford refers to "continual rumors" of Narragansett or conspiratorial action against the Pilgrims; it seems likely that this was a deliberate strategy on the part of the Natives, a kind of Algonquian disinformation campaign that both made the Pilgrims more grateful for Massasoit's friendship and kept them active players in the political scene (Bradford, *Of Plymouth Plantation,* 111).

6. Salisbury, *Manitou and Providence,* 119.

7. See Kamensky, *Governing the Tongue,* on the role of rumors and gossip in the early settlement period. The metaphor of breathing evokes Saul's persecution of the disciples, against whom he was "breathing out threatenings and slaughter" (Acts 9:1).

8. Winslow, *Good Newes from New-England,* 2; hereafter cited in the text.

9. As with many colonial translators, it is difficult at this remove to make claims about Tisquantum's motivation; good discussions of the situation in early Plymouth can be found in Salisbury, *Manitou and Providence;* Kupperman, *Indians and English;* and Vaughan, *New England Frontier.*

10. Bradford, *Of Plymouth Plantation,* 99. See also Winslow, *Good Newes from New-England,* 10. As Winslow reports in *Good Newes from New-England,* Algonquian hospitality customs also routed information through the sachem: "All travelers or strangers for the most part lodge at the *Sachim's,* when they come they tell him how long they will stay and to what place they go" (56).

11. Winslow, too, confesses that equivocation was a strategy: "notwithstanding our high words and loftie lookes towards them," the English were "still lying open to all casualty" (4).

12. Williams, *A Key into the Language of America,* 71. The same was true of indigenous networks in Virginia; in his *Generall Historie* John Smith reported having tested the rapidity and consistency of Native communications by deliberately starting a rumor and then traveling quickly upriver, where he heard the rumor repeated. See Smith, *Complete Writings,* 2:169.

13. Mourt, *A relation or jiournall,* 41–42.

14. Elsewhere in *Good Newes from New-England,* Winslow refers to Corbitant as "a notable politician, yet ful of merry iests & squibs, & neuer better pleased than when the like are returned againe vpon him" (32–33).

15. Winslow reports that some of those who came to see Massasoit were "by their report from a place not less than an hundred miles" (35). Hobomock, no doubt concerned about Massasoit, likely had a hand in the decision to start the trip; it was not uncommon for Algonquians to travel at night.

16. See Winslow, *Good Newes from New-England,* 5. See also Rath, *How Early America Sounded,* 183–84, on the similarities between today's Internet packet-switching technology and east coast

Native information systems. Movement through the woods while carrying a message was also, in conjunction with a material construct, part of an act of remembering or rerecording history. Winslow points out, "Instead of Records and Chronicles . . . where any remarkeable act is done, in memorie of it, either in the place, or by some path-way near adioyning, they make a round hole in the ground about a foote deepe, and as much over, which when others passing by behold, they enquire the cause and occasion of the same, which being once knowne, they are carefull to acquaint all men, as occasion serueth therewith. And least such holes should be filled, or grown vp by any accident, as men passe by they will oft renew the same; By which meanes many things of great Antiquitie are fresh in memory. So that as a man travelleth, if he can vnderstand his guide, his iourney will be the lesse tedious, by reason of the many historicall Discourses will be related vnto him." *Good Newes from New-England,* 61. The unique medium of the memory hole is a kind of inverse monument in its uniformity and subterranean emptiness. It seems only to impede travel for those unfamiliar with its social role (as a walking hazard for horses or people), but eases it for the initiated traveler. One might imagine the surface of southeastern New England as being like a giant compact disc—filled with identical holes that, when properly decoded, render a unique sound.

17. See Bradford, *Of Plymouth Plantation,* 88–89.

18. See, for example, Salisbury, *Manitou and Providence,* 129. Salisbury argues that because "bands were autonomous and revenge was largely a matter of personal and familial concern," the hatred for the Wessagusset settlers by a small number of Native men only "dovetailed with a less focused anti-English resentment among a large group of Indians. The result was the *appearance* of a conspiracy that Massasoit exploited to regain his position as Plymouth's only dependable Indian friend and that Plymouth itself used for conducting its armed intervention" (132).

19. Eliot, in a letter published in Winslow, *The Glorious Progress of the Gospel,* 11.

20. Cronon, *Changes in the Land,* 40.

21. Massasoit might have gotten infected without the help of the Dutch. See the list of diseases common in precontact America in Newman, "Aboriginal New World Epidemiology," especially 669.

22. See Andrews and Bharucha, "Review," 47; this is a review of Ramkumar and Rao, "Efficacy and Safety of Traditional Medical Therapies for Chronic Constipation." Winslow's "confection" may have been some kind of candied berry or, more likely, a fruit "conserve" (a general term that could include a range of preserves), perhaps of apple or lemon.

23. Samuel Eliot Morison and others have noted that Massasoit had constipation, but attribute it to various nondisease causes; "a bout of gluttony," Morison moralistically suggests in Bradford, *Of Plymouth Plantation,* 117n4. Shepard Krech discusses the difficulties of precise identification of diseases from early contact records, and of assessing kill rates or long-term effects of maladies, in *The Ecological Indian,* especially 73–99.

24. For a description of botulism and its etiology, see Centers for Disease Control and Prevention, *Botulism in the United States,* 1–43; and Hatheway, "Botulism."

25. Thompson, "Introduction," 3. See also Friedman, McQuaid, and Grendell, *Current Diagnosis and Treatment in Gastroenterology.*

26. See Schoenfeldt, *Bodies and Selves in Early Modern England;* Paster, *The Body Embarrassed;* and Craik, "Reading *Coryats Crudities.*"

27. Chaplin, "Natural Philosophy and an Early Racial Idiom in North America," 238. As Chaplin points out, Galenic theory was undergoing challenges both from Paracelsian approaches and a nascent germ theory during the seventeenth century. In Winslow's writing, however, humor theory appears in its most common form, mixing elements from natural philosophy with treatments adapted to humor theory from popular domestic manuals. For a collection of essays that demonstrate the breadth and implications of the debates among atomists, Paracelsians, Harveyites, Galenists, Baconians, and many others, see Debus, ed., *Science, Medicine, and Society in the Renaissance.* See also Kupperman, "Fear of Hot Climates in the Anglo-American Colonial Experience"; and the essays in Lindman and Tarter, eds., *A Centre of Wonders.*

28. For an extended contemporary treatise on Galenic health, see Elyot, *The Castle of Health.* Elyot's text was first published in the 1530s and was frequently reprinted.

29. Analysis of urine and feces had been the primary means of diagnosis for doctors for hundreds of years. Medical texts of the sixteenth and seventeenth centuries were dominated by discussions of digestion, because it was in the concoction, or the conversion of objects from the outside into fluids inside and into excrement, that the health of a person was understood to lie. See Siraisi, *Medieval and Early Renaissance Medicine.* On excrement, see Persels, "The Sorbonnic Trots"; and Persels and Ganim, ed., *Fecal Matters in Early Modern Literature and Art.*

30. Chaplin observes that medicine was a subset of the larger field of natural philosophy, the latter of which "sought to describe a wider range of phenomena and was accessible to a broader range of literate people" ("Natural Philosophy and an Early Racial Idiom in North America," 234).

31. Physical balance was, Schoenfeldt shows, imagined to implicate psychological balance as well; "the consuming subject was pressured . . . to conceive all acts of ingestion and excretion as very literal acts of self-fashioning" (*Bodies and Selves in Early Modern England*, 11). Paster *(The Body Embarrassed),* too, demonstrates that the belief in women as inherently "leaky vessels," unable to control their humoral balance, had important consequences for the development of women's agency and cultural conceptions of female subjectivity. In light of this use of humor theory to ground subjectivity, we might see Winslow's cure as, in part, an attempt to teach Massasoit English self-fashioning tactics for a man of his rank. Certainly Massasoit's mental balance was no less important to the Plymouthites than, from the English reader's standpoint, it would have been imagined to be for the Wampanoag.

32. Such an argument is made in Cushman, "Reasons and Considerations," included as the concluding letter in Mourt, *Mourt's Relation,* 91–92.

33. Current scholarship debates the duration and persuasiveness of the authorization of hereditary monarchy through the idea of the "king's two bodies" (the body natural and the body politic). But Winslow here engages the notion if only to suggest that the forces involved in maintaining political power may be more heterogeneous than the myth of the king's embodiment of authority through the people suggests. The king's "real" body is a vector for a population's will; his metaphorical body transcends his own and is the embodiment of power, divinely ordained or not. See Kantorowicz, *The King's Two Bodies;* but also see Douglas, *Natural Symbols,* especially 65–81.

34. Schoenfeldt, *Bodies and Selves in Early Modern England,* 29.

35. Bradford, *Of Plymouth Plantation,* 62.

36. Cressy, *Coming Over,* 222–23.

37. See ibid., 225.

38. Ibid., 216.

39. As Ian Steele has shown, communication became more predictable. Still, it is worth differentiating between the statistical verity that Steele demonstrates respecting the high percentage of ships and cargoes that reached their destinations and the impressions that Atlantic denizens had about seaborne transmission. Popular anxieties about airline travel, for example, do not conform to the statistical likelihood of hijacking or accident (Steele, *The English Atlantic).*

40. James Cudworth and Johanna Tuttle quoted in Cressy, *Coming Over,* 214.

41. The term is used by two writers cited by Cressy in ibid., 223.

42. Winslow's description of "miscarriage" causing him to be "hindred" here mixes strains of Galenic metaphor; as Paster points out, miscarriage and incontinence were considered evidence of women's natural inability to regulate flows properly by an English society anxious about gendered power. Winslow's challenge may have been to depict an Atlantic communications environment as much from a domestically English standpoint as possible. He represents the "leaky vessels" of news-bearing ships not as carrying information to competing imperial or commercial powers (often the real endpoint of a "miscarried" message) but merely as a hindrance to business destined to continue with proper management.

43. For the broad context of uses of civility in English imperial efforts and why they largely failed, see Oberg, *Dominion and Civility.*

44. Williams, *Correspondence,* 2:611.

45. See Chaplin, "Natural Philosophy," 248; and Bragdon, *Native Peoples of Southern New England.*

46. On emetics, see Silverman, "Indians, Missionaries, and Religious Translation," 149; Bragdon, *Native Peoples of Southern New England;* Winslow, *Good Newes from New-England,* 56. For a seventeenth-century account of American medicines, see Josselyn, *New-Englands rarities discovered. . . .* Historians of medicine in New England have argued that Native and English treatments were relatively compatible, and that the Americans' "approach encouraged the settlers to establish an independent tradition of prescribing a specific remedy for a specific ailment" (Gifford, "Botanic Remedies in Colonial Massachusetts," 269). See also Bradley, "Medical Practices of the New England Aborigines"; Calloway, *New Worlds for All,* 24–41; and Beinfield, "The Early New England Doctor."

47. Bragdon, *Native Peoples of Southern New England,* 18, 19. For a bibliography of works on woodlands spirituality and health in this period, see Bragdon, *The Columbia Guide to the American Indians of the Northeast,* 18–20. Kupperman, *Indians and English* observes structural similarities among Algonquian, English, and French conceptions of health and spirituality; see also Salwen, "Indians of Southern New England and Long Island"; Simmons, *Spirit of the New England Tribes;* R. Peters, *The Wampanoags;* and Weinstein-Farson, *The Wampanoag,* 45–46.

48. Salisbury points out that "the pow-wows would be the principal earthly adversaries in any Puritan missionary effort. Though later missionaries often disagreed with Winslow's evaluation of native religion, all followed him in placing primary emphasis on Hobbamock and the pow-wows as the root of native 'heathenism'" (*Manitou and Providence,* 138). Convincing the *pawwaws* to give up the devil as a means of curing seemed like a policy that would quickly spread Christian influence. But they were unpredictable in the communications system in part because they were, and sometimes still are, constitutively independent of the band or kinship political structure. By ranging across kinship groups, shamanic healers played an important role in maintaining both the legitimacy of the sachems' power (by exercising a brand of authority neither contained by the sachemship nor available to it except by persuasion) and the flexibility of intertribal relations (since unlike sachems, who get their authority *through* tribute or war relations, *pawwaws* could perform within different groups without being of them or responsible to them).

49. Dod and Cleaver, *A Godly Forme,* quoted in Wall, *Staging Domesticity,* 32. On the mixing of folk and Galenic logics in household manuals, see Schoenfeldt, *Bodies and Selves,* 37.

50. Korda, *Shakespeare's Domestic Economies,* 73, see also 7. Wall also shows that the sometimes painful remedies and violent nature of household work (with knives, blood, and animal body parts strewn throughout the kitchen) mixed threat with comfort in the English household. This dynamic might inform Winslow's depiction of himself administering conserves to Massasoit on the point of a knife. Becoming like the threatening but comforting housewife, Winslow introduces Massasoit to English-style domestic persuasion.

51. See Wall, *Staging Domesticity,* 46; Craik, "Reading *Coryats Crudities,*" 82. Trudy Eden observes that the English "highly regarded foods that exhibited a balance of heat and moisture, like sugar, because their elemental quality so closely resembled that of the sanguine person and thus of the perfect human body" (Eden, "Food, Assimilation, and the Malleability of the Human Body in Early Virginia," 32).

52. Dawson, *The good hvswifes Iewell,* 54. See similar recipes in *A Closet for Ladies and Gentlewomen,* 83, 144, 183; and in similar texts of the time, which frequently borrowed from each other.

53. Markham, *Countrey contentments.* On Winslow's early years and apprenticeship with stationer John Beale, see Bangs, *Pilgrim Edward Winslow,* 1–5.

54. Wall, *Staging Domesticity,* 28.

55. Winslow may have assembled his recipe using a combination of traditional and Galenic logics, or he may have learned a template for it through personal experience from a relative or one of his wives (first Elizabeth, who died shortly after the emigration, then Susanna). His use of strawberry leaves in the first broth is somewhat contradictory according to the pharmacopoeia of the day; they may have been intended to treat the swelling in Massasoit's mouth. John Gerard's popular *Herball* observes of strawberry leaves that "the decoction thereof strengtheneth the gummes, fasteneth the teeth, and is good to be held in the mouth, both against the inflammation or burning heate thereof, and also of the almonds of the throat: they stay the ouermuch flowing of the bloudy flix, and other issues of bloud" (Gerard, *The herbal*, 998). Markham's recipe for constipation recommends crushed herbs with white wine; Winslow's substitution of boiled water would have addressed the humoral logic of countering binding with heat and wetness (15). Sassafras, however, was reputed to break down obstructions, particularly of the kidney and bladder, when boiled; see Bright, *A treatise*, 110; Markham, *Countrey contentments*, 31, 33.

56. Winthrop, *Journal*, 124–25. The English sometimes used the term "sagamore" to refer to sachems.

57. See, for example, the recent review by Jenkins et al., "Probiotics."

58. Serres, *The Parasite*, 8.

59. In his influential essay "Identity in Mashpee," James Clifford warns that the body, figured as Winthrop does in "Modell of Christian Charity" or by humor theory, is hierarchically "organ"-ized, which is a risky trope for thinking about belonging. "The culture concept accommodates internal diversity and an 'organic' division of roles but not sharp contradictions, mutations, or emergences." Clifford warns that such a concept cannot see "contending or alternating futures" (Clifford, *Predicament of Culture*, 338). The parasite—always next to and linked to the body, emerging from and within it—might be a better, if less comforting, resource for thinking about social expression and its relation to power.

60. See Finch, "'Civilized' Bodies and the 'Savage' Environment of Early New Plymouth," especially 48.

61. Stallybrass and White, *Politics and Poetics of Transgression*, 192.

62. For model arguments about the relationship between symbolic and material economies, see Douglas and Isherwood, *The World of Goods;* Foucault, *Discipline and Punish;* and most pertinent to early New England, D. Murray, *Indian Giving.*

63. Paster, *The Body Embarrassed*, 7. For the larger scholarly discussion of the role of sexual difference in scientific discourse, see, among many others, Grosz, *Volatile Bodies;* Butler, *Gender Trouble;* Lacquer, *Making Sex;* and Foucault, *History of Sexuality.*

64. Winslow, *Good Newes from New-England*, 36. In a passage directly connecting the logic of preservation and consumption to the taking of physical space from Native Americans, Winslow writes, "wee haue enioyed such plentie as though the windowes of heauen had beene opened vnto vs. How few, weake, and raw were we at our first beginning, and there setling, in the middest of barbarous enemies? yet God wrought our peace for vs. How often haue wee beene at the pits brim, and in danger to be swallowed vp, yea, not knowing, till afterward that we were in perill? and yet God preserued vs: yea, and from how many that we yet know not of, he that knoweth all things can best tell: So that when I seriously consider of things, I cannot but thinke that God hath a purpose to giue that Land as an inheritance to our Nation, and great pittie it were that it should long lie in so desolate a state, considering it agreeth so well with the constitution of our bodies" (52). God here acts through Galenic logics, not allowing the raw to be swallowed up, preserving them for introduction into a place of ideal balance. Tensions remain, as Winslow's frequent claims of God's preference are contradicted by his sense of "pittie" that the union of English and America was not effected earlier. The trope of preservation has been by this point linked to Massasoit's body throughout the text, and a reader may be left wondering at the conflation of the complicated indigenous sociopolitical landscape depicted in *Good Newes from New-England* into the flat

"barbarous enemies." Though it sounds like a conclusion, Winslow follows this passage with his famously detailed ethnography of the Algonquians with whom he had become acquainted.

65. Robinson, letter included in Bradford, *Of Plymouth Plantation*, 197–98.

3. Forests of Gestures

1. Williams, *Correspondence*, 1:22, 58. While the manuscript of *A Key into the Language of America* might actually have been begun at sea on his way to England, Williams appears to have added to it on arrival, judging from references made within the text, such as an observation respecting long-haired Englishmen (49).

2. Keary, "Retelling the History of the Settlement of Providence"; D. Murray, *Indian Giving*; Felker, "Roger Williams's Uses of Legal Discourse"; Cesarini, "The Ambivalent Uses." Jonathan Beecher Field argues that for dissidents like Williams, the Atlantic provided important balancing power, making it more likely that appeals like his would be successful in London. Winslow's and Bradford's anxieties about the constipated Atlantic were perhaps being directly played on here, as Williams performs for his audience a metaphorical reveling in the release from orthodox Congregationalist oppression offered by his arrival in London (Field, "The Grounds of Dissent").

3. Miller, "Roger Williams."

4. Ivy Schweitzer's work has been particularly influential for my reading of Williams. According to Schweitzer, *A Key into the Language of America*'s dialogic form "does not subdue" the Narragansett language but instead "allows the two contradictory worlds implied by their linguistic representations to exist fruitfully side by side" (Schweitzer, *Work of Self-Representation*, 228). In shifting focus from the dynamics of race and selfhood to communications practices, I argue that in some ways *A Key* goes so far as to interarticulate these elements.

5. On Williams's self-deconstructing textuality, see Myles, "Dissent and the Frontier of Translation"; Murray, *Indian Giving*; and Wertheimer, "Roger Williams." Williams's challenge to textuality itself as a source of truth has a history of inducing such comparisons; even Perry Miller at one point reads Williams as a protoexistentialist (P. Miller, "Roger Williams," 24). On Williams's centrality for Native American ethnography, see Rubertone, *Grave Undertakings*, xiv–xv.

6. Pagden, *The Fall of Natural Man*.

7. See P. Miller, "Roger Williams" and *Roger Williams*; Rosenmeier, "The Teacher and the Witness"; and Felker, "Roger Williams's Uses of Legal Discourse."

8. Salisbury, *Manitou and Providence*, 197; Williams, *The bloudy tenent*, 114. This perspective may have been informed by the work of Francisco Vitoria; see Lepore, *The Name of War*, 109–10.

9. Salisbury, *Manitou and Providence*, 213.

10. Ibid., 213. For a time, Salisbury shows, they were right.

11. Among other provocative treatments of Williams's theology in relation to his Indian writings, see Wertheimer, "Roger Williams"; and T. Wood, "Kingdom Expectations."

12. Reinitz, "The Separatist Background of Roger Williams' Argument for Religious Toleration," 111. "Types," "shadows," and "figures" were the key categories of relational interpretation between the books of the Bible and subsequent Christian history. Reinitz suggests deep roots of the typological argument in separatist thinking; Williams's argument relies on the technicalities of typology, but also on the political history of persecution suffered by nonconformists. Certainly in *The hireling ministry none of Christs* Williams insists that there is no antitype in the New Testament for the punishment of heresy by civic force in the Old Testament, and uses the argument for which Reinitz finds a long genealogy—that the material punishments of the Old Testament were figurations of spiritual punishments in the New Testament.

13. E. Morgan, *Roger Williams*, 22, 51. Williams began publishing his insistence on the conversion-by-example approach at precisely the time that most Puritan colonies, in the wake of the Antinomian controversy, gave up on policies like those of the Massachusetts Bay colony charter,

which stated that "good life and orderlie conversation maie wynn and incite the natives" to Christianity, supplementing conversion by example with systematic support for and encouragement of a missionary program (Shurtleff, ed., *Records*, 1:17).

14. Williams, *Mr. Cottons letter*, 42. During the tumult of the English Civil War, Williams's insistence that since "those glorious *first ministeriall gifts* are ceased" proselytizing was unjustifiable was less strenuous than it would eventually become; "in these great Earthquakes," he wrote, "wherein it pleaseth God to shake foundations, civill and spirituall, such a Ministry of Christ Jesus may be sought after, whose proper worke is preaching, for converting and gathering of true penitents" (*The hireling ministry*, 17; *Mr. Cottons Letter*, 43). By 1652 his confidence had been restored: "I prejudice not an Externall *Test* and *Call*, which was at first and shall be againe in force at the *Resurrection* of the *Churches*. . . . But in the present *State* of things, I cannot but be humbly bold to say, that I know no other *True Sender*, but the most *Holy Spirit*" (*The hireling ministry*, 4).

15. Williams, *The hireling ministry*, 21. See 1 Corinthians 14:24–25.

16. Cesarini, "The Ambivalent Uses of Roger Williams' *A Key into the Language of America*," 483.

17. J. Robinson, "A Justification of Separation from the Church of England," 1:xliv–xlv. See also John Milton's characterization of religious truth as a "streaming fountain" that needed the protection of Parliament against restrictions on licensing in order to remain vital. Milton, *Areopagitica*, 26. See also David Lovejoy, *Religious Enthusiasm in the New World*.

18. Williams, *The hireling ministry*, 24.

19. Rubertone warns against an overreading of Narragansetts as always mobile, which has at times "inhibited and perhaps even prevented the exploration of Native peoples' attachments to place. Assumptions about Native mobility, as many historical analysts have noted, helped the English lay claim to Native land and justify its dispossession." She suggests the concept of Native homelands, which would embrace socially lived spaces, ecological forms (landscape and season), and ritual or cosmological understandings of space (Rubertone, *Grave Undertakings*, 66, 103). Darnell, "Rethinking the Concepts," describes Algonquian social strategies as "a process of subsistence-motivated expansion and contraction" (91).

20. On indigenous trade and political networks, see Sayre, *Les sauvages américains;* Turnbaugh, "Wide-Area Connections in Native North America"; Brooks, *The Common Pot;* and D. Murray, *Indian Giving*.

21. Williams, *Correspondence*, 1:150–51.

22. Axtell, *The European and the Indian*, 168–206.

23. Certeau, *The Practice of Everyday Life*, 99. See also Axtell, "The White Indians of Colonial America."

24. "I have travelled with neere 200. of them at once," Williams writes elsewhere in *A Key into the Language of America*, "neere 100. miles through the woods, every man carrying a *little Basket* of this at his *back*, and sometimes in a hollow *Leather Girdle* about his middle sufficient for a man three or foure daies" (11). For the context of English anxieties about the unconstrained movement of individuals during the era of the civil wars, see Hill, *World Turned Upside Down*, especially chapter 3, "Masterless Men."

25. For the debate in colonial studies over the relationship among metaphor, empire, and the notion of the "proper," see Cheyfitz, *The Poetics of Imperialism;* and Greenblatt, *Marvelous Possessions*.

26. Williams, *The hireling ministry*, A2v–A3r. The ambiguity here is typical of Williams; he calls on Paul, who distinguishes his own people from barbarians, but in this construction Williams might be rephrasing "English" as "Barbarians." As late as 1682 Williams insisted that his movements in Indian country were integral to his ability to maintain favor with the Narragansetts and thus that such mobility, as the root of friendship, was the only true basis of residency; see Williams, *An Affidavit*.

27. Williams, *Correspondence*, 1:307; Williams, *Complete Writings*, 3:209–10.

28. E. Morgan, *Roger Williams;* on Williams and theology, see also Gilpin, *The Millenarian Piety.* Myles, in "Dissent and the Frontier of Translation," discusses how Williams's poetry was shaped by his resistance to the *translatio studii et imperii* and the notion of England as a second Israel. The double connotation of *translation,* meaning "to move physically" and "to convert from one language to another," is at play in Williams's *A Key into the Language of America,* which for Myles critiques the foundations of imperial translation.

29. On the domestic English context for such critiques, see Hill, *World Turned Upside Down,* especially chapter 7.

30. Williams, *A Key into the Language of America,* 118; second quote from ibid., "To the Reader," n.p.; Perkins, *A Golden Chaine,* 1047.

31. On the theological debates dividing New England leaders, see Knight, *Orthodoxies in Massachusetts.* Knight considers Williams such a fringe figure that she does not factor him in her analysis, but Williams's notion of preparation situates him among the "internationalist" Puritans such as John Cotton, whose notions of church polity were grounded in a concern for global combat against the Antichrist. See also Delbanco, *Puritan Ordeal,* 49–52; and E. Morgan, *Visible Saints.*

32. Delbanco, *Puritan Ordeal,* explores in depth the centrality of the doctrine of preparation in Puritan theological debate. Williams's notion of preparation elaborated on his Cambridge brethren's insistence that God's love rather than man's self-discipline began the process of preparation. He broke preparation down into literal and theological (or roughly civic and religious) meanings of the term. Native mobility and basic forms of civility made them ripe both for conversion and for appreciating the distinction between God's world and man's. That distinction underwrote the separation of church and state; one had to be prepared both for civility and for salvation, but the two processes could inform each other under a rightly ordered government. American Indians were as such unlikely to become a "Nation"—that is, to confuse church and political order—once they began to hear the word of God.

33. Williams, *The bloudy tenet,* 25.

34. Bragdon, *Native People,* 40–41; see also Bragdon, *The Columbia Guide;* and Salwen, "Indians of Southern New England."

35. Bragdon, "'Emphattical Speech,'" 108. See also the account of Wampanoag "Indian taverns"—stick piles at path crossings—in Clifford, *Predicament of Culture,* 281.

36. Williams, *A Key into the Language of America,* 54. This reference to the Athenians, though possibly simply meant to refer to the passage in Acts, suggestively differentiates Williams's argument from the more common colonial allusion to Roman imperial governance. In the 1640s, as Nigel Smith and David Norbrook have emphasized, the Roman republic served as a historiographic prism for debates about English governance. Norbrook, *Writing the English Republic;* Smith, *Literature and Revolution in England.*

37. See, for example, D. Murray, *Indian Giving,* 98. Williams reports what is likely the original of this scene, and depicts himself using the same technology, in a letter to John Winthrop during the Pequot War (*Correspondence* 1:112–14). Similar uses of sticks had been recorded before; a peace envoy from Pequot to Massachusetts Bay in October 1634 "brought two bundles of sticks, whereby he signified how much beaver and otter skins he would give us" (Winthrop, *Journal,* 1:138–39).

38. Shagan, "The English Inquisition," 543. Shagan argues that because sovereignty has been for some time considered the "central issue of early modern political thought," there has resulted a "tendency to separate religious and constitutional issues" that keeps scholars from seeing the cluster of crucial issues between or beyond the categories of the theological and the legal-constitutional that faced the era's political theorists (542n4).

39. Felker has shown that Williams's views "derive at least as much from his attempt to apply the linguistic assumptions of the English common law to colonial situations" as they do from biblical typology. In *A Key into the Language of America,* Williams "extended and refined his legal

hermeneutics . . . which reveals his understanding of the crucial role of language in evaluating the accuracy of any ostensible relation to the truth" ("Roger Williams's Uses of Legal Discourse," 624–25). Williams would have received a legal argument and sanction for his theological claims about the ideal relationship between church and state from his mentor Edward Coke's approach to the question of the monarchy's relation to law. Indeed, in his embrace of radical typology, he may have been pursuing a logic of reading as much informed by Coke's controversial approach to law and the monarchy as a sweeping Separatist indulgence in exegesis. Williams's insistence on Native American sovereignty was both more radical than the Puritans imagined (though radical enough to get him deported) and a complex interweaving of legal and theological arguments. The association with Coke is also the unlikely, if historically provocative, narrative emphasis of Settle, *I, Roger Williams*.

40. Williams, *The hireling ministry*, 34. Loyalty oaths drew just as much fire: in 1665–66, the Providence Plantations General Assembly passed a bill allowing individuals, in declaring, to modify the oaths of engagement or allegiance required to obtain freeholder status because so many owners had dissented for reasons of conscience from taking the oath. See Bartlett, *Records*, 2:141–42. On oaths in New Haven, see Marcus, "'Due Execution of the Generall Rules of Righteousness.'"

41. Coke, "Of Oaths Before and Ecclesiastical Judge Ex Officio" and "No man shall be examined on secret opinions," in *Selected Writings and Speeches*, 432. This text resulted from a 1606 consultation in which Coke participated; it was published in volume 12 of his *Reports* in 1656. See also Shapiro, *Probability and Certainty in Seventeenth-Century England*, especially 186.

42. Dickson, *The Financial Revolution in England*, 350, 364.

43. Williams to John Winthrop, 20 August 1637, in Williams, *Correspondence*, 1:112.

44. Williams, *Correspondence*, 1:234, 1:79.

45. Ibid., 1:163.

46. Ibid., 1:126, 2:538.

47. Dexter emigrated with Williams in the wake of the controversy over Williams's subsequent publication, *The bloudy tenet*. Whether or not Williams had in mind the possibility of starting a press at Providence—aware that, as A. J. Liebling famously put it, the "freedom of the press belongs to whoever owns one"—is unknown. But Williams and Dexter would remain friends and political comrades in Rhode Island for forty years. Further evidence of Williams's attention to communications systems in the establishment of English civil society within Narragansett country, Dexter's presence offered Williams the experience and imagination of a veteran of the pamphlet wars and political wrangling of London in the early days of the Civil War. Dexter served as secretary, treasurer, and eventually president of Providence Plantations.

48. Wroth, "Variations in Five Copies of Roger Williams' *A Key into the Language of America*." Copies in other libraries show even more variants, and more combinations of them, than reported by Wroth. Information on Dexter comes from Swan, *Gregory Dexter;* and Bowen, *The Providence Oath*. Richard Oulton and Gregory Dexter were partners for some time; during their partnership they printed works by Williams's friends John Milton and Henry Vane. See also the discussion of the printing of *A Key into the Language of America* in Teunissen and Hinz, ed., *A Key into the Language of America*, 70–80.

49. Cotton, *The Doctrine of the Church*, title page.

50. Massachusetts Historical Society, *Letters and Papers of Roger Williams*. LaFantasie's introduction to the *Correspondence* contains an account of the informational networks, epistolary and otherwise, in which Williams himself participated.

51. D. Murray, *Indian Giving*, 96.

52. Canup quoted in ibid., 97.

53. Ibid., 79.

54. For an overview of seventeenth- and eighteenth-century colonial vocabularies in the context of debates about philology, race, and culture, see Laura J. Murray, "Vocabularies of Native

American Languages," especially 604–5; see also Schweitzer, *Work of Self-Representation*. On *A Key into the Language of America*'s similarities to Comenius's *Janua Linguarum* (1631), see Myles, "Dissent and the Frontier of Translation," 96.

55. John Considine, in "Narrative and Persuasion in Early Modern English Dictionaries and Phrasebooks," demonstrates that the use of dialogue in phrase books, particularly multilingual ones, had a wide precedent in Europe. See also Bart, *Antichi vocabolari plurilingui*. Considine doubts that such texts were useful for actual linguistic acquisition or translation. Instead, because their structures suggested the universality and translatability of language, they reinforced moral and religious lessons that would more likely have been the reading focus for an early modern user.

56. See Gutjahr, "The Letter(s) of the Law."

57. This is not to say that Williams and Dexter did not face practical limitations in their rendition of Narragansett; because of the notational scheme Williams chose, roman was no doubt the least visually confusing typeface. Yet the renditions of Narragansett terms in italics in the observational sections of Williams's text are reasonably clear, while in overall appearance, as in much seventeenth-century English printing, the book suffers from often confounding clunkiness.

58. Considine, "Narrative and Persuasion in Early Modern English Dictionaries and Phrasebooks," 196.

59. A. Wood, *Athenae Oxonienses;* Cooper, *Thesaurus linguae Romanae;* Cooper's work was reprinted throughout the sixteenth century.

60. Michel de Certeau has influentially insisted that during this time, in the wake of Calvinist thinking about language and divinity, "The dictionary becomes a theological instrument. Just as religious language is perverted by a usage which is 'discomfiting to get to know' and which refers to unfathomable intentions or 'heart,' now, situated on the very line that demarcated the rift of the universe, translation lets primitive reality pass into Western discourse. All that is needed is to have one language 'converted' into another" (Certeau, *The Writing of History,* 223). Yet as Edward Gray points out, there was considerable contest over this idea beyond the Catholic-Protestant conflict (Gray, *New World Babel*). What I argue here about Williams and the national dictionary furthermore suggests that the tie of language, nation, and eschatology is not instrumental in any straightforward way—or in merely the seventeenth-century meaning of "instrument" as Certeau too playfully uses it here.

61. Myles, "Dissent and the Frontier of Translation," 99.

62. Certeau, *Practice of Everyday Life,* 105.

63. Keith Stavely argues that Williams's reliance on the biblical figure of the enclosed garden—the church of the godly set apart within the wilderness of the world—underwrote a more material "anti-expansionist emphasis" in his politics that nonetheless never found full expression in his writings ("Roger Williams and the Enclosed Gardens of New England," 259–60).

64. Certeau, *Practice of Everyday Life,* 103.

65. See Simmons, *Cautantowwit's House.*

66. Not discussed explicitly in what follows, but crucial in the understanding of Narragansett history, is Turnbaugh, "Assessing the Significance of European Goods" and "Community, Commodities, and the Concept of Property." Quotations from Williams are frequent in the section of the Pequot Museum (discussed in chapter 4) that addresses how the objects in the exhibit of a contact-era Pequot village were reconstructed—that is, in what is functionally the sources section of the museum. Also quoted, although less frequently, are Giovanni da Verrazano, John Brereton, William Wood, Daniel Gookin, and Edward Winslow.

67. See R. Peters, *The Wampanoags of Mashpee.*

68. See, for example, Lindsay, "Tribe That Greeted Pilgrims"; and Axtell, *The European and the Indian,* 110–11. The literature on Native North American sovereignty claims is vast and contentious. It participates in global debates about indigenous rights. Studies that have informed the analysis here include Weaver, *Other Words;* Kroeber, ed., *Native American Persistence and Resurgence;*

Harris, *Making Native Space;* Krupat, *Red Matters;* and Clifford, "Identity in Mashpee," in *Predicament of Culture,* 277–346.

69. See also the work of Ives Goddard, Paul Robinson, Jack Campisi, Dean Snow, William Turnbaugh, and Patricia Rubertone.

70. Clifford, *Predicament of Culture,* 40.

71. Bragdon, *Native People of Southern New England,* xvii. Bragdon develops these arguments in other essays; see "Vernacular Literacy and Massachusett World View" and "Gender as a Social Category in Native Southern New England." Bragdon's unwillingness to pin down the constituencies of culture and identity and how they relate to change may well be a tactic that responds to, as it preempts, judicial demands for concrete definitions of these controversial concepts.

72. Rubertone, *Grave Undertakings,* 127. Rubertone offers a trenchant and thorough summary of the development of Williams's reputation as a forerunner of U.S. democracy through a series of historical and biographical accounts beginning in the early nineteenth century. Her analysis also emphasizes the ways in which Narragansett social protocols likely precluded Williams's seeing the complexity of the group's gender roles and religious practices. The tension between change and coherence exhibited in Rubertone also characterizes P. Robinson et al., "Preliminary Biocultural Interpretations." Williams's *An Affidavit* offers insight into divisive Narragansett politics in the late seventeenth century. Despite his negative estimation of several sachems of the time, Williams never relinquishes his insistence on Narragansett sovereignty in this document.

73. For a similar emphasis on the coherence of Narragansett culture in the history of philosophy, see S. Pratt, *Native Pragmatism.* On sovereignty and evidence, see, among others, Jaimes, "Federal Indian Identification Policy"; Weiner, "Diaspora, Materialism, Tradition"; and Sparke, "A Map That Roared."

74. *Cherokee Nation v. Georgia,* 30 U.S. 1 (1831), 17.

75. Thomas, "Cultural Change on the Southern New England Frontier," 138. Thomas's findings suggest considerable fissures even in the comparatively small societies of the Connecticut River valley. Politically and economically, unity was often difficult to find or produce. The evidence for trade goods and subsistence patterns in archaeological sites and court records and the history of military alliances in the region suggest that indigenous Connecticut River valley leaders disagreed over the question of how best to maintain control over their regional status.

76. Silverman, "Indians, Missionaries, and Religious Translation," 146, 174. Salisbury agrees with Silverman that rather than causing "a loss of Native cultural identity, Christianity—especially as practices beyond the purview of the missionaries—may actually have served to sustain and reinforce that identity for some Indians, and to have strengthened rather than weakened their resistance to cultural genocide." Such a declaration, for all its elegance, depends on an ambiguous definition of "culture" and as a result may dodge, rather than answer, the key question of the relationship between political and cultural sovereignty. The demographics of affiliative aesthetics often, at times constitutively, transgress those of political belonging (Salisbury, "'I Loved the Place of My Dwelling,'" 113). On the problematic term "conversion," see also Salisbury, "Embracing Ambiguity."

77. See Sekatau and Herndon, "Recovering Gendered Political Histories"; and Rubertone, *Grave Undertakings.* D. Murray, in *Indian Giving,* observes that *A Key into the Language of America*'s "word lists reflect . . . hard bargaining and mistrust rather than concord" (111).

78. See the range of approaches to indigenous self-determination among Womack, *Red on Red;* Alfred, *Peace, Power, Righteousness;* Warrior, *Tribal Secrets;* Mihesuah, *Indigenous American Women;* and Seed, *American Pentimento.* Michael Elliott and Annette Kolodny point out that the national legitimacy of the United States is threatened by Native American literature and history if they are taken to be "literature" and "history" by Western understandings of those categories. "The many versions of American prehistory are perhaps best understood not as faulty anthropology or inept archaeology," Kolodny writes, but instead "as narrative sites of an enduring conflict over claims to the same living space by radically different cultures." Elliott and Kolodny argue for

a strategic use of origin narratives, since, as Kolodny observes, "While narratives of prehistory have previously served the interests of Euro-American nation building, another version of those narratives may yet serve the interests of Native American tribal rebuilding" (Kolodny, "Fictions of American Prehistory," 716). Such an understanding, based on consensual self-definition within a tribal organization, imagines indigenous self-determination as embracing fluid cultures, not merely ones that look continuous from the perspective of outsiders (Elliott, "Coyote Comes to the *Norton*").

79. James Clifford, discussing Thomas Biolsi's argument that multiple definitions of sovereignty function simultaneously within and among tribes currently seeking recognition or land, describes the concept's use as having a "strategic complexity." See Biolsi, "Imagined Geographies"; and Clifford, "Varieties of Indigenous Experience," 217.

80. D. Murray, *Indian Giving*, 93.

81. Williams, *Complete Writings*, 4:103.

82. E. Morgan, *Roger Williams*, 142.

4. Multimedia Combat and the Pequot War

1. The Pequots controlled the area between the Mystic and the Connecticut rivers at the height of their influence in the seventeenth century. Today they exist in two tribes, the federally recognized Western or Mashantucket Pequots (near Ledyard), on whom this essay will focus, and the Eastern Pequot Indian Tribe (near North Stonington). The Mashantucket Pequots were granted recognition by federal legislation in 1983. The Eastern Pequots were granted preliminary recognition by the Bureau of Indian Affairs, but this was repealed in October 2005. At the time of this writing the tribe was seeking an appeal and a reversal of the decision.

2. Lepore, *The Name of War*, 67.

3. "Ultimately," Lepore writes, "all Indian explanations for or interpretations of the war were dismissed—'these Heathenish Stories are conconant to their Barbarous Crueltie, and ought to be valued accordingly'—because they compromised the justness of the colonists' own cause" (ibid., 119). My reading suggests that the English attempted to dismiss Native explanations and interpretations because they compromised the English ontology of communication itself by troubling the notion that truth could be discerned from falsehood.

4. Mihesuah and Wilson, introduction to *Indigenizing the Academy*, 4. This argument has also been made influentially by some postcolonial theorists. Indigenous or anticolonial narratives "often themselves bespeak an antihistorical consciousness," Dipesh Chakrabarty argues, in that they "entail subject positions and configurations of memory that challenge and undermine the subject that speaks in the name of history" ("Postcoloniality and the Artifice of History," 10–11). This is no less true of the form of Algonquian society, its notions of interdependence, and its communal systems for archiving knowledge than of the societies of which Chakrabarty writes. Such arguments call for a different way of thinking about history, one more conscious of the fact that academic history tends to declare certain kinds of evidence real and certain stories about progress or consciousness to be more valid than others. At the least, contradiction, circularity, and irresovability must take a new place in this history.

5. On the history of Native New England since the colonial era, see among many others Grumet, ed., *Northeastern Indian Lives*; Den Ouden, *Beyond Conquest*; Hauptman and Wherry, eds., *The Pequots in Southern New England*; Weinstein, ed., *Enduring Traditions*; and Peters, *The Wampanoags of Mashpee*.

6. See Allen, *Off the Reservation*; Cook-Lynn, *Why I Can't Read Wallace Stegner*; Weaver, *That the People Might Live*; and Womack, *Red on Red*.

7. My approach to museums in this chapter owes much to Wallach, *Exhibiting Contradiction*.

8. Smith, "The Terrible Nearness of Distant Places," 393, 388–89.

9. On artful Algonquian combat, see Chaplin, *Subject Matter*, 108. But for evidence that Native conflict did sanction indiscriminate killing in some cases, see Lee, "Peace Chiefs and Blood Revenge." Chaplin also argues in *Subject Matter* that the English came to think of Native bodies as artificial in the sense that they were technologically enhanced during upbringing; this perception would have been fueled by the experience of the Pequot War (244). Chaplin argues that the English "worried over a negative outcome in open competition; they preferred to be the gatherers of military intelligence, not the hapless objects of others' surveillance" (111). But from this she concludes that the colonies "took initial shape in a zone of military encounter, where Indians and English may have allowed their cultures selectively to bleed into each other so that they could get on with the task of shedding each other's blood" (115). Here I focus Chaplin's reading practice on a particular war to suggest a slightly more complex picture, in which the investments of the audiences and the publishers involved in the public parts of the war—in action and in published versions of it—were more various.

10. Slotkin, *Regeneration through Violence*, 77.

11. For a survey of the argument using political and military explanations for the war's cruelty, see Hirsch, "The Collision of Military Cultures in Seventeenth-Century New England"; and Karr, "'Why Should You Be So Furious?'" Karr argues that the Pequots were considered an "internal foe" by Puritans and could thus be attacked using those more extreme measures reserved for enemies with whom diplomatic relations were imagined to be unsustainable, a common practice of the time in European warfare.

12. Fromson, *Hitting the Jackpot*, 186.

13. Rath, *How Early America Sounded*, 170.

14. One of the signs at the entrance to the Pequot War exhibit declares, "There is no single cause, no simple answer" to why the Pequot War happened, encouraging visitors who read this sign to look for tensions rather than simple explanations. For an alternative filmic representation of the battle, see *Mystic Voices*, an Emmy award-winning documentary written and produced by Charles Clemmons and Guy Perrotta, funded by the International Documentary Association, which is not associated with any tribal organization. This film closely follows the interpretations of the war offered in the foundational work by Francis Jennings, *The Invasion of America*, and in the study by Alfred A. Cave, *The Pequot War*. "Massacre at Mystic," a segment of the History Channel's series *10 Days That Unexpectedly Changed America*, shows a full and explicit reversal of the moral terms in which the Pequot War was cast in early histories. If until the twentieth century the Puritans were characterized as the spiritually superior victors over savage, materialistic Pequots, here the episode's Web site reports that "the deeply spiritual Pequots survived through co-existence with their environment" while "the settlers sneaked into the Pequot fort at Mystic planning to kill the Indians in their beds and plunder their property." The online discussion boards, featuring viewer reactions to the segment, offer an excellent glimpse of the passion and the anxieties that the Pequot War and the question of Native identity provoke. See discussion boards for "Massacre at Mystic: May 26, 1637," at the History Channel's Web site, http://www.history.com.

15. Paul Chaat Smith, discussing his involvement with the Smithsonian's National Museum of the American Indian (NMAI), observes that he argued that such a focus should be the conscious strategy of the museum, such that visitors would "see that understanding the process of how the stories were gathered is crucial to understanding the stories themselves" ("The Terrible Nearness of Distant Places," 322). Smith laments that this approach was not fully deployed in the NMAI; as I argue below, it seems only partially evident in the Mashantucket Pequot Museum. Randolph Starn, summarizing recent evolutions of museology, observes that such perspectival strategies "jostle unevenly with liberal and professional ideals of 'balance' enjoining both respect for cultural differences and consensual standards" ("A Historian's Brief Guide to New Museum Studies," paragraph 36).

16. Robert Gross pointed out to me that the question might be taken as an irreverent remark reflecting the visitors' shrewd awareness of the postmodern mixing of media. Certainly such

inclusions align the Pequot Museum with what has been termed the Disneyfication of the museum or what Timothy W. Luke terms the promotion of "entertainmentalities"—though as others point out, the deliberate evocation of wonder and absorption in museums has a long tradition, going back at least to the early modern era's *wunderkammers* or cabinets of curiosity. See R. Starn, "A Historian's Brief Guide to New Museum Studies," paragraphs 41–42; Luke, *Museum Politics,* 15. The contest over museum design has class overtones, as the theme park, associated by some observers with low culture, contends with the disciplinary model of the museum as rationalizer of the masses. New museum designs blur the boundaries of education and entertainment and raise tensions among the different parties who stand to gain or lose authority from exhibitions.

17. Mary Lawlor writes that "the mannequin faces . . . invest the museum with a certain playfulness" ("Identity in Mashantucket," 168). Other reviewers, like Jill Knight Weinberger and Mike Allen, are stunned by the effort and expense that went into the exhibit; for them its uncanniness emerges from the oddity of such excess in a Native American museum—a class of institution usually underfunded and more likely to be dominated by artifactual material than reconstructions. See Weinberger, "The Mashantucket Pequot Museum and Research Center"; and Allen, "Casino Riches." By my unscientific count, the Pequot village reconstruction was more likely to hold the attention of audiences for long periods of time, while what might be considered the most confrontational exhibit, a theater running a documentary of the tribe's pursuit and winning of federal recognition, was empty each time I visited it, on two separate occasions (November 2005 and April 2006). The mannequins are an unusual tactic; the NMAI and Plimoth Plantation, the two museums most locally and directly competing with the Mashantucket Pequot Museum, do not use such figures. At the least, for museumgoers who know the history of "live Indian" exhibits in, for example, Alfred Kroeber's museum of anthropology in San Francisco or the American Museum of Natural History, the first impression is of a confrontationally ironic twist on the tendency of museums to present Native people as objects, frozen in the past, equivalent to dinosaurs or other extinct natural entities. See O. Starn, *Ishi's Brain,* especially 181–83.

18. The literature on the Pequot War is vast. John W. De Forest was the first to attempt a comprehensive history, in *History of the Indians of Connecticut.* See the critique of De Forest in Paul Pasquaretta, *Gambling and Survival in Native North America,* 86–88. Influential treatments of the war include Cave, *The Pequot War;* Jennings, *The Invasion of America;* Slotkin, *Regeneration through Violence;* Pearce, *Savagism and Civilization;* Vaughan, *New England Frontier;* and Salisbury, *Manitou and Providence,* especially 203–24.

19. Bradford, *Of Plymouth Plantation,* 73, hereafter cited in the text. On the circulation of Bradford's manuscript among colonial readers before its first complete print publication in the nineteenth century, see D. Anderson, *William Bradford's Books.* Anderson justifiably insists on the spelling *Of Plimmoth Plantation,* from Bradford's manuscript; I have chosen to use Morison's edition since it is common and I devote less attention to Bradford's manuscript's physical properties than to those of other texts under analysis here.

20. The analysis of violent interactions is only one part of a broader interest in communications systems in Bradford's narrative. As recent scholarship suggests, Bradford studied both the economic systems to which Plymouth was subject and the nature of the communications between God and man. Morison's edition, Douglas Anderson points out, hides the communications history of Plymouth; in Bradford's design this was in fact highlighted, one of the central dramas of the text, as letters map out the movement of communication and trust across the Atlantic and around American space. Bradford also wrote dialogues, directed at younger and second-generation colonists, to model proper communications with their elders, and late in life he took up the study of Hebrew in order to read biblical texts in, as he understood it, as close to the "language of God" as possible. See D. Anderson, *William Bradford's Books,* 197; Read, "Silent Partners"; and Burnham, *Folded Selves,* 46–67.

21. Simmons, "The Mystic Voice," 154.

22. On trapping and war, see Malone, *The Skulking Way of War,* 21. Malone here also describes a common Algonquian use of a landscape bordered on one side by a natural barrier to guide opponents into a position more advantageous for attack, not unlike the situation the Pilgrims faced on the shoreline of Cape Cod.

23. "Noyses" (of nonhuman animal or instrumental origin) and "Voyces" (of human origin) were distinguished from each other in Renaissance English thought. Bradford switches from using the term "noise in Newfoundland" to describe the sound to saying it was made by "the same voices" the party had heard before. See Rath, *How Early America Sounded,* 3–6; and on wolf and dog sounds in particular, Coleman, *Vicious.*

24. See also Winslow's account of this incident, quoted in Bangs, *Pilgrim Edward Winslow,* 21.

25. Tooker, ed., *Native North American Spirituality of the Eastern Woodlands,* 53–54; this narrative was originally recorded by John Arthur Gibson in 1900 and published in a different version in Hewitt, *Iroquoian Cosmology,* 479–87.

26. Hoffer compares English and Algonquian ways of seeing, hearing, and smelling woodlands in *Sensory Worlds in Early America,* 63.

27. Malone, *The Skulking Way of War,* 21, 70. For a revision of Malone's account, see Lee, "Peace Chiefs ad Blood Revenge." Local Algonquians, Winslow reported, also liked to fight in bad weather—no doubt particularly when they were out to kill and kidnap rather than to impress. Rain and thunder took fire (and for a time firearms) out of play, masked scents and sounds, and even made texture problematic by rendering the ground and weapons slippery. It enhanced the advantages of surprise; knowing one was going to fight in the rain gave one time to grease bow strings, wrap grips, and approach the enemy from the driest ground.

28. Such a distinction, in fact, might be argued to be untenable if we are to take east coast Algonquian spirituality seriously; that is, the attackers might have considered themselves to *be* wolves. Tooker observes that, for seventeenth-century American Indians of the east coast and for some of their descendants, animals could transform into each other, while "humans, both living and dead, may take on the form of animals while their vital part remains unchanged. Such instances of metamorphosis are reported to have taken place in contemporary times as well as in myths" (*Native North American Spirituality of the Eastern Woodlands,* 27). Daniel Richter, in *Facing East from Indian Country,* has discussed the difficulties of writing history that takes such transformations into account, difficulties similar to ones faced in the reconstruction of Puritan notions of witchcraft and possession by the devil. As A. Irving Hallowell advises, we can at least use the absence of animal-human-spirit boundaries to rethink the parameters of Native expectations about appearances and truths: what appear to be people "may be friendly and help me when I need them," he writes from a speculative first-person Anishinaabe perspective, "but, at the same time, I have to be prepared for hostile acts, too. I must be cautious in my relations with other 'persons' because appearances may be deceptive" ("Ojibwa Ontology," 43).

29. In an analysis of what he terms colonial acoustemology, Bruce R. Smith writes that for early modern English people, the "*sounds* of another culture . . . penetrate 'in here' and threaten to overwhelm the listener's sense of well-being. Cries of war and wails of mourning seem to have been two signal occasions when English speakers felt their hold on language to be slipping." Smith compares the English reactions to Irish, Algonquian, and African sounds to conclude that scholars must use an ecological framework when approaching representations of cultures in contact (*The Acoustic World,* 287–341, quoted 328).

30. The March 22, 1622, attack on English settlements in Virginia, which exposed the weaknesses of English understandings both of Native communications systems and of their protocols for violence, was a key event for New England settlers. Early on they tried to learn from the negative example of the Virginia settlers, but in ways that sometimes conflicted. For Myles Standish and other military men, the conclusion was that Indians were not to be trusted and that preemptive violence, or at least constant preparation for it, were to be the norm. For Thomas Morton, Edward

Winslow, and other settlers, the lesson was that English traditions of grappling over the control of communications flows would need to be extended to include Native polities and their semiotic systems.

31. Gardener, "Leift Lion Gardener," 129.

32. Pasquaretta, *Gambling and Survival in Native North America*, 19; on Underhill see Shelley, *John Underhill;* and Cave, *The Pequot War*, 140–67. On the broader context of tensions between military men and the religious authorities in New England, see Breen, *Transgressing the Bounds.*

33. Plymouth resisted Massachusetts Bay's insistence that it participate in the war, believing that the Bay was misrepresenting the case against the Pequots and overextending its authority. The establishment of Fort Saybrook happened under the auspices of the controversial Warwick Patent, by which a group of patentees laid claim to large stretches of the southern New England coast. John Winthrop Jr. was named "governor" of the Connecticut River claim, which was quickly co-opted by Connecticut and Massachusetts Bay. The information in my account of Underhill's role in the war comes from Underhill, *Newes from America;* Cave, *The Pequot War;* Hauptman and Wherry, ed., *The Pequots in Southern New England;* and Jennings, *The Invasion of America.*

34. Higginson, quoted in Cave, *The Pequot War,* 169.

35. Underhill, though commissioned by the Warwick patentees, retained his Massachusetts Bay title ("muster master," one he considered insulting) during the 1637 campaign—further indication of the complex set of affiliations military men could generate. Though lacking much battle experience, Underhill had at least learned some formal military tactics (his father had fought in the Dutch wars) and gained some experience fighting American Indians. See Cave, *The Pequot War,* 141.

36. Scholars disagree about whether Underhill's narrative was designed to restore him to good standing in Massachusetts or whether it insinuates an Antinomian position, arguing that the godly of any stripe who come to plant in America will be able to find a suitable community. Slotkin, *Regeneration through Violence,* 70; Pasquaretta, *Gambling and Survival in Native North America,* 20–22. While Underhill was denied the land he expected to receive in reward from Massachusetts Bay, the publication event of the Pequot War was certainly a lucrative one for Underhill in his career as an Indian fighter.

37. See U.S. Department of Defense, *Information Operations Roadmap,* especially appendices B and C, 70–71. The report also recommends that the U.S. military generate the capability to "provide maximum control of the entire electromagnetic spectrum"—which would include the control of all light and heat, for example, in anything considered a battle space. At http://www.gwu .edu/~nsarchiv/NSAEBB/NSAEBB177/info_ops_roadmap.pdf, 61 (accessed 30 October 2003).

38. See Deleuze and Guattari, *A Thousand Plateaus.*

39. Both of the other first-person accounts of the Pequot War use such an assertion to distinguish the professional domain of the military leader. John Mason declares that "the more an Enterprize is dissembled and kept secret, the more facile to put in Execution" (Mason, *A Brief History,* 3). Gardener's narrative ends with the advice to young soldiers that "policy is needful in wars as well as strength" (Gardener, "Leift Lion Gardener his relation of the Pequot Warres," 149). Details in these accounts suggest that the Pequots and the English were less ciphers to each other than they have been depicted by historians. Gardener includes comments that demonstrate the interpenetration of English and Pequot society in the years leading up to the conflict, including Pequots who recognize him by his voice and "an Indian from Pequit, whose name was Cocommithus, who had lived at Plimoth, and could speak good English" (Gardener, "Leift Lion Gardener," 124).

40. Formally, Underhill's narrative begins as a war narrative, then becomes a captivity narrative as he recounts the imprisonment of two female Connecticut settlers by the Pequots. In the midst of the captivity narrative is nested a prospectus of settlement areas for English colonists, after which follows a lengthy sermon giving way to the conclusion of the war narrative. Richard Slotkin's analysis of the formal qualities of the narrative has been influential; in this reading

Underhill both others the Native as savage and implies that the virgin land of America is held captive by uncivilized Indians, inviting participation by his English readers in the larger project of which the war was a part. See Slotkin, *Regeneration through Violence.*

41. Salwen, "Indians of Southern New England and Long Island"; and Cave, *The Pequot War,* 64.

42. Underhill, *Newes from America,* 4, hereafter cited in the text.

43. See Pasquaretta, *Gambling and Survival,* 24–25.

44. For a comparable scene in the colonial south, see Lee Miller's interpretation of Ralph Lane's 1586 trip on the Roanoke River in *Roanoke,* especially 117. For a fuller discussion of the social history of the senses in this period, see Hoffer, *Sensory Worlds in Early America;* and Rath, *How Early America Sounded.*

45. Gardener claims it was nine hours before the English moved. Later, Gardener would respond to a Pequot request for negotiation by playing on the Pequot ambassador's claim, telling a different Pequot spokesperson that "we knew not the Indians one from another" ("Leift Lion Gardener," 132). Gardener's account does not make clear that this is an ironic rhetorical reversal, but in general, Gardener appears to have been much more savvy about local tactics in warfare and Native negotiating protocols than were the other captains. On Williams's request for distinguishing marks for Native allies, see Chaplin, *Subject Matter,* 269.

46. See an analysis of this scene in the context of gender and colonial military cultures in Chaplin, *Subject Matter,* 254; and a discussion of the history of wartime sartorial theft in Hoffer, *Sensory Worlds in Early America,* 85. Similar jibes and the use of dead Englishmen's clothes are reported by Gardener ("Leift Lion Gardener"). Roger Williams reports the theft of clothes from living captives—even undergarments unlikely to make an intimidating visual impression—as a common practice during the war; at one point it was reported that "at Monahiganick there are neere 300, who have bound and robd our men (even of the very covering of their Secret parts) as they have past from Qunnticut hether" (*Correspondence,* 1:146). See also Axtell, *The European and the Indian,* 297–311.

47. Kibbey, *The Interpretation of Material Shapes in Puritanism,* especially 44–64. Laurie Shannon identifies a "Protestant semiology of dress" in John Foxe's *Book of Martyrs* that similarly focuses on the "danger of being falsely covered" as a key component of Protestant understandings of how persons relate to clothes (Shannon, "'His Apparel Was Done upon Him,'" 193–94). On the connection between human figures and violence in Protestant thought, see Mueller, "Pain, Persecution, and the Construction of Selfhood in Foxe's *Acts and Movements.*"

48. Gordon Sayre has shown that clothes were also crucial parts of the colonial economy. Mary Rowlandson's narrative of her captivity during King Philip's War—in which she is made to manufacture English-style clothes for her captors—shows the persistence of this tactic among the region's warriors. See Sayre, *Les sauvages américains,* chapter 4, "Clothing, Money, and Writing"; and Rowlandson, *The Soveraignty & Goodness of God.* The defeat at Mystic, though sometimes depicted as having broken the spirit of the Pequots, did not put an end to tactics based on mockery. Even in a late engagement at Pawcatuck after the Pequots had been considerably dispersed and diminished in population, Mason reports that "we could see the Indians running up and down Jeering of us" along the east shore of a river (*A Brief History of the Pequot War,* 18).

49. Hoffer, *Sensory Worlds in Early America,* 70.

50. A marginal note on page 37 of Underhill's text indicates that the map comes "before the booke," though copies in current collections are not always configured this way. At this time the engraving and printing of such figures was still an expensive and comparatively uncommon undertaking in London. Because books were at times sold in sheets, rather than bound, and the figure was likely printed at a separate time, the marginal note may indicate a suggestion for binding rather than evidence of a normal state of *Newes from America.*

51. In his journal, Winthrop noted suspicions about Underhill's spiritual state, including the wry observation that the muster master reported receiving inspiration from God under the influence

of "the creature called tobacco." Underhill was also accused of dallying with the wife of a neighbor in Massachusetts. See Winthrop, *Journal*, 1:275–76.

52. Underhill's figure, I am arguing, was taking control of the temporal sequence to make a claim for his heroism and for his authoritative knowledge of the battle's events. But the image's correspondence to what actually happened in the battle is unclear, from a historian's perspective. The figure does not simply reveal history but shows instead how Underhill has co-opted the battle's temporal sequence to construct a certain kind of story using both text and image.

53. Underhill's figure does not conform to any of the written descriptions of the entry to the fort when oriented with the top to the north or to the west, as were most common in colonial maps. Mason claims that he led his troops up to an entrance "on the North East Side" (*A Brief History of the Pequot War*, 7, 9); Underhill says that his own approach was from the south (*Newes from America*, 37).

54. The circular shape of the palisade recalls two other important early modern figures for English readers: the "wooden O" of the Globe Theatre and the circular city that was used to emblematize the senses. Images of that city, of course, contain not two but five entrances. The narrative I have been describing may also draw on the notion of the theater of memory. See F. Yates, *The Art of Memory;* Hoffer, *Sensory Worlds in Early America;* and B. Smith, *The Acoustic World of Early Modern England*, especially 206–45.

55. The museum was designed by New York's Polshek and Partners, headed by James Polshek (previously head of the school of architecture at Columbia). According to Brett Fromson, the design was created in consultation with and given final approval by the tribe. Historian Jack Campisi and archaeologist Kevin McBride (currently the museum's director of research) were involved from an early stage. Little notice has been paid to the connection between Underhill's figure and the museum's design; it emphasizes both the key Algonquian spiritual and historical theme of emergence (much of the museum is underground; visitors descend into and then out of it) and a more technological notion of defensive military design. See Fromson, *Hitting the Jackpot*, 178–82.

56. Vizenor's scholarship represents a sustained and nuanced engagement with the question of the relationship between a poststructuralist critical mode and Native American studies; see also Krupat, "Post-Structuralism and Oral Literature." For readings of the museum through the lens of postmodernism, see Uriarte, "Imagining the Nation with House Odds"; Lawlor, "Identity in Mashantucket"; and Harkin, "Staged Encounters." Harkin suggests that a postmodern tourist sensibility, one interested in play and the problems, rather than the comforts, of authenticity is a target for the generation of images of Pequotness at Mashantucket. The postmodern sensibility, then, is an audience relation; rather than being an overdetermining consciousness, it is more like a generic expectation. This helps distinguish between the representations of Indianness at the museum and those at the casino, which are more generic and are dominated, as in most casinos, more by images of local landscape, flora, and fauna than by particular references to tribal history.

57. James Clifford suggests that in Native American museum spaces today messages are "delivered, performed, within an ongoing contact history" (*Routes*, 193). The Pequot Museum is a national museum, and it decenters the national context of mainstream U.S. collections by suggesting that all such collections deploy an idea of the universal in the interests of the national. The museum promotes a negotiation over definitions of relationship. But Clifford nonetheless refers to such a dynamic as "a postmodern marketing of heritage" (218). Not all performances, however, are postmodern. I suggest that such a pedagogical or contact dynamic of objects, relationships, and images can emerge out of a tribal past as much as being an adaptation to a late capitalist Western present.

58. See Eisler, *Revenge of the Pequots;* Fromson, *Hitting the Jackpot;* Benedict, *Without Reservation.* The investigative television program *60 Minutes* also produced a segment, featuring Benedict, on Pequot gaming industries. See "Wampum Wonderland," narrated by Steve Kroft, *60 Minutes*, CBS, 18 September 1994.

59. Eisler, *Revenge of the Pequots*, 242. For a succinct example of a somewhat extreme negative reaction to the Pequots from within the Native American community, see Delphine Red Shirt, "These Are Not Indians." Similar issues face the Lumbee tribe and others. See Blu, *The Lumbee Problem*; and Rountree, *Pocahontas's People*. Abramoff's firm was employed by many tribes, including the Pequots and the Mashpees, to lobby for reservation gaming interests.

60. Clifford, "Identity in Mashpee," in Clifford, *Predicament of Culture*, 277–346; Starn, *Ishi's Brain*, 203. Gerald Vizenor has described the desire for "pure blooded" tribal foundations as "sentimental monogenism" (*Crossbloods*, vii). Elsewhere, Vizenor has similarly emphasized the performative elements of Indianness, the way Native representations disrupt U.S. mythologies, in terms that draw on the notion of simulation as something not completely controlled by the simulator: "We are postindian storiers at the curtains of that stubborn simulation of the *indian* as savage, and the *indian* as a pure and curative tradition. The *indian* is a simulation, an invention, and the name could be the last grand prize at a casino" (Vizenor and Lee, *Postindian Conversations*, 21).

61. See Tench and Kranish, "Mashpees Near Federal Recognition"; and Adams, "Mohegan Books Show $3 Billion Impact from Reversed Recognitions." Even domestic investment by Native groups can pit a company or individual against a state or locality, as in the case of Fess Parker's offer to develop private land in conjunction with the Santa Ynez Chumash tribe. See Bunting, "Plan's Death Doesn't Kill Land Debate." Benedict, whose account is flawed by myopia about Native history and a lack of engagement with the complexity of tribal definitions, nonetheless offers a succinct account of the international funding of Pequot development (*Without Reservation*, 182, 213). See also Fromson, *Hitting the Jackpot*, 125.

62. See Adams, "Foxwoods Works to Keep Up." At the time of this writing, the Mashantucket Pequots had just beaten out Donald Trump for a slot-machine casino license in Philadelphia. On aboriginal property rights and the problem of investment in land held in U.S. trust, see Seed, *American Pentimento*, 185. On the way casino conflicts are heralded in reservation political battles over environmental issues from mining to the disposal of hazardous waste—a debate also involving foreign investments and questions about tribal definition—see Krech, *The Ecological Indian*, 211–29.

63. See also McMullen, "Canny about Conflict."

64. Eisler, *Revenge of the Pequots*, 185. On the Pequot emphasis on households over other affiliative concepts, see Starna, "The Pequots in the Early Seventeenth Century." On the Mohegans and the Pequots, see Oberg, *Uncas*; Den Ouden, *Beyond Conquest*; and E. Johnson, "Uncas and the Politics of Contact."

65. Neal Salisbury calls this the "wampum revolution" (*Manitou and Providence*, 147–48). See also P. Robinson, "Lost Opportunities."

66. Ceci, "Native Wampum as a Peripheral Resource in the Seventeenth-Century World System," 60–61. See also McBride, "The Source and Mother of the Fur Trade."

67. *Cherokee Nation v. Georgia*, 30 U.S. 1 (1831).

68. For discussions of the concept of sovereignty in Native American scholarship and politics, see among others Mohawk, ed., *Exiled in the Land of the Free*; Alfred, *Peace, Power, Righteousness*; and, in a broad context of indigenous studies, Barker, ed., *Sovereignty Matters*.

69. Clifford, *Predicament of Culture*, 343. McMullen calls "coversion" the process by which, "trying to manage information about themselves, New England's native people restricted use of identifying symbols to avoid recognition and appear, superficially, to be like non-natives" ("What's Wrong with This Picture?" 135). In the case of the Pequots, I am suggesting the possibility that this strategy may not be limited to colonial or postcolonial relations. For the broader context of sociological and anthropological debate on this question, see Goffman, *The Presentation of Self in Everyday Life*; and Harrison, "Identity as a Scarce Resource."

70. West quoted in M. Allen, "Casino Riches Build an Indian Museum with 'Everything.'"

71. See Mignolo, *Darker Side of the Renaissance*; Brotherston, *Book of the Fourth World*, 47; Tooker, *Native North American Spirituality of the Eastern Woodlands*; Tinker, *Missionary Conquest*;

Simmons, *Spirit of the New England Tribes*. McMullen suggests that we look at cyclical resurgence as enabled by the temporary lodging of tribe-specific ways or values in Pan-Indian or regional groups that formed in the wake of dispossession ("What's Wrong with This Picture?" 134).

72. In the legal community the concept of property is now commonly taught in terms of a bundle of rights that can be undone and rearranged depending on the needs of a variety of potential owners or interests in a single thing taken to be property. See Waldron, *Right to Private Property*.

73. See *Kelo v. City of New London*, 545 U.S. 469 (2005).

74. Hauptman goes so far as to call the tribe's activities "state-building in the grandest sense" ("The Pequots in Southern New England, 78). For discussions of reciprocity and gifting in Algonquian cultures, see Murray, *Indian Giving*.

75. Apess, *On Our Own Ground*, 157. See among other excellent analyses of Apess's strategies, Pasquaretta, *Gambling and Survival in Native North America*, 85; Brooks, *The Common Pot*, 163–218; Dannenberg, "'Where, then, shall we place the hero of the wilderness?'" 80; and Warrior, *People and the Word*, 1–47.

76. Eisler, *Revenge of the Pequots*.

Coda

1. See Berman, *All That Is Solid Melts into Air*; Huyssen, *After the Great Divide*; and Harvey, *Condition of Postmodernity*.

2. See, among others, Bauer, *Cultural Geography of Colonial American Literatures*; Egan, *Authorizing Experience*; Shapin and Schaffer, *Leviathan and the Air-Pump*; and M. Pratt, *Imperial Eyes*. My account of technology as a social relation that complicates the usual idea of modernity is inspired by Latour, *We Have Never Been Modern*.

3. Babylon and HumanID were listed on the DARPA Web site under the now subdivided Information Awareness Office. For reasons that are perhaps obvious, DARPA does not maintain a complete public archive; some past versions of the site are available at the Internet Archive. These projects are generally known as Rapid Multilingual Support (RMS) programs. U.S. DARPA Babylon project description referenced from http://www.darpa.mil/iao/Babylon.htm (accessed 20 November 2002). U.S. DARPA Human ID at a Distance project from http://www.darpa.mil/iao/HID.htm (accessed 20 November 2002).

4. GALE (Global Autonomous Language Exploitation) project, at http://www.darpa.mil/ipto/solicitations/closed/05–28_PIP.htm (accessed 23 April 2006).

5. Harvey, *Justice, Nature, and the Geography of Difference*, 7–8.

6. Williams, "Christians make not Christians," title page.

7. That this context is important to Tremblay's work is suggested by the titles of similar works, such as her basket *Waiting for New Red Visions among All the Images of Black and White on the Silver Screen* (2004), exhibited at the Froelick Gallery, Portland, Oregon, April 2006.

Bibliography

Abrahams, Roger D. "Antick Dispositions and the Perilous Politics of Culture: Costume and Culture in Jacobean England and America." *Journal of American Folklore* 111 (1998): 115–32.

Adams, Jim. "Foxwoods Works to Keep Up." *Indian Country Today,* 29 November 2005. http://www.indiancountrytoday.com/content.cfm?id=1096411983.

———. "Mohegan Books Show $3 Billion Impact from Reversed Recognitions." *Indian Country Today,* 29 November 2005. http://www.indiancountrytoday.com/content.cfm?id=1096411984.

Agnew, Jean-Christophe. *Worlds Apart: The Market and the Theatre in Anglo-American Thought, 1550–1750.* New York: Cambridge University Press, 1986.

Alfred, Taiaiake. *Peace, Power, Righteousness: An Indigenous Manifesto.* New York: Oxford University Press, 1999.

Allen, Mike. "Casino Riches Build an Indian Museum with 'Everything.'" *New York Times,* Late East Coast ed., 10 August 1998, A1.

Allen, Paula Gunn. *Off the Reservation: Reflections on Boundary-Busting, Border-Crossing Loose Canons.* Boston: Beacon, 1998.

Allison, Antony Francis, and D. M. Rogers. *The Contemporary Printed Literature of the English Counter-Reformation between 1558 and 1640: An Annotated Catalogue.* 2 vols. Brookfield, Vt.: Gower, 1989–94.

Amory, Hugh. *Bibliography and the Book Trades: Studies in the Print Culture of Early New England.* Edited by David D. Hall. Philadelphia: University of Pennsylvania Press, 2005.

Amory, Hugh, and David D. Hall. *A History of the Book in America.* Vol. 1, *The Colonial Book in the Atlantic World.* New York: Cambridge University Press, 2000.

Anderson, Douglas. *William Bradford's Books: Of Plimmoth Plantation and the Printed Word.* Baltimore, Md.: Johns Hopkins University Press, 2003.

Anderson, Virginia DeJohn. *Creatures of Empire: How Domestic Animals Transformed Early America.* Oxford: Oxford University Press, 2004.

Andrews, Christopher, and A. M. Bharucha. "Review: Good Evidence Supports Polyethelene Glycol and Tegaserod for Constipation." *ACP Journal Club* 143, no. 2 (September–October 2005): 47.

Apess, William. *On Our Own Ground: The Complete Writings of William Apess, A Pequot.* Edited by Barry O'Connell. Amherst: University of Massachusetts Press, 1992.

Axtell, James. "Babel of Tongues: Communicating with the Indians in Eastern North America." In *The Language Encounter in the Americas, 1492–1800,* edited by Edward G. Gray and Norman Fiering, 15–60. New York: Berghan, 2000.

———. *The European and the Indian: Essays in the Ethnohistory of Colonial North America.* New York: Oxford University Press, 1981.

———. "The White Indians of Colonial America." *William and Mary Quarterly* 32, no. 1 (January 1975): 55–88.

Baker, Nicholson. *Double Fold: The Assault on Libraries and Paper.* New York: Random House, 2001.

Bangs, Jeremy Dupertuis. *Pilgrim Edward Winslow: New England's First International Diplomat.* Boston: New England Historic Genealogical Society, 2004.

Barker, Joanne, ed. *Sovereignty Matters: Locations of Contestation and Possibility in Indigenous Struggles for Self-determination.* Lincoln: University of Nebraska Press, 2005.

Bart, Alda Rossebastiano. *Antichi vocabolari plurilingui d'uso popolare: La tradizione del 'solentissimo vochabuolista.'* Alexandria: Edizioni dell'Orso, 1984.

Bartlett, John Russell. *Records of the Colony of Rhode Island and Providence Plantations.* 7 vols. Providence, R.I.: Alfred Anthony, 1856–1862.

Baudrillard, Jean. *Simulacra and Simulation.* Translated by Sheila Faria Glaser. Ann Arbor: University of Michigan Press, 1994.

Bauer, Ralph. *The Cultural Geography of Colonial American Literatures: Empire, Travel, Modernity.* New York: Cambridge University Press, 2003.

Beinfield, Malcolm S. "The Early New England Doctor: An Adaptation to a Provincial Environment." *Yale Journal of Biology and Medicine* 15 (1942–3): 271–88.

Benedict, Jeff. *Without Reservation: How a Controversial Indian Tribe Rose to Power and Built the World's Largest Casino.* New York: Harper Perennial, 2001.

Besnier, Nico. "Literacy and the Notion of Person on Nukulaelae Atoll." *American Anthropologist,* n.s., 93, no. 3 (September 1991): 570–87.

The Bible, that is, The holy Scriptures conteined in the Olde and Newe Testament. . . . London: Christopher Barker, 1599 [actually Amsterdam: Stam, 1630s–40s].

Biolsi, Thomas. "Imagined Geographies: Sovereignty, Indigenous Space, and American Indian Struggles." *American Ethnologist* 32, no. 2 (2005): 239–59.

Blu, Karen I. *The Lumbee Problem: The Making of an American Indian People.* Cambridge: Cambridge University Press, 1980.

Boon, James A. *Other Tribes, Other Scribes: Symbolic Anthropology in the Comparative Study of Cultures, Histories, Religions, and Texts.* New York: Cambridge University Press, 1983.

Bowen, Richard Le Baron. *The Providence Oath of Allegiance and Its Signers, 1651–2.* Concord, N.H.: Rumford, 1943.

Bradford, William. *Of Plymouth Plantation, 1620–1647.* Edited by Samuel Eliot Morison. New York: Modern Library, 1967.

Bradley, W. T. "Medical Practices of the New England Aborigines." *Journal of the American Pharmaceutical Association* 25, no. 2 (1936): 138–47.

Bragdon, Kathleen J. *The Columbia Guide to the American Indians of the Northeast.* New York: Columbia University Press, 2001.

———. "'Emphattical Speech and Great Action': An Analysis of Seventeenth-Century Native Speech Events Described in Early Sources." *Man in the Northeast,* no. 33 (1987): 101–11.

———. "Gender as a Social Category in Native Southern New England." *Ethnohistory* 43, no. 4 (1996): 573–92.

———. *Native People of Southern New England, 1500–1650.* Norman: University of Oklahoma Press, 1996.

———. "Vernacular Literacy and Massachusett World View, 1650–1750." In *Algonkians of New England: Past and Present*, 26–34. Dublin Seminar for New England Folklife, no. 16. Boston: Boston University, 1991.

Breen, Louise A. *Transgressing the Bounds: Subversive Enterprises among the Puritan Elite in Massachusetts, 1630–1692*. New York: Oxford University Press, 2001.

Bremer, Francis. "Increase Mather's Friends: The Trans-Atlantic Congregational Network of the Seventeenth Century." *Proceedings of the American Antiquarian Society* 94, pt. 1 (1984): 59–96.

Bright, Timothie. *A treatise, wherein is declared the sufficiencie of English medicines, for cure of all diseases, cured with medicines*. London, 1615.

Brooks, Lisa. *The Common Pot: The Recovery of Native Space in the Northeast*. Minneapolis: University of Minnesota Press, 2008.

Brotherston, Gordon. *The Book of the Fourth World: Reading the Native Americas through Their Literature*. New York: Cambridge University Press, 1992.

Brown, Matthew P. "'BOSTON SOB/NOT': Elegiac Performance in Early New England and Materialist Studies of the Book." *American Quarterly* 50, no. 2 (1998): 306–39.

———. *The Pilgrim and the Bee: Reading Rituals and Book Culture in Early New England*. Philadelphia: University of Pennsylvania Press, 2007.

Brown, Michael F. "Sovereignty's Betrayals." *Indigenous Experience Today*. Edited by Marisol de la Cadena and Orin Starn. New York: Berg, 2007.

Brown, Richard. *Knowledge Is Power: The Diffusion of Information in Early America, 1700–1865*. New York: Oxford University Press, 1991.

Bunting, Glenn F. "Plan's Death Doesn't Kill Land Debate." *Los Angeles Times*, 2 October 2005, B1.

Burnham, Michelle. *Folded Selves: Colonial New England Writing in the World System*. Lebanon, N.H.: University Press of New England, 2007.

Burton, Henry. *A divine tragedie lately acted, or A collection of sundry memorable examples of Gods judgements upon Sabbath-breakers, and other like libertines, in their unlawfull sports, happening within the realme of England, in the compass only of two yeares last past*. Amsterdam: J. F. Stam, 1636.

Bushnell, David. "The Treatment of the Indians in Plymouth Colony." In *New England Encounters: Indians and Euroamericans, ca. 1600–1850*, edited by Alden T. Vaughan, 59–83. Boston: Northeastern University Press, 1999.

Bushnell, Rebecca. *Green Desire: Imagining Early Modern English Gardens*. Ithaca, N.Y.: Cornell University Press, 2003.

Butler, Judith. *Bodies That Matter: On the Discursive Limits of "Sex."* New York: Routledge, 1993.

———. *Gender Trouble: Feminism and the Subversion of Identity*. New York: Routledge, 1990.

Calloway, Colin G. *New Worlds for All: Indians, Europeans, and the Remaking of Early America*. Baltimore, Md.: Johns Hopkins University Press, 1997.

Cartelli, Thomas. "Transplanting Disorder: The Construction of Misrule in Morton's *New English Canaan* and Bradford's *Of Plymouth Plantation*." *English Literary Renaissance* 27, no. 2 (1997): 258–81.

Cave, Alfred A. *The Pequot War*. Amherst: University of Massachusetts Press, 1996.

Ceci, Lynn. "Native Wampum as a Peripheral Resource in the Seventeenth-Century World System." In *The Pequots in Southern New England: The Fall and Rise of an American Indian Nation*, edited by Laurence M. Hauptman and James Wherry, 48–64. Norman: University of Oklahoma Press, 1990.

Centers for Disease Control and Prevention. *Botulism in the United States, 1899–1996: Handbook for Epidemiologists, Clinicians, and Laboratory Workers*. Atlanta: CDC, 1998.

Certeau, Michel de. *The Practice of Everyday Life*. Berkeley: University of California Press, 1984.

———. *The Writing of History*. New York: Columbia University Press, 1992.

Cesarini, J. Patrick. "The Ambivalent Uses of Roger Williams's *A Key into the Language of America*." *Early American Literature* 38 (2003): 469–94.

Chakrabarty, Dipesh. "Postcoloniality and the Artifice of History: Who Speaks for 'Indian' Pasts?" *Representations* 37 (Winter 1992): 1–26.

Chaplin, Joyce E. "Natural Philosophy and an Early Racial Idiom in North America: Comparing English and Indian Bodies." *William and Mary Quarterly* 54, no. 1 (January 1997): 229–252.

———. *Subject Matter: Technology, the Body, and Science on the Anglo-American Frontier, 1500–1676.* Cambridge, Mass.: Harvard University Press, 2001.

Chartier, Roger. *Forms and Meanings: Texts, Performances, and Audiences from Codex to Computer.* Philadelphia: University of Pennsylvania Press, 1995.

Cheyfitz, Eric. *The Poetics of Imperialism: Translation and Colonization from "The Tempest" to Tarzan.* Philadelphia: University of Pennsylvania Press, 1997.

Child, John. *New England's Jonas Cast Up in London. Tracts and Other Papers, Relating Principally to the Origin, Settlement, and Progress of the Colonies in North America, From the Discovery of the Country to the Year 1776.* Vol. 4. Peter Force, coll. New York: Peter Smith, 1947.

Cleaver, Robert, and John Dod. *A Godly Forme of Houshold Government for the ordering of priuate families, according to the direction of Gods word.* London, 1621.

Clifford, James. *The Predicament of Culture: Twentieth-Century Literature, Ethnography, and Art.* Cambridge, Mass.: Harvard University Press, 1988.

———. *Routes: Travel and Translation in the Late Twentieth Century.* Cambridge, Mass.: Harvard University Press, 1997.

———. "Varieties of Indigenous Experience: Diasporas, Homelands, Sovereignties." In *Indigenous Experience Today,* edited by Marisol de la Cadena and Orin Starn, 197–224. New York: Berg, 2007.

A Closet for Ladies and Gentlewomen. Or, the Art of Preserving, Conserving, and Candying. London: Arthur Johnson, 1611.

Cohen, Daniel A. *Pillars of Salt, Monuments of Grace: New England Crime Literature and the Origins of American Popular Culture, 1674–1860.* New York: Oxford University Press, 1993.

Coke, Edward. *The Selected Writings and Speeches of Sir Edward Coke.* 3 vols. Edited by Steve Sheppard. Indianapolis: Liberty Fund, 2004.

Coleman, Jon T. *Vicious: Wolves and Men in America.* New Haven, Conn.: Yale University Press, 2004.

Connors, Donald F. *Thomas Morton.* New York: Twayne, 1969.

Considine, John. "Narrative and Persuasion in Early Modern English Dictionaries and Phrasebooks." *Review of English Studies* 52 (May 2001): 195–206.

Cook-Lynn, Elizabeth. *Why I Can't Read Wallace Stegner and Other Essays: A Tribal Voice.* Madison: University of Wisconsin Press, 1996.

Cooper, Thomas. *Thesaurus linguae Romanae & Britannicae tam accurate congestus.* London, 1565.

Cotton, John. *The Doctrine of the Church, to which are committed the keys of the kingdome of Heaven wherein is demonstrated by way of question and answere what a visible church is according to the order of the Gospel.* London, 1643.

Craik, Katharine A. "Reading *Coryats Crudities* (1611)." *Studies in English Literature* 44, no. 1 (Winter 2004): 77–96.

Cressy, David. *Coming Over: Migration and Communication between England and New England in the Seventeenth Century.* New York: Cambridge University Press, 1987.

Cronon, William. *Changes in the Land: Indians, Colonists, and the Ecology of New England.* New York: Hill and Wang, 1983.

Daniels, Bruce. *Puritans at Play: Leisure and Recreation in Colonial New England.* New York: St. Martin's, 1996.

Dannenberg, Anne Marie. "'Where, then, shall we place the hero of the wilderness?': William Apess's Eulogy on King Philip and Doctrines of Racial Destiny." In *Early Native American Writing: New Critical Essays,* edited by Helen Jaskoski, 66–82. New York: Cambridge University Press, 1996.

Darnell, Regna. "Rethinking the Concepts of Band and Tribe, Community and Nation: An Accordion Model of Nomadic Native American Social Organization." In *Papers of the Twenty-Ninth Algonquian Conference,* edited by David H. Pentland, 90–105. Winnipeg: University of Manitoba, 1999.

Darnton, Robert. "An Early Information Society: News and the Media in Eighteenth-Century Paris." Presidential Address to the American Historical Association. *American Historical Review* 105, no. 1 (February 2000): 1–35.

———. "The Heresies of Bibliography." *New York Review of Books,* 29 May 2003, 43–45.

———. *Literary Underground of the Old Regime.* Cambridge, Mass.: Harvard University Press, 2005.

———. "Peasants Tell Tales: The Meaning of Mother Goose." In *The Great Cat Massacre and Other Episodes in French Cultural History,* 9–74. New York: Basic Books, 1999.

Davidson, Cathy N. *Revolution and the Word: The Rise of the Novel in America.* Rev. ed. Oxford: Oxford University Press, 2004.

Dawson, Thomas. *The good hvswifes Iewell. Wherein is to bee found most excellent and rare Deuices, for conceits in Cookery, found out by the practise of Thomas Dawson.* London, 1610.

Debus, Allen G., ed. *Science, Medicine, and Society in the Renaissance: Essays to Honor Walter Pagel,* 2 vols. New York: Science History Publications, 1972.

De Forest, John W. *History of the Indians of Connecticut from the Earliest Known Period to 1850.* Hartford, Conn.: W. J. Hamersley, 1851.

Delbanco, Andrew. *The Puritan Ordeal.* Cambridge, Mass.: Harvard University Press, 1989.

Deleuze, Gilles, and Felix Guattari. *A Thousand Plateaus: Capitalism and Schizophrenia.* Translated by Brian Massumi. Minneapolis: University of Minnesota Press, 1987.

Deloria, Philip J. "American Indians, American Studies, and the ASA." *American Quarterly* 55, no. 4 (December 2003): 669–80.

Deloria, Vine, Jr. *Custer Died for Your Sins: An Indian Manifesto.* Norman: University of Oklahoma Press, 1988 [1969].

Demos, John. "The Maypole of Merry Mount." *American Heritage* 37, no. 6 (October–November 1986): 82–87.

Dempsey, Jack. "Reading the Revels: The Riddle of May Day in *New English Canaan.*" *Early American Literature* 34, no. 3 (1999): 283–312.

Den Ouden, Amy E. *Beyond Conquest: Native Peoples and the Struggle for History in New England.* Lincoln: University of Nebraska Press, 2005.

Derrida, Jacques. *Paper Machine.* Stanford, Calif.: Stanford University Press, 2005.

———. "Signature Event Context." In *A Derrida Reader: Between the Blinds,* edited by Peggy Kamuf, 80–111. New York: Columbia University Press, 1991.

Diamond, Jared. *Guns, Germs, and Steel: The Fates of Human Societies.* New York: W.W. Norton, 1997.

Dickson, P. G. M. *The Financial Revolution in England: A Study in the Development of Public Credit.* New York: St. Martin's Press, 1967.

Douglas, Mary. *Natural Symbols: Explorations in Cosmology.* New York: Pantheon, 1970.

Douglas, Mary, and Baron Isherwood. *The World of Goods.* New York: Basic, 1979.

Drucker, Johanna. *Figuring the Word: Essays on Books, Writing, and Visual Poetics.* New York: Granary Books, 1998.

Edelman, Lee. *Homographesis: Essays in Gay Literary and Cultural Theory.* New York: Routledge, 1994.

Eden, Trudy. "Food, Assimilation, and the Malleability of the Human Body in Early Virginia." In *A Centre of Wonders: The Body in Early America,* edited by Janet Moore Lindman and Michele Lise Tarter, 29–42. Ithaca, N.Y.: Cornell University Press, 2001.

Egan, Jim. *Authorizing Experience: Refigurations of the Body Politic in Seventeenth-Century New England Writing.* Princeton, N.J.: Princeton University Press, 1999.

Eisler, Kim Isaac. *Revenge of the Pequots: How a Small Native American Tribe Created the World's Most Profitable Casino.* Lincoln, Neb.: Bison, 2002.

Elliott, Michael. "Coyote Comes to the *Norton*: Indigenous Oral Narrative and American Literary History." *American Literature* 75, no. 4 (2003): 723–49.

Elyot, Thomas. *The Castle of Health.* London, 1610.

Felker, Christopher D. "Roger Williams's Uses of Legal Discourse: Testing Authority in Early New England." *New England Quarterly* 63, no. 4 (December 1990): 624–48.

Field, Jonathan Beecher. "The Grounds of Dissent: Heresies and Colonies in New England, 1636–1663." PhD diss., University of Chicago, 2004.

Finch, Martha L. "'Civilized' Bodies and the 'Savage' Environment of Early New Plymouth." In *A Centre of Wonders: The Body in Early America,* edited by Janet Moore Lindman and Michele Lise Tarter, 43–59. Ithaca, N.Y.: Cornell University Press, 2001.

Finnegan, Ruth. *Communicating: The Multiple Modes of Human Interconnection.* New York: Routledge, 2002.

———. *Literacy and Orality: Studies in the Technology of Communication.* New York: Blackwell, 1988.

Fliegelman, Jay. *Declaring Independence: Jefferson, Natural Language, and the Culture of Performance.* Stanford, Calif.: Stanford University Press, 1994.

Force, Peter. *Tracts and Other Papers Relating Principally to the Origin, Settlement, and Progress of the Colonies in North America: From the Discovery of the Country to the Year 1776.* Vol. 2. Washington, D.C.: Peter Force, 1838.

Foucault, Michel. *Discipline and Punish: The Birth of the Prison.* Translated by Alan Sheridan. New York: Pantheon, 1977.

———. *The History of Sexuality: An Introduction.* Translated by Robert Hurley. New York: Pantheon, 1978.

———. "Technologies of the Self." In *Technologies of the Self: A Seminar with Michel Foucault,* edited by L. H. Martin, H. Gutman, and P. H. Hutton, 16–49. London: Tavistock Press, 1988.

Friedman, Scott L., Kenneth R. McQuaid, and James H. Grendell. *Current Diagnosis and Treatment in Gastroenterology.* New York: McGraw-Hill Medical, 2002.

Fromson, Brett Duval. *Hitting the Jackpot: The Inside Story of the Richest Indian Tribe in History.* New York: Grove, 2003.

Fuller, Thomas. *The History of the Worthies of England, who for parts and learning have been eminent in the several counties: together with an historical narrative of the native commodities and rarities in each county.* 2 vols. London, 1662.

Fumerton, Patricia. "Not Home: Alehouses, Ballads, and the Vagrant Husband in Early Modern England." *Journal of Medieval and Early Modern Studies* 32, no. 3 (Fall 2002): 493–518.

Gardener, Lion. "Leift Lion Gardener his relation of the Pequot Warres." In *History of the Pequot War: The Contemporary Accounts of Mason, Underhill, Vincent, and Gardener,* edited by Charles Orr. New York: AMS Press, 1981.

Gates, Henry Louis, Jr. *The Signifying Monkey: A Theory of African-American Literary Criticism.* New York: Oxford University Press, 1988.

Gerard, John. *The herbal, or Generall historie of plantes.* London, 1633.

Gifford, George E., Jr. "Botanic Remedies in Colonial Massachusetts, 1620–1820." In *Medicine in Colonial Massachusetts,* edited by Philip Cash, Eric H. Christianson, and J. Worth Estes, 263–88. Boston: Colonial Society of Massachusetts, 1980.

Gilpin, W. Clark. *The Millenarian Piety of Roger Williams.* Chicago: University of Chicago Press, 1979.

Goddard, Ives, and Kathleen Bragdon, eds. *Native Writings in Massachusett.* Philadelphia: American Philosophical Society, 1988.

Goffman, Erving. *The Presentation of Self in Everyday Life.* Garden City, N.J.: Doubleday, 1959.

Goody, Jack, and Ian Watt. "The Consequences of Literacy." In *Perspectives on Literacy,* edited by Eugene R. Kintgen, Barry M. Kroll, and Mike Rose, 3–27. Carbondale: Southern Illinois University Press, 1988.

Gordis, Lisa. *Opening Scripture: Bible Reading and Interpretive Authority in Puritan New England.* Chicago: University of Chicago Press, 2003.

Gray, Edward G. *New World Babel: Languages and Nations in Early America.* Princeton, N.J.: Princeton University Press, 1999.

Greenblatt, Stephen. *Learning to Curse: Essays in Early Modern Culture.* New York: Routledge, 1990.

———. *Marvelous Possessions: The Wonder of the New World.* Chicago: University of Chicago Press, 1991.

———. "Racial Memory and Literary History." *PMLA* 116, no. 1 (January 2001): 48–63.

Grosz, Elizabeth. *Volatile Bodies: Toward a Corporeal Feminism.* Bloomington: Indiana University Press, 1994.

Grumet, Robert S., ed. *Northeastern Indian Lives, 1632–1816.* Amherst: University of Massachusetts Press, 1996.

Gura, Philip. *A Glimpse of Sion's Glory: Puritan Radicalism in New England, 1620–1660.* Middletown, Conn.: Wesleyan University Press, 1984.

Gustafson, Sandra M. *Eloquence Is Power: Oratory and Performance in Early America.* Chapel Hill: University of North Carolina Press, 2000.

Gutjahr, Paul C. "The Letter(s) of the Law: Four Centuries of Typography in the King James Bible." In *Illuminating Letters: Typography and Literary Interpretation,* edited by Gutjahr and Megan L. Benton, 17–44. Amherst: University of Massachusetts Press, 2001.

Habermas, Jürgen. *The Structural Transformation of the Public Sphere: An Inquiry into the Status of a Bourgeois Category.* Cambridge, Mass.: MIT Press, 1989.

———. *The Theory of Communicative Action.* Boston: Beacon Press, 1984.

Hall, David D. *Cultures of Print: Essays in the History of the Book.* Amherst: University of Massachusetts Press, 1996.

———. *Worlds of Wonder, Days of Judgment: Popular Religious Belief in Early New England.* Cambridge, Mass.: Harvard University Press, 1990.

Hall, Kim F. *Things of Darkness: Economies of Race and Gender in Early Modern England.* Ithaca, N.Y.: Cornell University Press, 1995.

Hallowell, A. Irving. "Ojibwa Ontology, Behavior, and World View." In *Culture in History: Essays in Honor of Paul Radin,* edited by Stanley Diamond, 19–52. New York: Columbia University Press, 1960.

Harkin, Michael. "Staged Encounters: Postmodern Tourism and Aboriginal People." *Ethnohistory* 50, no. 3 (2003): 575–85.

Harris, Cole. *Making Native Space: Colonialism, Resistance, and Reserves in British Columbia.* Vancouver: University of British Columbia Press, 2003.

Harrison, Simon. "Identity as a Scarce Resource." *Social Anthropology* 7, no. 3 (1999): 239–51.

Harvey, David. *The Condition of Postmodernity: An Enquiry into the Origins of Cultural Change.* New York: Blackwell, 1990.

———. *Justice, Nature, and the Geography of Difference.* Cambridge, Mass.: Blackwell, 1996.

Hatheway, C. L. "Botulism: The Present Status of the Disease." *Current Topics in Microbiology and Immunology* 195 (1995): 55–75.

Hauptman, Laurence M., and James Wherry, eds. *The Pequots in Southern New England: The Fall and Rise of an American Indian Nation.* Norman: University of Oklahoma Press, 1990.

Heath, Shirley Brice. "The Functions and Use of Literacy." *Journal of Communication* 30 (Winter 1980): 123–33.

Hewitt, J. N. B. "Iroquoian Cosmology: Second Part." *Annual Report of the Bureau of American Ethnology* 43, 1928.

Hill, Christopher. *The World Turned Upside Down: Radical Ideas during the English Revolution.* London: Temple Smith, 1972.

Hirsch, Adam. "The Collision of Military Cultures in Seventeenth-Century New England." *Journal of American History* 74 (March 1988): 1187–212.

Hoffer, Peter Charles. *Sensory Worlds in Early America.* Baltimore, Md.: Johns Hopkins University Press, 2003.

Huyssen, Andreas. *After the Great Divide: Modernism, Mass Culture, and Postmodernism.* Bloomington: Indiana University Press, 1986.

Jaenen, Cornelius J. "Native Oral and Inscribed Discourse." In *History of the Book in Canada,* vol. 1, *Beginnings to 1840,* edited by Patricia Lockhart Fleming, Giles Gallichan, and Yvan Lamonde, 13–21. Toronto: University of Toronto Press, 2004.

Jaimes, M. Annette. "Federal Indian Identification Policy: A Usurpation of Indigenous Sovereignty in North America." In *The State of Native America: Genocide, Colonization, and Resistance,* edited by M. Annette Jaimes, 123–38. Boston: South End Press, 1992.

Jehlen, Myra. "History before the Fact, or Captain John Smith's Unfinished Symphony." *Critical Inquiry* 19 (Summer 1993): 677–92.

Jenkins, B. et al. "Probiotics: A Practical Review of Their Role in Specific Clinical Scenarios." *Nutrition in Clinical Practice* 20, no. 2 (April 2005): 262–70.

Jennings, Francis. *The Invasion of America: Indians, Colonialism, and the Cant of Conquest.* New York: W. W. Norton, 1976.

Johns, Adrian. *The Nature of the Book: Print and Knowledge in the Making.* Chicago: University of Chicago Press, 1998.

Johnson, A. J. "J. F. Stam, Amsterdam, and English Bibles." *Library* 5, no. 9 (1954): 185–93.

Johnson, Eric S. "Uncas and the Politics of Contact." In *Northeastern Indian Lives, 1632–1816,* edited by Robert Steven Grumet, 29–47. Amherst: University of Massachusetts Press, 1996.

Josselyn, John. *New-Englands rarities discovered in birds, beasts, fishes, serpents, and plants of that country.* London, 1672.

Kamensky, Jane. *Governing the Tongue: The Politics of Speech in Early New England.* New York: Oxford University Press, 1997.

Kantorowicz, Ernst. *The King's Two Bodies: A Study in Mediaeval Political Theology.* Princeton, N.J.: Princeton University Press, 1957.

Karr, Ronald Dale. "'Why Should You Be So Furious?': The Violence of the Pequot War." *Journal of American History* 85, no. 3 (December 1998): 876–909.

Keary, Anne. "Retelling the History of the Settlement of Providence: Speech, Writing, and Cultural Interaction on Narragansett Bay." *New England Quarterly* 69, no. 2 (June 1996): 250–86.

Kibbey, Anne. *The Interpretation of Material Shapes in Puritanism: A Study of Rhetoric, Prejudice, and Violence.* New York: Cambridge University Press, 1986.

Kittler, Friedrich A. *Discourse Networks, 1800/1900.* Translated by Michael Metteer and Chris Cullens. Stanford, Calif.: Stanford University Press, 1990.

Knight, Janice. *Orthodoxies in Massachusetts: Rereading American Puritanism.* Cambridge, Mass.: Harvard University Press, 1994.

Kolodny, Annette. "Fictions of American Prehistory: Indians, Archaeology, and National Origin Myths." *American Literature* 75, no. 4 (2003): 693–721.

Korda, Natasha. *Shakespeare's Domestic Economies: Gender and Property in Early Modern England.* Philadelphia: University of Pennsylvania Press, 2002.

Krech, Shepard. *The Ecological Indian: Myth and History.* New York: W. W. Norton, 1999.

Krim, Arthur J. "Acculturation of the New England Landscape: Native and English Toponymy of Eastern Massachusetts." In *New England Prospect: Maps, Place Names, and the Historical Landscape,* edited by Peter Benes, 69–88. Boston: Boston University Press, 1980.

Kroeber, Karl, ed. *Native American Persistence and Resurgence*. Durham, N.C.: Duke University Press, 1994.

Krupat, Arnold. "Post-Structuralism and Oral Literature." In *Recovering the Word: Essays on Native American Literature*, edited by Brian Swann and Arnold Krupat, 113–28. Berkeley: University of California Press, 1987.

———. *Red Matters: Native American Studies*. Berkeley: University of California Press, 2000.

———. *The Turn to the Native: Studies in Criticism and Culture*. Lincoln: University of Nebraska Press, 1996.

Kupperman, Karen Ordahl. "Fear of Hot Climates in the Anglo-American Colonial Experience." *William and Mary Quarterly* 41, no. 2 (April 1984): 213–40.

———. *Indians and English: Facing Off in Early America*. Ithaca, N.Y.: Cornell University Press, 2000.

———. *Settling with the Indians: The Meeting of English and Indian Cultures in America, 1580–1640*. Totowa, N.J.: Rowman and Littlefield, 1980.

———. "Thomas Morton, Historian." *New England Quarterly* 50, no. 4 (1977). 660–64.

Lacquer, Thomas. *Making Sex: Body and Gender from the Greeks to Freud*. Cambridge, Mass.: Harvard University Press, 1990.

Latour, Bruno. *We Have Never Been Modern*. Translated by Catherine Porter. Cambridge, Mass.: Harvard University Press, 1993.

Laud, William. *The Works of the Most Reverend Father in God, William Laud D.D.* 7 vols. Oxford: J. H. Parker, 1847–1860.

Lawlor, Mary. "Identity in Mashantucket." *American Quarterly* 57, no. 1 (2005): 153–77.

Lechford, Thomas. *Plain-Dealing, or News from New-England*. Boston: Wiggin & Lunt, 1867.

Lee, Wayne E. "Peace Chiefs and Blood Revenge: Patterns of Restraint in Native American Warfare, 1500–1800." *Journal of Military History* 71 (July 2007): 701–41.

Lefebvre, Henri. *The Production of Space*. Oxford: Blackwell, 1991.

Le Mayre, Marten. *The Dutch schoolemaster, Wherein is shewed the true and perfect way to learne the Dutch tongue, to the fartherance of all those which would gladlie learne it*. London, 1606.

Lepore, Jill. *The Name of War: King Philip's War and the Origins of American Identity*. New York: Knopf, 1998.

Lienhard, Martin. "Las prácticas textuales indígenas: aproximaciones a un nuevo objeto de investigación." *Nuevo Texto Crítico* 7, no. 14–15 (July 1994–June 1995).

———. *La voz y su huella: Escritura y conflicto étnico-social en América Latina, 1492–1988*. Hanover, N.H.: Ediciones del Norte, 1991.

Lindman, Janet Moore, and Michele Lise Tarter, eds. *A Centre of Wonders: The Body in Early America*. Ithaca, N.Y.: Cornell University Press, 2001.

Lindsay, Jay. "Tribe That Greeted Pilgrims Nears End of Recognition Fight." Associated Press, 5 August 2005. http://www.ap.org.

Lipking, Lawrence. "The Marginal Gloss: Notes and Asides on Poe, Valéry, 'The Ancient Mariner,' the Ordeal of the Margin, *Storiella as She Is Syung*, Versions of Leonardo, and the Plight of Modern Criticism." *Critical Inquiry* 3, no. 4 (Summer 1977): 609–55.

Lockridge, Kenneth A. *A New England Town: The First Hundred Years, Dedham, Massachusetts, 1636–1736*. New York: Norton, 1970.

Looby, Christopher. *Voicing America: Language, Literary Form, and the Origins of the United States*. Chicago: University of Chicago Press, 1996.

Lovejoy, David. *Religious Enthusiasm in the New World: Heresy to Revolution*. Cambridge. Mass.: Harvard University Press, 1985.

Luhmann, Niklas. *Social Systems*. Stanford, Calif.: Stanford University Press, 1995.

Luke, Timothy W. *Museum Politics: Power Plays at the Exhibition*. Minneapolis: University of Minnesota Press, 2002.

Lyons, Scott Richard. "Rhetorical Sovereignty: What Do American Indians Want from Writing?" *College Composition and Communication* 51, no. 3 (February 2000): 447–68.

Major, Minor Wallace. "Thomas Morton and His *New English Canaan*." PhD diss., University of Colorado, 1957.

———. "William Bradford versus Thomas Morton." *Early American Literature* 5, no. 2 (1970): 1–13.

Malone, Patrick M. *The Skulking Way of War: Technology and Tactics among the New England Indians.* New York: Madison Books, 1991.

Marcus, Gail Sussman. "'Due Execution of the Generall Rules of Righteousnesse': Criminal Procedure in New Haven Town and Colony, 1638–1658." In *Saints and Revolutionaries: Essays on Early American History,* edited by David D. Hall, John M. Murrin, and Thad W. Tate, 99–137. New York: Norton, 1984.

Markham, Gervase. *Countrey contentments, in two bookes.* London: John Beale, 1615.

Masayesva, Victor. *Imagining Indians.* Produced and directed by Victor Masayesva. VHS. V. Masayesva, 1992.

Mason, John. *A Brief History of the Pequot War: Especially Of the memorable Taking of their Fort at Mistick in Connecticut in 1637.* Boston: S. Kneeland and T. Green, 1736.

Massachusetts Historical Society. *Letters and Papers of Roger Williams, 1629–1682.* Boston: Massachusetts Historical Society, 1924.

"Massacre at Mystic." *Ten Days That Unexpectedly Changed America.* Produced by Susan Werbe; directed by James Moll. History Channel, 2006.

McBride, Kevin. "The Source and Mother of the Fur Trade: Native-Dutch Relations in Eastern New Netherland." In *Enduring Traditions: The Native Peoples of New England,* edited by Laurie Weinstein, 33–51. Westport, Conn.: Bergin & Garvey, 1994.

McKenzie, D. F. *Bibliography and the Sociology of Texts.* Cambridge: Cambridge University Press, 1999.

McLuhan, Eric, and Frank Zingrone, eds. *Essential McLuhan.* New York: Basic, 1995.

McMullen, Ann. "Canny about Conflict: Nativism, Revitalization, and the Invention of Tradition in Native Southeastern New England." In *Reassessing Revitalization Movements: Perspectives from North America and the Pacific Islands,* edited by Michael E. Harkin, 261–77. Lincoln: University of Nebraska Press, 2004.

———. "What's Wrong with This Picture?: Context, Coversion, Survival, and the Development of Regional Native Cultures and Pan-Indianism in Southeastern New England." In *Enduring Traditions: The Native Peoples of New England,* edited by Laurie Weinstein, 118–50. Westport, Conn.: Bergin & Garvey, 1994.

McWilliams, John. *New England's Crises and Cultural Memory: Literature, Politics, History, Religion, 1620–1860.* New York: Cambridge University Press, 2004.

Mehrer, Mark W., and James M. Collins. "Household Archaeology at Cahokia and in Its Hinterlands." In *Mississippian Communities and Households,* edited by J. Daniel Rogers and Bruce D. Smith, 32–57. Tuscaloosa: University of Alabama Press, 1995.

Merrell, James H. *The Indians' New World: Catawbas and Their Neighbors from European Contact through the Era of Removal.* New York: W. W. Norton, 1989.

Mignolo, Walter. *The Darker Side of the Renaissance: Literacy, Territoriality, and Colonization.* Ann Arbor: University of Michigan Press, 1995.

Mihesuah, Devon A. *Indigenous American Women: Decolonization, Empowerment, Activism.* Lincoln: Bison, 2003.

Mihesuah, Devon A., and Angela Wilson, eds. *Indigenizing the Academy: Transforming Scholarship and Empowering Communities,* 1–15. Lincoln: University of Nebraska Press, 2004.

Miller, Lee. *Roanoke: Solving the Mystery of the Lost Colony.* New York: Penguin, 2002.

Miller, Perry. *The New England Mind: The Seventeenth Century.* Cambridge, Mass.: Harvard University Press, 1939.

———. "Roger Williams: An Essay in Interpretation." In *The Complete Writings of Roger Williams*, 7:5–25. New York: Russell & Russell, 1963.

———. *Roger Williams: His Contribution to the American Tradition*. New York: Atheneum, 1966.

Milton, John. *Areopagitica; a speech of Mr. John Milton for the liberty of unlicens'd printing, to the Parlament of England*. London, 1644.

Mohawk, John, ed. *Exiled in the Land of the Free: Democracy, the Indian Nations, and the U.S. Constitution*. Santa Fe: Clear Light, 1992.

Monaghan, E. Jennifer. *Learning to Read and Write in Colonial America*. Amherst: University of Massachusetts Press, 2005.

Morgan, Edmund S. *Roger Williams: The Church and the State*. New York: Norton, 1967.

———. *Visible Saints: The History of a Puritan Idea*. Ithaca, N.Y.: Cornell University Press, 1974.

Morgan, John. *Godly Learning: Puritan Attitudes towards Reason, Learning, and Education, 1560–1640*. Cambridge: Cambridge University Press, 1986.

Morton, Thomas. *New English Canaan*. Edited by Jack Dempsey. Scituate, Mass.: Digital Scanning, 2000.

———. *New English Canaan, or New Canaan, containing an Abstract of New England*. London: Charles Green, 1632; Amsterdam: J. F. Stam, 1637.

Mouffe, Chantal. *The Democratic Paradox*. New York: Verso, 2000.

Mourt, G. *Mourt's Relation: A Journal of the Pilgrims at Plymouth*. Edited by Dwight Heath. Bedford, Mass.: Applewood, 1963.

———. *A relation or iournall of the beginning and proceedings of the English plantation setled at Plimoth in New England*. London, 1622.

Mueller, Janel M. "Pain, Persecution, and the Construction of Selfhood in Foxe's *Acts and Monuments*." In *Religion and Culture in Renaissance England*, edited by Claire McEachern and Debora Shuger, 161–87. Cambridge: Cambridge University Press, 1997.

Murphy, Edith. "'A Rich Widow, Now to Be Tane Up or Laid Downe': Solving the Riddle of Thomas Morton's 'Rise Oedipeus.'" *William and Mary Quarterly* 53, no. 4 (October 1996): 755–68.

Murray, David. *Forked Tongues: Speech, Writing, and Representation in North American Indian Texts*. Bloomington: Indiana University Press, 1991.

———. *Indian Giving: Economies of Power in Indian-White Exchanges*. Amherst: University of Massachusetts Press, 2000.

Murray, John J. "The Cultural Impact of the Flemish Low Countries on Sixteenth- and Seventeenth-Century England." *American Historical Review* 62, no. 4 (July 1957), 837–54.

Murray, Laura J. "Vocabularies of Native American Languages: A Literary and Historical Approach to an Elusive Genre." *American Quarterly* 53, no. 4 (December 2001): 590–623.

Myles, Anne G. "Dissent and the Frontier of Translation: Roger Williams's *A Key into the Language of America*." In *Possible Pasts: Becoming Colonial in Early America*, edited by Robert Blair St. George, 88–108. Ithaca, N.Y.: Cornell University Press, 2000.

Mystic Voices: The Story of the Pequot War. Produced and directed by Charles Clemmons and Guy Perrotta. Mystic Voices, LLC, 2004.

Nash, Alice. "'Antic Deportments and Indian Postures': Embodiment in the Seventeenth-Century Anglo-Algonquian World." In *A Centre of Wonders: The Body in Early America*, edited by Janet Moore Lindman and Michele Lise Tarter, 163–75. Ithaca, N.Y.: Cornell University Press, 2001.

Nelson, Dana D. "From Manitoba to Patagonia." *American Literary History* 15, no. 2 (Summer 2003): 367–94.

Newman, Andrew. "On The Literacy Frontier: Early American Letters at their Limits." PhD diss., University of California, Irvine, 2004.

Newman, Mark, Albert-László Barabási, and Duncan J. Watts, eds. *The Structure and Dynamics of Networks*. Princeton, N.J.: Princeton University Press, 2006.

Newman, Marshall T. "Aboriginal New World Epidemiology and Medical Care, and the Impact of Old World Disease Imports." *American Journal of Physical Anthropology* 45, no. 3, pt. 2 (1976): 667–72.

Norbrook, David. *Writing the English Republic: Poetry, Rhetoric, and Politics, 1627–1660.* Cambridge: Cambridge University Press, 1999.

Oberg, Michael Leroy. *Dominion and Civility: English Imperialism and Native America, 1585–1685.* Ithaca, N.Y.: Cornell University Press, 2003.

———. *Uncas: First of the Mohegans.* Ithaca, N.Y.: Cornell University Press, 2003.

Ong, Walter J. *Orality and Literacy: The Technologizing of the Word.* London: Routledge, 2001 [1982].

Pagden, Anthony. *The Fall of Natural Man: The American Indian and the Origins of Comparative Ethnology.* New York: Cambridge University Press, 1982.

Pasquaretta, Paul. *Gambling and Survival in Native North America.* Tucson: University of Arizona Press, 2003.

Paster, Gail Kern. *The Body Embarrassed: Drama and the Disciplines of Shame in Early Modern England.* Ithaca, N.Y.: Cornell University Press, 1993.

Patterson, Annabel. *Censorship and Interpretation: The Conditions of Writing and Reading in Early Modern England.* Madison: University of Wisconsin Press, 1984.

Pauketat, Timothy R. *The Ascent of Chiefs: Cahokia and Mississippian Politics in Native North America.* Tuscaloosa: University of Alabama Press, 1994.

Pearce, Roy Harvey. *Savagism and Civilization: A Study of the Indian and the American Mind.* Baltimore, Md.: Johns Hopkins University Press, 1967.

Perkins, William. *A Golden Chaine, or The description of theologie containing the order of the causes of saluation and damnation, according to Gods word.* Cambridge, 1600.

Persels, Jeff. "The Sorbonnic Trots: Staging the Intestinal Distress of the Roman Catholic Church in French Reform Theater." *Renaissance Quarterly* 56, no. 4 (Winter 2003): 1089–111.

Persels, Jeff, and Russell Ganim, ed. *Fecal Matters in Early Modern Literature and Art: Studies in Scatology.* Burlington, Vt.: Ashgate, 2004.

Peters, John Durham. *Speaking into the Air: A History of the Idea of Communication.* Chicago: University of Chicago Press, 1999.

Peters, Russell M. *The Wampanoags of Mashpee: An Indian Perspective on American History.* Somerville, Mass.: Nimrod Press, 1987.

Pfister, Joel and Nancy Schnog. *Inventing the Psychological: Toward a Cultural History of Emotional Life in America.* New Haven, Conn.: Yale University Press, 1997.

Pratt, Mary Louise. *Imperial Eyes: Travel Writing and Acculturation.* London: Routledge, 1992.

Pratt, Scott L. *Native Pragmatism: Rethinking the Roots of American Philosophy.* Bloomington: Indiana University Press, 2002.

Prempart, James. *A Historicall Relation of the famous Siege of the Citie called the Bvsse.* Amsterdam: Jan Fredericksz Stam, 1630.

Pulitano, Elvira. *Toward a Native American Critical Theory.* Lincoln: University of Nebraska Press, 2003.

Quilligan, Maureen, ed. "Renaissance Materialities." Special issue, *Journal of Medieval and Early Modern Studies* 32, no. 3 (Fall 2002).

Ramkumar, D., and S. S. Rao. "Efficacy and Safety of Traditional Medical Therapies for Chronic Constipation: Systematic Review." *American Journal of Gastroenterology* 100 (2005): 936–71.

Ranlet, Philip. "The Lord of Misrule: Thomas Morton of Merry Mount." *New England Historical and Genealogical Register* 134 (October 1980): 282–90.

Rath, Richard Cullen. *How Early America Sounded.* Ithaca, N.Y.: Cornell University Press, 2003.

Read, David. "Silent Partners: Historical Representation in William Bradford's *Of Plymouth Plantation.*" *Early American Literature* 33 (1998): 291–314.

Red Shirt, Delphine. "These Are Not Indians." *American Indian Quarterly* 26, no. 4 (2002): 643–44.

Reinitz, Richard. "The Separatist Background of Roger Williams' Argument for Religious Toleration." In *Typology and Early American Literature*, edited by Sacvan Bercovitch, 107–37. Amherst: University of Massachusetts Press, 1972.

Rice, Grantland S. *Transformation of Authorship in America*. Chicago: University of Chicago Press, 1997.

Richter, Daniel K. *Facing East from Indian Country: A Native History of Early America*. Cambridge, Mass.: Harvard University Press, 2001.

———. *The Ordeal of the Longhouse: The Peoples of the Iroquois League in the Era of European Colonization*. Chapel Hill: University of North Carolina Press, 1992.

Rigal, Laura. *The American Manufactory: Art, Labor, and the World of Things in the Early Republic*. Princeton, N.J.: Princeton University Press, 1998.

Robinson, John. "A Justification of Separation from the Church of England." In vol. 2 of *The Works of John Robinson*, edited by Robert Ashton, 3 vols. London, 1851.

Robinson, Paul A. "Lost Opportunities: Miantonomi and the English in Seventeenth-Century Narragansett Country." In *Northeastern Indian Lives, 1632–1816*, edited by Robert Steven Grumet, 13–28. Amherst: University of Massachussetts Press, 1996.

Robinson, Paul A., et al. "Preliminary Biocultural Interpretations from a Seventeenth-Century Narragansett Indian Cemetery in Rhode Island." In *Cultures in Contact: The Impact of European Contacts on Native American Cultural Institutions A.D. 1000–1800*, edited by William W. Fitzhugh, 107–30. Washington, D.C.: Smithsonian, 1985.

Rosenmeier, Jesper. "The Teacher and the Witness: John Cotton and Roger Williams." *William and Mary Quarterly* 25 (1968): 408–31.

Round, Phillip H. *By Nature and by Custom Cursed: Transatlantic Civil Discourse and New England Cultural Production, 1620–1660*. Amherst: University of Massachusetts Press, 1999.

Rountree, Helen C. *Pocahontas's People: The Powhatan Indians of Virginia through Four Centuries*. Norman: University of Oklahoma Press, 1990.

Rowlandson, Mary. *The Soveraignty & Goodness of God, together, with the faithfulness of his promises displayed; being a narrative of the captivity and restauration of Mrs. Mary Rowlandson*. Cambridge, Mass. Bay Colony, 1682.

Rubertone, Patricia. *Grave Undertakings: An Archaeology of Roger Williams and the Narragansett Indians*. Washington, D.C.: Smithsonian Institution, 2001.

Salisbury, Neal. "Embracing Ambiguity: Native Peoples and Christianity in Seventeenth-Century North America." *Ethnohistory* 50, no. 2 (Spring 2003): 247–59.

———. "'I Loved the Place of My Dwelling': Puritan Missionaries and Native Americans in Seventeenth-Century Southern New England." In *Inequality in Early America*, edited by Carla G. Pestana and Sharon V. Salinger, 111–33. Hanover, N.H.: University Press of New England, 1999.

———. *Manitou and Providence: Indians, Europeans, and the Making of New England, 1500–1643*. New York: Oxford University Press, 1982.

Salomon, Frank. *The Cord Keepers: Khipus and Cultural Life in a Peruvian Village*. Durham, N.C.: Duke University Press, 2004.

Salwen, Bert. "Indians of Southern New England and Long Island: Early Period." In *Handbook of North American Indians*, vol. 15, edited by Bruce G. Trigger, 160–76. Washington, D.C.: Smithsonian Institution, 1978.

Sayre, Gordon. *Les sauvages américains: Representations of Native Americans in French and English Colonial Literature*. Chapel Hill: University of North Carolina Press, 1997.

Schmidt, Benjamin. *Innocence Abroad: The Dutch Imagination in the New World, 1570–1670*. New York: Cambridge University Press, 2001.

Schoenfeldt, Michael. *Bodies and Selves in Early Modern England: Physiology and Inwardness in Spenser, Shakespeare, Herbert, and Milton*. Cambridge: Cambridge University Press, 1999.

Schweitzer, Ivy. *The Work of Self-Representation: Lyric Poetry in Colonial New England.* Chapel Hill: University of North Carolina Press, 1991.

Seed, Patricia. *American Pentimento: The Invention of Indians and the Pursuit of Riches.* Minneapolis: University of Minnesota Press, 2001.

Sekatau, Ella Wilcox, and Ruth Wallis Herndon. "Recovering Gendered Political Histories: Local Struggles and Native Women's Resistance in Colonial Southern New England." In *Reinterpreting New England Indians and the Colonial Experience,* edited by Colin G. Calloway and Neal Salisbury, 137–73. Charlottesville: University of Virginia Press, 2003.

Serres, Michel. *The Parasite.* Trans. Lawrence R. Schehr. Baltimore, Md.: Johns Hopkins University Press, 1982.

Settle, Mary Lee. *I, Roger Williams.* New York: Norton, 2002.

Shagan, Ethan. "The English Inquisition: Constitutional Conflict and Ecclesiastical Law in the 1590s." *Historical Journal* 47, no. 3 (2004): 541–65.

Shannon, Laurie. "'His Apparel Was Done upon Him': Rites of Personage in Foxe's *Book of Martyrs.*" *Shakespeare Studies* 28 (2000): 193–98.

Shapin, Steven, and Simon Schaffer. *Leviathan and the Air-Pump: Hobbes, Boyle, and the Experimental Life.* Princeton, N.J.: Princeton University Press, 1989.

Shapiro, Barbara. *Probability and Certainty in Seventeenth-Century England.* Princeton, N.J.: Princeton University Press, 1983.

Shea, Daniel B. "'Our Professed Old Adversary': Thomas Morton and the Naming of New England." *Early American Literature* 23, no. 1 (1988): 52–69.

Shelley, Henry C. *John Underhill: Captain of New England and New Netherland.* New York: D. Appleton, 1932.

Shields, David. *Civil Tongues and Polite Letters in British America.* Chapel Hill: University of North Carolina Press, 1997.

Shurtleff, Nathaniel B., ed. *Records of the Governor and Company of the Massachusetts Bay in New England.* 5 vols. Boston, 1853–54.

Silverman, David. "Indians, Missionaries, and Religious Translation: Creating Wampanoag Christianity in Seventeenth-Century Martha's Vineyard." *William and Mary Quarterly* 62, no. 2 (April 2005): 141–74.

Simmons, William S. *Cautantowwit's House: An Indian Burial Ground on the Island of Conanicut in Narragansett Bay.* Providence, R.I.: Brown University Press, 1970.

———. "The Mystic Voice: Pequot Folklore from the Seventeenth Century to the Present." In *The Pequots in Southern New England: The Fall and Rise of an American Indian Nation,* edited by Laurence M. Hauptman and James D. Wherry, 141–76. Norman: University of Oklahoma Press, 1990.

———. *Spirit of the New England Tribes: Indian History and Folklore, 1620–1984.* Amherst, Mass.: University Press of New England, 1986.

Siraisi, Nancy G. *Medieval and Early Renaissance Medicine: An Introduction to Knowledge and Practice.* Chicago: University of Chicago Press, 1990.

Slights, William W. E. "The Edifying Margins of Renaissance English Books." *Renaissance Quarterly* 42, no. 4 (Winter 1989): 682–716.

Slotkin, Richard. *Regeneration through Violence: The Mythology of the American Frontier, 1600–1860.* Norman: University of Oklahoma Press, 1973.

Smith, Bruce R. *The Acoustic World of Early Modern England: Attending to the O-Factor.* Chicago: University of Chicago Press, 1999.

Smith, John. *Complete Writings of Captain John Smith (1580–1631).* 3 vols. Edited by Philip L. Barbour. Chapel Hill: University of North Carolina Press, 1986.

Smith, Nigel. *Literature and Revolution in England, 1640–1660.* New Haven, Conn.: Yale University Press, 1994.

Smith, Paul Chaat. "The Terrible Nearness of Distant Places: Making History at the National Museum of the American Indian." In *Indigenous Experience Today,* edited by Marisol de la Cadena and Orin Starn, 379–96. New York: Berg, 2007.

Snow, Dean R. *The Archaeology of New England.* New York: Academic Press, 1980.

Sparke, Matthew. "A Map That Roared and an Original Atlas: Canada, Cartography, and the Narration of Nation." *Annals of the Association of American Geographers* 88, no. 3 (1998): 463–95.

Sprunger, Keith. *Trumpets from the Tower: English Puritan Printing in the Netherlands, 1600–1640.* New York: E. J. Brill, 1994.

Spufford, Margaret. *Small Books and Pleasant Histories: Popular Fiction and Its Readership in Seventeenth-Century England.* Athens: University of Georgia Press, 1982.

Stallybrass, Peter, and Allon White. *The Politics and Poetics of Transgression.* Ithaca, N.Y.: Cornell University Press, 1986.

Starn, Orin. *Ishi's Brain: In Search of America's Last "Wild" Indian.* New York: W. W. Norton, 2001.

Starn, Randolph. "A Historian's Brief Guide to New Museum Studies." *American Historical Review* 110, no. 1 (February 2005), http://www.historycooperative.org/journals/ahr/110.1/starn.html (accessed 21 July 2006).

Starna, William A. "The Pequots in the Early Seventeenth Century." In *The Pequots in Southern New England: The Fall and Rise of an American Indian Nation,* edited by Laurence M. Hauptman and James Wherry, 33–47. Norman: University of Oklahoma Press, 1990.

Stavely, Keith. "Roger Williams and the Enclosed Gardens of New England." In *Puritanism: Transatlantic Perspectives on a Seventeenth-Century Anglo-American Faith,* edited by Francis J. Bremer, 257–74. Boston: Massachusetts Historical Society, 1993.

Stearns, Raymond Phineas. "The New England Way in Holland." *New England Quarterly* 6, no. 4 (December 1933): 747–92.

Steedman, Caroline. *Dust: The Archive and Cultural History.* New Brunswick, N.J.: Rutgers University Press, 2002.

Steele, Ian K. *The English Atlantic, 1675–1740: An Exploration of Communication and Community.* New York: Oxford University Press, 1986.

Sternberg, Paul R. "The Publication of Thomas Morton's *New English Canaan* Reconsidered." *Papers of the Bibliographical Society of America* 80, no. 3 (1986): 369–74.

St. George, Robert Blair. *Conversing by Signs: Poetics of Implication in Colonial New England Culture.* Chapel Hill: University of North Carolina Press, 1998.

Street, Brian. *Literacy in Theory and Practice.* New York: Cambridge University Press, 1984.

Sturtevant, William C., ed. *Handbook of North American Indians.* Vol. 15. Washington, D.C.: Smithsonian Institution, 1978.

Sullivan, Lynne P. "Mississippian Households and Community Organization in Eastern Tennessee." In *Mississippian Communities and Households,* edited by J. Daniel Rogers and Bruce D. Smith, 99–123. Tuscaloosa: University of Alabama Press, 1995.

Swan, Bradford F. *Gregory Dexter of London and New England, 1610–1700.* Rochester, N.Y.: Leo Hart, 1949.

Swann, Brian and Arnold Krupat, eds. *Recovering the Word: Essays on Native American Literature.* Berkeley: University of California Press, 1987.

Tench, Megan and Michael Kranish. "Mashpees Near Federal Recognition." *Boston Globe,* 1 April 2006, http://www.boston.com/news/local/articles/2006/04/01/mashpees_near_federal_recognition/.

Teunissen, John J., and Evelyn J. Hinz, ed. *A Key into the Language of America.* Detroit: Wayne State University Press, 1973.

Teuton, Christopher B. "Theorizing American Indian Literature: Applying Oral Concepts to Written Traditions." In *Reasoning Together,* edited by Craig S. Womak, Daniel Heath Justice, and Christopher B. Teuton, 193–215. Norman: University of Oklahoma, 2008.

Thomas, Peter A. "Cultural Change on the Southern New England Frontier, 1630–1665." In *Cultures in Contact: The Impact of European Contacts on Native American Cultural Institutions, A.D. 1000–1800,* edited by William W. Fitzhugh, 131–61. Washington, D.C.: Smithsonian Institute Press, 1985.

Thompson, W. G. "Introduction." In *First Principles of Gastroenterology: The Basics of Disease and an Approach to Management,* edited by A. B. R. Thomson and E. A. Shaffer. Toronto: University of Toronto Press, 1992.

Tinker, George. *Missionary Conquest: The Gospel and Native American Cultural Genocide.* Minneapolis: Fortress Press, 1993.

Todorov, Tzvetan. *The Conquest of America: The Question of the Other.* New York: Harper & Row, 1984.

Tooker, Elisabeth, ed. *Native North American Spirituality of the Eastern Woodlands: Sacred Myths, Dreams, Visions, Speeches, Healing Formulas, Rituals and Ceremonials.* Mahwah, N.J.: Paulist Press, 1979.

Trent, Robert F. "The Concept of Mannerism." In *New England Begins: The Seventeenth Century,* 3 vols., edited by Jonathan L. Fairbanks and Robert F. Trent, 3:368–412. Boston: Museum of Fine Arts, 1982.

Tribble, Evelyn B. *Margins and Marginality: The Printed Page in Early Modern England.* Charlottesville: University Press of Virginia, 1993.

Turnbaugh, William A. "Assessing the Significance of European Goods in Seventeenth-Century Narragansett Society." In *Ethnohistory and Archaeology: Approaches to Postcontact Change in the Americas,* edited by J. Daniel Rogers and Samuel Wilson, 133–60. New York: Plenum, 1993.

———. "Community, Commodities, and the Concept of Property in Seventeenth-century Narragansett Society." In *Archaeology of Eastern North America: Papers in Honor of Stephen Williams,* edited by James Stoltman, 285–95. Archaeological Report 25. Jackson: Mississippi Department of Archives and History, 1993.

———. "Wide-Area Connections in Native North America." *American Indian Culture and Research Journal* 1, no. 4 (1976): 22–28.

Tuvill, D. *The Dove and the Serpent, in which is contained a large description of all such points and principles, as tend either to conversation, or, negotiation.* London, 1614.

Underhill, John. *Newes from America, or A new and experimentall discoverie of New England containing, a true relation of their war-like proceedings these two yeares last past, with a figure of the Indian fort, or palizado.* London, 1638.

Uriarte, John J. Bodinger de. "Imagining the Nation with House Odds: Representing American Indian Identity at Mashantucket." *Ethnohistory* 50, no. 3 (2003): 549–65.

Urton, Gary. "From Knots to Narratives: Reconstructing the Art of Historical Record Keeping in the Andes from Spanish Transcriptions of Inka *Khipus." Ethnohistory* 45, no. 3 (Summer 1998): 409–38.

Vaughan, Alden T. *New England Frontier: Puritans and Indians, 1620–1675.* 3rd ed. Norman: Oklahoma University Press, 1995.

Vizenor, Gerald. *Crossbloods: Bone Courts, Bingo, and Other Reports.* Minneapolis: University of Minnesota Press, 1990.

———. *Manifest Manners: Postindian Warriors of Survivance.* Hanover, N.H.: University Press of New England, 1994.

Vizenor, Gerald, and A. Robert Lee. *Postindian Conversations.* Lincoln: University of Nebraska Press, 1999.

Wald, Priscilla. *Constituting Americans: Cultural Anxiety and Narrative Form.* Durham, N.C.: Duke University Press, 1995.

Waldron, Jeremy. *The Right to Private Property.* Oxford, England: Clarendon Press, 1988.

Wall, Wendy. *Staging Domesticity: Household Work and English Identity in Early Modern Drama.* New York: Cambridge University Press, 2002.

Wallace, Anthony F. C. *The Death and Rebirth of the Seneca*. New York: Vintage, 1972.

Wallach, Alan. *Exhibiting Contradiction: Essays on the Art Museum in the United States*. Amherst: University of Massachusetts Press, 1998.

Warkentin, Germaine. "In Search of 'The Word of the Other': Aboriginal Sign Systems and the History of the Book in Canada." *Book History* 2 (1999): 1–27.

Warrior, Robert Allen. *The People and the World: Reading Native Nonfiction*. Minneapolis: University of Minnesota Press, 2005.

———. *Tribal Secrets: Recovering American Indian Intellectual Traditions*. Minneapolis: University of Minnesota Press, 1994.

Weaver, Jace. *Other Words: American Indian Literature, Law, and Culture*. Norman: University of Oklahoma Press, 2001.

———. *That the People Might Live: Native American Literatures and Native American Community*. New York: Oxford University Press, 1997.

Weinberger, Jill Knight. "The Mashantucket Pequot Museum and Research Center." *American History* 35, no. 4 (October 2000): 16.

Weiner, James. "Diaspora, Materialism, Tradition: Anthropological Issues in the Recent High Court Appeal of the Yorta Yorta." *Land, Rights, Laws: Issues of Native Title* 2, issue paper no. 18 (2002): 1–12.

Weinstein, Laurie, ed. *Enduring Traditions: The Native Peoples of New England*. Westport, Conn.: Bergin & Garvey, 1994.

Weinstein-Farson, Laurie. *The Wampanoag*. New York: Chelsea House, 1989.

Wertheimer, Eric. "Roger Williams, Perry Miller, and Indians." *Arizona Quarterly* 50, no. 2 (Summer 1994): 1–18.

Weston, Thomas. *History of the Town of Middleboro, Massachusetts*. Boston, Mass.: Houghton Mifflin, 1906.

White, Richard. *The Middle Ground: Indians, Empires, and Republics in the Great Lakes Region, 1650–1815*. New York: Cambridge University Press, 1991.

Williams, Roger. *An Affidavit by Roger Williams in His Handwriting*. Providence: Rhode Island Historical Society, 1976.

———. *The bloudy tenent, of persecution, for cause of conscience, discussed, in a conference betweene truth and peace*. London, 1644.

———. *Christenings make not Christians, or A Briefe Discourse concerning that name Heathen, commonly given to the Indians*. London: Jane Coe, 1645.

———. *The Complete Writings of Roger Williams*. 7 vols. New York: Russell & Russell, 1963.

———. *The Correspondence of Roger Williams*. 2 vols. Edited by Glenn LaFantasie. Hanover, N.H.: Brown University Press, 1988.

———. *The hireling ministry none of Christs, or, A discourse touching the propagating the Gospel of Christ Jesus*. London, 1652.

———. *A Key into the Language of America*. London: Gregory Dexter, 1643.

———. *Mr. Cottons letter lately printed, examined and answered*. London, 1644.

Wilson, Angela Cavender. "Reclaiming Our Humanity: Decolonization and the Recovery of Indigenous Knowledge." In *Indigenizing the Academy: Transforming Scholarship and Empowering Communities*, edited by Devon Abbott Mihesuah and Angela Cavender Wilson, 69–87. Lincoln: University of Nebraska Press, 2004.

Winslow, Edward. *The Glorious Progress of the Gospel, amongst the Indians in New England*. London, 1649.

———. *Good Newes from New-England, or A true Relation of things very remarkable at the Plantation of Plimoth in New-England*. London: John Bellamy, 1624.

Winthrop, John. *The Journal of John Winthrop, 1630–1649*. 2 vols. Edited by Richard S. Dunn, James Savage, and Laetitia Yeandle. Cambridge, Mass.: Harvard University Press, 1996.

Wogan, Peter. "Perceptions of European Literacy in Early Contact Situations." *Ethnohistory* 41, no. 3 (Summer 1994): 407–29.

Womack, Craig. *Red on Red: Native American Literary Separatism*. Minneapolis: University of Minnesota Press, 1999.

Wood, Anthony. *Athenae Oxonienses, an exact history of all the writers and bishops who have had their education in the most ancient and famous University of Oxford, from the fifteenth year of King Henry the Seventh, Dom. 1500, to the end of the year 1690*. London, 1691.

Wood, Timothy L. "Kingdom Expectations: The Native American in the Puritan Missiology of John Winthrop and Roger Williams." *Fides et Historia* 32, no. 1 (Winter–Spring 2000): 39–49.

Woodfield, Denis B. *Surreptitious Printing in England, 1550–1640*. New York: Bibliographical Society of America, 1973.

Wroth, Lawrence. "Variations in Five Copies of Roger Williams' *Key into the Language of America*." *Collections of the Rhode Island Historical Society* 29, no. 2 (1936): 120–21.

Wyss, Hilary. *Writing Indians: Literacy, Christianity, and Native Community in Early America*. Amherst: University of Massachusetts Press, 2000.

Yates, Frances. *The Art of Memory*. Chicago: University of Chicago Press, 1966.

Yates, Julian. *Error, Misuse, Failure: Object Lessons from the English Renaissance*. Minneapolis: University of Minnesota Press, 2003.

Zuckerman, Michael. "Pilgrims in the Wilderness: Community, Modernity, and the Maypole at Merry Mount." *New England Quarterly* 50, no. 2 (1977): 255–77.

Index

Abramoff, Jack, 160
Algonquians, 1, 19, 126, 144, 205n28; communications media, 6, 145; literacy and reading interest among, 2, 35–36, 38–39, 41, 43, 49; multimedia combat techniques, 27–28, 149–51, 203n9
Allen, Paula Gunn, 10, 131, 134, 166
Americans. *See* Native Americans
Amsterdam. *See* Dutch print culture
animal communication, 142, 150, 160, 167–68, 205n23
animal-human metamorphosis, 205n28
anxiety, 29–30, 74, 135, 140, 150, 159, 170, 183n19
Apess, William, 165–66
archives, 13, 16–17
assimilation, 157–66. *See also* simulation
authentication, 17, 43, 69, 110–11
Axtell, James, 19–20, 49, 103

Babylon project, 171, 210n3
Barabási, Albert-László, 9
baskets, Native, 176
Baudrillard, Jean: *Simulacra and Simulation,* 159–60
Berkhofer, Robert, 19
Besnier, Nico, 185n42
Bible (Geneva 1587 ed.), 99, 100, 104

bibliography, bibliographic approaches, 13, 16, 17
Blackfoot students, 5
Block Island, 148, 149–51
bodily flows, 77, 82. *See also* humoral theory of disease
body as medium: as the body politic, 73–74, 89–90, 193n33; as a medium, 174, 183n13; Native bodies, 203n9
Book of Common Prayer, 35–37, 99
books: early modern dictionaries and phrase books, 121–22, 200n55, 200n60; of emblems, 115, 117; history of, 5–6, 11, 30, 182n10; as a multimedia form, 7; and oral traditions, 12–19. *See also* text as medium
botulism, 75–76
Bourdieu, Pierre, 181n3
bowel problems, 26, 27; somatic metaphors, 78–81. *See also* Massasoit's curing
Bradford, William, 78, 204n20; deer trap incident, 3–4, 12, 140–41; objections to Morton, 39–40
Bradford, William. *See also* Mourt, G. (pseud.); *Of Plymouth Plantation*
Bragdon, Kathleen, 44, 46, 47–48, 83–84, 107–8; on ecological influences, 125–26; on social structure, 189n45

Matt Cohen is associate professor of English at the University of Texas at Austin.